HAND-LIST OF
ANGLO-SAXON NON-RUNIC
INSCRIPTIONS

HAND-LIST OF
ANGLO-SAXON
NON-RUNIC
INSCRIPTIONS

ELISABETH OKASHA

School of English and American Studies
University of East Anglia

CAMBRIDGE
AT THE UNIVERSITY PRESS
1971

Published by the Syndics of the Cambridge University Press
Bentley House, 200 Euston Road, London NW1 2DB
American Branch: 32 East 57th Street, New York, N.Y.10022

© Cambridge University Press 1971

Library of Congress Catalogue Card Number: 75-129934

ISBN: 0 521 07904 7

Printed in Great Britain
at the University Printing House, Cambridge
(Brooke Crutchley, University Printer)

دائماً دائماً

CONTENTS

HAND-LIST

Guide to the Entries   43

CONTENTS

PREFACE

In the course of compiling this Hand-list I have visited over one hundred parish churches and cathedrals in which inscriptions are preserved. I should like to thank the incumbents of these churches, and the Deans and Chapters of the cathedrals, for their permission to study and photograph. I am also grateful to the directors and staff of the museums in which inscriptions are preserved for permission to work there and for their unfailing courtesy; these museums are listed in Index II, to which should be added Tullie House Museum, Carlisle. One stone, Wycliffe, is in private possession and I am most grateful to Mr C. U. Peat for his kindness and hospitality to me while studying it. My sincere thanks are also due to the staff of the University Libraries of Aberdeen and Cambridge, and of the Reading Room, the Department of Medieval and Later Antiquities, and the Department of Coins and Medals, all of the British Museum.

I should like to acknowledge the financial help received for travel and the collection of photographs from: the Board of Graduate Studies, University of Cambridge; the Carnegie Trust for the Universities of Scotland; the Colt Fund of the Society for Medieval Archaeology; Newnham College, Cambridge; the Scottish Education Department; and the University of Aberdeen.

Part of this Hand-list was compiled as a Ph.D. thesis submitted to the University of Cambridge. It is a great pleasure to express my gratitude to Dr R. I. Page, Corpus Christi College, who supervised my work as a research student and has continued to give me every possible assistance. Many scholars of various disciplines, especially in the Universities of Aberdeen and Cambridge, have helped me in the course of this work, to all of whom I am extremely grateful. Help over particular points is acknowledged in the foot-notes and in addition I should like to record my especial thanks to the following: Mr M. Biddle, Dr J. M. Cooper, Professor B. Dickins, Mr M. Dolley, Mr P. Grierson, Mr H. Hargreaves, Mrs B. Trengove, Mrs L. E. Webster, Professor D. Whitelock, Mr D. M. Wilson. Cambridge University Press have dealt competently and patiently with a difficult manuscript, and I am particularly grateful to Mrs A. M. J. Blackburn, Mrs J. Godden and Mr R. J. Hollick for their help.

Finally I should like to thank my husband, to whom this book is dedicated, for his encouragement and help, his stimulating criticism, and his unfailing patience with a working wife.

ACKNOWLEDGEMENTS

Acknowledgement is due to the following holders of copyright for permission to reproduce photographs: A.C.L. Bruxelles, 17c; the Society of Antiquaries of London, 44, 72; the Museum of Antiquities, Newcastle upon Tyne, 2a, 2b, 2c, 39, 46, 62; the Department of Antiquities, Ashmolean Museum, Oxford, 4a, 4b, 4c, 14a, 14b, 19a, 19b, 28, 29, 106a, 106b, 106c, 154, 156; Chanoine Léon Blouet, 93; the British Museum, 6, 9, 13a, 13b, 13c, 13d, 20a, 20b, 20c, 20d, 27, 30, 33, 35a, 36, 37, 38, 45, 47, 49, 50, 66a, 66b, 66c, 66d, 70a, 70b, 70c, 100, 104a, 104b, 107a, 107b, 107c, 109a, 109b, 114, 115a, 115b, 115c, 115d, 117, 119, 123, 124, 125, 126, 127, 128, 129, 130, 131, 132, 133, 134, 136–7, 155a, 155b, 155c, 155d; the late G. Baldwin Brown, 42; A. J. D. Buckley, Esq., 87; the Castle Museum, Norwich, 5a, 5b, 5c; Mrs G. W. Copeland, 101; the Courtauld Institute of Art, London, W.1, 59, 60a, 63, 85, 92; J. D. Cowen, Esq., 144; P. M. Dalley, Esq., 89; the Dean and Chapter, Durham Cathedral, 34a, 34b, 35b, 35c, 40, 48, 54, 145; the Dean and Chapter, Winchester Cathedral, 141; East Yorkshire Local History Society, 1; B. J. N. Edwards, Esq., 68a, 68b, 68c, 68d; O. Fein, Esq., 105; Miss K. Galbraith, 58; Messrs Gibson and Son, Hexham, 23a, 23b; Hampshire Field Club and Archaeological Society, 135; A. Hidalgo Jnr., 113; the Ipswich Museums Committee, 60b, 60c; Rev. M. Lucas, 67; Professor A. D. Mainds, 25; C. S. Middleton, Esq., 112; National Monuments Record (Crown Copyright), 11, 52, 56, 57, 64, 69a, 98, 111, 150, 151, 152, 153; Newent P.C.C. and City Museum and Art Gallery, Gloucester, 94c; Dr R. I. Page, 74, 75, 76, 77, 78, 79, 80, 81, 82, 83, 84, 88, 99, 116; Rev. Dr T. E. Peacock, 61; S. Pitcher, Esq., 94a, 94b, 94d; Reading Museum and Art Gallery, 118; Canon M. H. Ridgway, 32, 149; Royal Commission on Historical Monuments (Scotland), 10; Rev. R. T. G. Sharp, 31; the Spa Director, Bath, 7a, 7b; the Sunderland Museum, 91; Professor A. C. Thomas, 3; University Museum of Archaeology and Ethnology, Cambridge, 90, 97; Victoria and Albert Museum, 86, 103, 158; Winchester Excavations Committee, 138, 139, 140, 142; the Yorkshire Museum, York, 102, 147, 148.

I am also grateful to the University Library, Cambridge, the Bodleian Library, Oxford, G. W. Hare, Esq., R. H. Hayes, Esq., J. E. Hedley, Esq., Fisk Moore, Esq., Edward Reeves, Esq., and D. M. Smith, Esq. for providing photographs.

ABBREVIATIONS OF JOURNAL AND SERIES TITLES

AASR   *Associated Architectural Societies' Reports and Papers*
Acad.   *The Academy*
Acta Arch.   *Acta Archaeologica*
Anal. Bolland.   *Analecta Bollandiana*
Angl.   *Anglia*
Angl. Beib.   *Beiblatt zur Anglia*
Ann. Rpt. Council Yorks. Philos. Soc.   *Annual Report of the Council of the Yorkshire Philosophical Society*
Annales de la Soc. d'Arch. de Bruxelles   *Annales de la Société r. d'Archéologie de Bruxelles*
Antiq.   *Antiquity*
Antiq. Annaler   *Antiqvariske Annaler*
Antiq. J.   *The Antiquaries Journal*
Antiq. Rep. The Antiquarian Repertory
Antiquary   *The Antiquary*
Arch.   *Archaeologia*
Arch. Ael.   *Archaeologia Aeliana*
Arch. Camb.   *Archæologia Cambrensis*
Arch. Cant.   *Archaeologia Cantiana*
Arch. J.   *The Archaeological Journal*
Arch. Scot.   *Archaeologia Scotica*
Archiv   *Archiv für das Studium der Neueren Sprachen*
Art Bulletin   *The Art Bulletin*
Athenæum   *The Athenæum*
BMQ   *The British Museum Quarterly*
Brit. Num. J.   *The British Numismatic Journal and Proceedings of the British Numismatic Society*
Bucks. Berks. Oxon. Arch. J.   *The Bucks., Berks. and Oxon. Archæological Journal*
Builder   *The Builder*
Burl. Mag. The Burlington Magazine for Connoisseurs
CWAAS   *Cumberland and Westmoreland Antiquarian and Archaeological Society*
Camb. Antiq. Comms.   *Cambridge Antiquarian Communications*
Durh. Univ. J.   *The Durham University Journal*
EETS   *Early English Text Society*
EPNS   *English Place-name Society*
Ecclesiologist   *The Ecclesiologist*
Eng. Hist. Review   *The English Historical Review*
Essays & Studies   *Essays and Studies by Members of the English Association*
Essex Arch. Soc.   *Essex Archaeological Society*
Eurasia Sept. Antiq.   *Eurasia Septentrionalis Antiqua*
Fenland N & Q   *Fenland Notes and Queries*

ABBREVIATIONS

Gents. Mag.   The Gentleman's Magazine

Hampshire N & Q   Hampshire Notes and Queries

History Northumberland   The History of Northumberland

JBAA   The Journal of the British Archaeological Association

JEGP   The Journal of English and Germanic Philology

J. Royal Inst. Cornwall   Journal of the Royal Institution of Cornwall

J. Warburg Courtauld Insts.   Journal of the Warburg and Courtauld Institutes

Listener   The Listener

Lund Stud. Eng.   Lund Studies in English

MLR   The Modern Language Review

Mag. Art   The Magazine of Art

Med. Aev.   Medium Aevum

Med. Arch.   Medieval Archaeology

N & Q   Notes and Queries

Neuphil. Mitteil.   Neuphilologische Mitteilungen

Norsk Tidsskrift   Norsk Tidsskrift for Sprogvidenskap

Notices Proc. Royal Inst. G. B.   Notices of the Proceedings at the Meetings of the Members of the Royal Institution of Great Britain

Num. Chr.   The Numismatic Chronicle

PMLA   Proceedings of the Modern Language Association of America

Papers Proc. Hamps. Field Club Arch. Soc.   Papers and Proceedings of the Hampshire Field Club and Archæological Society

Philos. Trans.   Philosophical Transactions

Proc. Berw. Nat. Club   Proceedings of the Berwickshire Naturalists' Club

Proc. Brit. Acad.   Proceedings of the British Academy

Proc. Bury W. Suffolk Arch. Inst.   Proceedings of the Bury and West Suffolk Archaeological Institute

Proc. Geol. Polyt. Soc. WR Yorks.   Proceedings of the Geological and Polytechnic Society of the West Riding of Yorkshire

Proc. Oxf. Hist. Soc.   Proceedings of the Oxford Historical Society

Proc. Royal Arch. Inst.   Proceedings at the Annual Meeting of the Royal Archaeological Institute of Great Britain and Ireland

Proc. Soc. Ant. Lon.   Proceedings of the Society of Antiquaries of London

Proc. Soc. Ant. Newc.   Proceedings of the Society of Antiquaries of Newcastle

Proc. Soc. Ant. Scot.   Proceedings of the Society of Antiquaries of Scotland

Proc. Som. Arch. Nat. Hist. Soc.   Proceedings of the Somersetshire Archæological and Natural History Society

Proc. Suff. Inst. Arch.   Proceedings of the Suffolk Institute of Archæology

Reliq.   The Reliquary

Royal Arch. Inst.   Royal Archaeological Institute of Great Britain and Ireland

Royal Num. Soc. Special Publications   Special Publications of the Royal Numismatic Society

Saga-Book   The Saga-Book of the Viking Society for Northern Research

Stud. Conserv.   Studies in Conservation

Stud. Neophil.   Studia Neophilologica

ABBREVIATIONS

Stud. Phil.   *Studies in Philology*

Suff. Arch. Assoc. Orig. Papers   *Suffolk Archaeological Association Original Papers*

Surtees Soc.   *Surtees Society*

Sussex Arch. Colls.   *Sussex Archaeological Collections*

Sussex N & Q   *Sussex Notes and Queries*

TBGAS   *Transactions of the Bristol and Gloucestershire Archæological Society*

TCWAAS   *Transactions of the Cumberland and Westmoreland Antiquarian and Archaeological Society*

Toc H J.   *Toc H Journal*

Trans. A.A. Soc. Durh. North.   *Transactions of the Architectural and Archaeological Society of Durham and Northumberland*

Trans. Camb. Bibl. Soc.   *Transactions of the Cambridge Bibliographical Society*

Trans. Connecticut Acad. Arts Sciences   *Transactions of the Connecticut Academy of Arts and Sciences*

Trans. Devon Assoc. Adv. Sc. Lit. Art   *The Transactions of the Devonshire Association for the Advancement of Science, Literature and Art*

Trans. Dumfr. Galloway Nat. Hist. Ant. Soc.   *Transactions of the Dumfriesshire and Galloway Natural History and Antiquarian Society*

Trans. ER Antiq. Soc.   *Transactions of the East Riding Antiquarian Society*

Trans. Lancs. Ches. Antiq. Soc.   *Transactions of the Lancashire and Cheshire Antiquarian Society*

Trans. Phil. Soc.   *Transactions of the Philological Society*

Trans. Yorks. Dial. Soc.   *Transactions of the Yorkshire Dialect Society*

VCH   *The Victoria History of the Counties of England*

YAJ   *The Yorkshire Archaeological and Topographical Journal*

Yale Stud. Eng.   *Yale Studies in English*

INTRODUCTION

1 GENERAL

As the title implies, this Hand-list is a corpus of all known Anglo-Saxon, non-runic, inscribed objects. The limits of the Anglo-Saxon period are taken to be *c.* A.D. 450 to *c.* A.D 1100. Any object inscribed with both a runic and a non-runic text is included in the Hand-list. Seal-dies are included since they are single objects unlike the multiple copies of seals made from them. For this reason, seals and coins are excluded from the Hand-list; however seal-dies and coin-brooches, which are included, are often very similar to, or identical with, contemporary seals and coins.

Inscribed objects are denoted in the Hand-list by the name of their place of finding in modern times and, where necessary, are numbered e.g. Canterbury I, Canterbury II. Where an object contains two or more texts these are denoted thus, Canterbury i, Canterbury ii. On occasion these are, of course, combined e.g. Canterbury I ii, Canterbury II i. Different texts are distinguished on the basis of both their content and their positioning on the object. New subject matter introduced without being on a new line or on a different part of the object is not taken as a new text; the same subject matter in a new position is not so considered either.

The Hand-list includes inscriptions now lost but known to have been in existence after A.D. 1800, and such inscriptions are listed in Index IB. The date 1800 is arbitrary and is chosen for convenience only. All extant inscriptions have been personally examined by the author except for some of those preserved outside Britain (Cologne, Mortain and one side of Auzon).

Anglo-Saxon non-runic inscriptions are defined here as comprising inscriptions:

i   with texts in Old English, regardless of provenance,
ii with texts in Latin but including an Old English personal name, regardless of provenance,
iii with contemporary texts wholly in Latin, found in the Old English speaking area.

Inscriptions with texts in Latin but including a Celtic personal name are excluded, even if they were found in the Old English speaking area. It is not always certain whether or not some inscriptions with texts wholly in Latin date from the Anglo-Saxon period; this is particularly so in the case of objects dating from the later period. Such inscriptions are included in the Hand-list if they have been described as Anglo-Saxon and the opposite case has not been conclusively proved. Doubtful inscriptions which have been excluded from the body of the Hand-list for one of the above reasons are listed in Index III.

Inscribed objects are frequently of stone and comprise carved and uncarved crosses and slabs, also fonts and sun-dials. Non-stone inscriptions are generally of metal, although there are also inscribed objects of clay, ivory, whale-bone and wood. The inscriptions occur on: altars, bell-moulds, brooches, caskets, censer-covers, chess-men, coffins and coffin-plates, crosses, crucifixes, jewels, reliquaries, rings, seal-dies, strap-end coverings, sun-dials, weapons and weaving implements.

The texts of the vast majority of the inscriptions appear to be primary; that is, the object was intended from inception to contain the text. Where there is no evidence to the contrary, texts are assumed to be primary. Bishopstone, Chester-le-Street and Manchester have texts which are probably not primary. In addition, Lincoln I, Jarrow III and York VII contain texts inscribed on re-used Romano-British stones.

Other possibly non-primary texts are Ardwall ii, Canterbury IV, Newent i, Wallingford I i, and York IV. In addition, some of the small gravestones known as name-stones, for instance from Hartlepool, Lindisfarne, Monkwearmouth and Wensley, may have been mass-produced with names added later as necessary.

2 LOCALISATION AND DISTRIBUTION OF INSCRIPTIONS

The distribution of inscriptions is shown in Maps 1 and 2. Stones are relatively non-portable and can usually be assumed to have remained in the area in which they were inscribed. The following stones were certainly found *in situ*: Bishopstone, Breamore I, Hartlepool O, III, IV, V, Winchester I and York VII; others were probably *in situ*: Canterbury IV, Hartlepool VI, VII, and Kirkdale; and others possibly so: Hartlepool VIII, Lincoln I, Little Billing, Newent and Winchester III.

Old English texts are assumed to be written in the dialect of their find-place, unless there is evidence to the contrary. This is based on one of two assumptions, either that carvers were working from a written copy or that they spoke the local dialect. However these assumptions may not be altogether reliable. Although carvers may sometimes have been local men, perhaps employed on a full-time basis by a local monastery, it seems probable that many were itinerant. There is no evidence to show whether or not a written exemplum was used. It seems unlikely that long texts like Kirkdale or Deerhurst I would be carved directly; on the other hand, if a written exemplum were used, one might expect careful planning of space, which is demonstrably not the case, at least on Kirkdale. With the exceptions of Brussels I and Sutton, non-stone inscriptions in Old English contain texts too short to indicate their dialect. Skilled work in precious metals was presumably done to order at some centre of craftsmanship; *a priori* it seems likely that such texts would be worked from a written exemplum, but again there is little evidence.

Map 1 shows the distribution of inscribed stones. The majority of these, about 80 per cent, were found in the north of England.[1] This distribution pattern is closely paralleled by the distribution of Old English runic inscriptions on stone,[2] and of Anglo-Saxon carved stones, about 72 per cent of which occur in the north.[3] In direct contrast, the majority of remaining Anglo-Saxon stone churches or parts of churches are in the south of England.[4] The reason for this distinction between stones and stone churches is not altogether clear, especially since some stones, for example sun-dials and those with dedication texts, are found in association with churches. Differences in date may partly account for it. Again, it is possible that stone might be imported to an area more readily for the building of a church than for the erection of a personal memorial, though the reverse case is also arguable.

The distinction shown in Map 1 is explicable in a variety of ways. It may be partly accidental, in that known monastic sites, like Hartlepool, Lindisfarne and Whitby, are liable to be excavated. It is only at such monasteries that the series of several stones have been found. But of course there are also known monastic sites in the south. It may be partly historical; the appearance in the north of all the early stones is explicable in view of the fact that the northern kingdoms were probably more advanced culturally in the seventh and eighth centuries. Further reasons have been suggested, notably that of Clapham that the greater density of population in the south throughout the Middle Ages resulted in more destruction and re-use of earlier stones.[5]

But there is also a cogent geological reason to help account for this distribution. For stone to be inscribable, and to stand a reasonable chance of survival in this state, it must be of a relatively high hardness, and be comparatively non-reactant with rain, a weak acid solution. Such stone exists in large quantities in the north but is relatively scarce in the south. However, all the stones were not subject to the same conditions after inscribing; stones preserved indoors and, to a lesser extent, underground, are more likely to survive with their inscriptions intact, whatever their composition. Stone was probably imported from the north of England, Scotland and Wales and, in the late period, from the Continent. It has not proved feasible to obtain a geo-

---

1 'North' is taken to mean that area of England north of a line from the north of the Wash to the mouth of the Dee at Chester.

2 R. I. Page, in a personal communication.　　　　3 Allen (1889), 221–32, esp. 225.

4 Taylor, H. M. & Taylor, J. (1965), map inside covers.　　　5 Clapham (1930), 67–8.

logical description of every inscribed stone; until this is done for every Anglo-Saxon carved and inscribed stone, and for every stone church, any estimate of the position remains incomplete. It might turn out that early carvers used local stone while later ones were able to import, or that stone was imported for some uses and not for others.

Non-stone objects are generally portable and their find-places are therefore of less importance than those of stones, though Durham II was found *in situ*. However the distribution of non-stone inscriptions in Britain, shown on Map 2, does confirm that the distribution pattern of Map 1 is not of inscribed objects *per se*, but of inscribed stones. Seven non-stone inscriptions are of uncertain or unknown provenance; Essex, Lancashire, Suffolk, the 'eadward' brooch, the 'eawen' ring, the 'sigerie' ring, the 'ðancas' ring, and the V&A crucifix. Finally, five inscriptions were found outside Britain: Auzon, Brussels I, Mortain and Rome I, II.

3 PRINCIPLES OF DATING OF INSCRIPTIONS

The vast majority of the inscriptions in the Hand-list date from *c.* A.D. 700 to *c.* A.D. 1100, although it is possible that some of the late texts could in fact date from the early years of the twelfth century. Some early texts have been alleged to be of seventh century date. There seems, however, to be no evidence to support a date in the seventh century for any texts except Jarrow I, Durham I and probably Durham II.[1] The reason for this lack of very early texts, especially in Northumbria, is not altogether clear. Each object is separately dated with the exception of the series of stones from Hartlepool, Lindisfarne and Whitby. The date of each of the stones in these series is based on the collective evidence of all the stones of the series.

Wherever possible, an object is dated on both indirect and direct evidence. Indirect evidence comprises formulaic comparison of the text with other similar ones, and the architectural or historical dating of a church where the object does not form part of its fabric. Direct evidence comprises: linguistic dating of the text where it is in Old English; epigraphic dating of the text; artistic dating of the carving or decoration of the object; archaeological dating of the object when found during controlled excavation; historical dating of the object; architectural dating of the fabric of which the object forms part. In the case of linguistic dating, it is possible that with the use of set formulae the language became formalised, or on occasion even archaised. However, this has not been proved in the case of any specific text,

---

[1] See entries numbered 61, 34, 35.

and is not therefore taken into account for the purposes of dating. The principles of epigraphic dating are explained in detail elsewhere.[1] Archaeological and artistic datings are based on the opinions of authorities in these fields.

4 FORMULAE OF TEXTS

Each of the texts under discussion, excluding those that are fragmentary or illegible, employs one or more of the following formulae.

Dedication formulae

Although it is hazardous to generalise from only eight examples, it might seem that the Anglo-Saxon church had no set dedication formula, since these texts all differ from each other. They all date from the tenth to eleventh century, with the exception of Jarrow I which is dated A.D. 685. This is probably fortuitous, since churches are known to have been built throughout the period. The examples are: Aldbrough, Deerhurst I, Jarrow I, Kirkdale i, York I, and probably Deerhurst II, Ipswich II and Lincoln I. Canterbury IV may also have been a dedication text, although it is now too fragmentary to be certain.

Descriptive formulae

These texts can be divided into three categories, depending on what is being described. Some individual resemblances occur within the types, but there are no set formulae. The texts are of all dates.

Type *a*: texts referring to the object itself. The examples are: Brussels I iii, Canterbury II i, Crowland, Eye, Great Edstone ii, Kirkdale ii, Orpington i, ii, iii, Wallingford I i, ii, Weeke and possibly Sinnington.

Type *b*: texts referring to carving or decoration on the object. The examples are: Auzon, Bishop Auckland i, ii, Brussels I i, Canterbury III ii, Dewsbury II, Dewsbury III i, ii, Durham I (all texts), Inglesham, Ipswich I i, ii, Ipswich III i, ii, Jarrow III, Mortain i, ii, North Elmham i, ii, Ruthwell (all texts), Sherburn i, York IV, V&A crucifix i, probably Norham I and possibly Sulgrave.

Type *c*: texts referring outside the object. The examples are: Bath i, ii, Bossington, Breamore I, Canterbury I i, Driffield, Hartlepool VI i, Newent ii (former part), Sandford, Swindon (latter part), and possibly Attleborough, Billingham ii and Manchester.

[1] Okasha (1968), 321–38.

Maker and owner formulae

These texts refer to the object in the first person and also contain the name of the maker or the owner of the object, or both. Athelney and the 'sigerie' ring contain a variant, a commissioner formula. The majority of the texts are on metal objects, presumably since these were more readily personalised than stones. The texts all date from the ninth century onwards, suggesting that these formulae were more popular in the later period. There are also similar runic texts, for example Bridekirk and Kirkheaton. The non-runic examples are: Alnmouth i, Athelney, Bodsham, Brussels I ii, Canterbury I i, Cuxton, Exeter, Great Edstone i, Kirkdale iii, Lancashire, Pershore, Sittingbourne i, ii, Wallingford II i, ii, 'sigerie' ring and probably 'eawen' ring. Similar texts are Canterbury II ii, Little Billing, Stratfield Mortimer (latter part) and Sutton i which also has a Christian curse. Suffolk i, ii may also have maker and owner formulae. Some descriptive and memorial texts are similar but have no personal pronoun, e.g. Brussels I iii (latter part) and Lanteglos.

Memorial formulae

There are three varieties of memorial formula used in the texts, as well as some miscellaneous texts which do not fit into any of the categories. The Old English texts use a set formula which is also found fairly frequently on runic stones. It may occur in a simple or a more elaborate, poetic, form. All the examples date from the eighth to ninth century, and all come from the Anglian dialect areas: Dewsbury I, Falstone, Wycliffe, Yarm, and probable Carlisle I, Gainford and Thornhill.

Some texts, mainly from the eighth and ninth centuries, employ an *ora pro* formula: Billingham i, Hartlepool IV, Hartlepool V i, ii, Lancaster I, Lancaster II, York VII, probably York V, and possibly Birtley. Three texts have a 'here lies' formula: Monkwearmouth II, Whitchurch and Winchester I. The remaining, miscellaneous, texts are: Canterbury III i, Durham II i, Haddenham, London I, Stratfield Mortimer (former part), York II, York III; probably Lanteglos, Norham II, Winchester III, York VIII; and possibly Alnmouth ii, Caistor, Hackness, Hartlepool O, Jarrow II, Manchester and Whitby III.

Personal names

A large group of texts contain only one or two Old English names, some with a Latin title. There are many similar runic examples. Several of these are the small gravestones known as 'name-stones', which contain only a cross and a text on one face;

some of these were probably placed inside the grave. Some name-stones have a slightly longer text, for example Birtley, Hartlepool IV and Hartlepool V (see above, under *Memorial formulae*). All the name-stones date from the eighth to the ninth century and come from the Anglian dialect areas. The examples with this formula are: Hartlepool III, Hartlepool VI ii, Hartlepool VII, Hartlepool VIII, Hexham I, Lindisfarne I, Lindisfarne II, Wensley I, Wensley II; probably Lindisfarne VII, Lindisfarne X, Monkwearmouth I; and possibly Lindisfarne VIII. Some of the other stones containing only a personal name may be related to the series of name-stones, and were probably commemorative. They are: Ardwall, Bishopstone, Chester-le-Street, Newent i, ii (latter part), Ripon, Whitby IV, Whitby XIV; probably Plymstock, Whitby VII, Workington; and possibly Knells.

The other texts in this group are on brooches and rings. Wilson suggested that those rings containing royal names are less likely to be personal possessions than royal gifts.[1] These are Laverstock and Sherburn ii. Some of the other texts are, or contain, coins or coin-copies: Canterbury I, Rome II, Winchester IV, 'eadward' brooch, and probably Rome I, Winchester II. In addition Attleborough and Bossington may have been influenced by coins. The names on Llysfaen, Swindon (former part) and possibly Essex are presumably those of the owners.

[1] Wilson, D. M. (1964), 56.

GENERAL BIBLIOGRAPHY

INTRODUCTION

The General Bibliography gives in full every reference quoted in abbreviated form in the Hand-list. Authors are quoted with their first names appearing as initials, and these are normalised; this is because of the considerable inconsistency of usage especially among nineteenth-century authors. The latest editions of all works are used except where an early date is of significance, as in a find-report. Anonymous authors are denoted (—) (1900) etc., but this list is kept to a minimum by using an author's name even if he is only mentioned in Proceedings. The dates given for periodicals are of the year to which the volume refers, failing which, the year of publication. Where 'Proceedings' occurs in the title, this refers to Proceedings of the Society in whose Journal it appears. Where this is not the case, it is made clear, e.g. 'Proceedings of the Committee'. If the title of an article appears differently on the Contents page and heading the article, the former is used.

The particular bibliographies referring to each inscription are in the form author (date), page reference, e.g. Jones (1877), 54. Editions of early authors appear under the author's name and the date of the edition, e.g. Bede (1950). Bede's *Historia Ecclesiastica* is also quoted by book (II) and chapter (2). In the cases, however, where an editor entirely recasts a work, this appears under the editor's name. e.g. Gough (1806). Illustrations, whether showing the text or not, are all noted as 'figs.'; these are numbered, as in the work, only if they are otherwise difficult to locate. For references to *BCS* see Birch (1883–93).

These individual bibliographies are comprehensive in that they contain every reference known to the author which discusses or illustrates the text. They are, however, selective, in that they exclude: unpublished works; bibliographical listings; works not mentioning the text of the object; works only mentioning a runic text on objects containing both; and reviews, unless they also make an original contribution. On the other hand, any published work falling into one of these categories is included if it is illustrated, contains the first reference to an object, gives a significant discussion of the object's dating or artistry, or is otherwise considered important.

Each entry contains an individual bibliography except for the series of stones from Hartlepool and Lindisfarne. Many works treat these series as groups and a general bibliography of each series is therefore given, preceding the entries. The individual stones dealt with in the works are given after each reference. The word 'general' in this context refers either to all the stones of the series, or to the series in general.

The illustrations mentioned are of the stones referred to in the work, unless further details are given. An illustrated article described as 'general' thus illustrates all the stones. For example, 'Collingwood, W. G. (1903–4), 223 & fig. (General; fig. of IV)' means that Collingwood's work deals with the series in general and illustrates stone IV; 'Brown, G. B. (1919), 195–228 & figs. (General)' means that Brown's work deals with and illustrates all the stones in the series. The series of Whitby stones have individual bibliographies, but the one general article is noted.

GENERAL BIBLIOGRAPHY

For an explanation of the abbreviations used, see pp. xiii–xv.

Åberg, N. F. (1943), *The Occident and the Orient in the Art of the Seventh Century* I. Kungl. Vitterhets Historie och Antikvitets Akademiens Handlingar LVI (i). Stockholm.

Addison, F., *et al.* (1865), 'The Saxon Inscription at Beckermont'. *Arch. Ael.* NS VI, 60–2.

Akerman, J. Y. (1847), *An Archaeological Index to Remains of Antiquity of the Celtic, Romano-British, and Anglo-Saxon Periods*. London.

Allen, J. R. (1883–4), 'Notes on Early Christian Symbolism'. *Proc. Soc. Ant. Scot.* NS VI, 380–464.

Allen, J. R. (1887), *Early Christian Symbolism in Great Britain and Ireland before the thirteenth century*. London.

Allen, J. R. (1889), *The Monumental History of the Early British Church*. London.

Allen, J. R. (1890), 'The Early Sculptured Stones of the West Riding of Yorkshire'. *JBAA* XLVI, 288–310.

Allen, J. R. (1891), 'Descriptive Catalogue of the Early Christian Sculptured Stones of the West Riding of Yorkshire'. *JBAA* XLVII, 156–71, 225–46.

Allen, J. R. (1903), 'Early Christian Art and Inscriptions'. *VCH Hampshire* II, 233–49. London.

Allen, J. R. (1906a), 'The Thurible of Godric'. *Reliq.* NS XII, 50–3.

Allen, J. R. (1906b), 'Early Christian Art'. *VCH Northamptonshire* II, 187–99. London.

Allen, J. R. and Browne, G. F. (1885), 'The Crosses at Ilkley. Part III (Conclusion)'. *JBAA* XLI, 333–58.

Anderson, J. (1881), *Scotland in Early Christian Times* 2nd series. Edinburgh.

André, J. L. (1879–80), 'Notes on Religious and other Inscriptions...'. *Reliq.* XX, 75–80.

André, J. L. (1883–4), 'Notes on Finger Rings'. *Reliq.* XXIV, 1–10.

Andrews, W. J. (1926), in *Hampshire Observer* 2 October 1926, 9.

Anscombe, A. (1926–7), 'The Ring of Bishop Eolla'. *Sussex N & Q* I, 136–9.

Arbman, H. (1958), 'Die Kremsmünsterer Leuchter'. *Meddelanden från Lunds Universitets Historiska Museum*, 170–92.

Archer, J. W. (1849), in 'Proceedings' 1 June 1849. *Arch. J.* VI, 289.

d'Ardenne, S. T. R. O. (1939), 'The Old English Inscription on the Brussels Cross'. *English Studies* XXI, 145–64, 271–2.

Axon, W. E. A. (1905), 'The "Angel Stone" in Manchester Cathedral'. *JBAA* NS XI, 169–71.

Bæksted, A. (1943), *Runerne: Deres Historie og Brug*. Copenhagen.

Baker, G. (1822–30), *The History and Antiquities of the County of Northampton* I. London.

Bakka, E. (1966), 'The Alfred Jewel and Sight'. *Antiq. J.* XLVI, 277–82.

Barnes, H. (1832), 'Account of the discovery of the Matrix of an Anglo-Saxon Seal'. *Arch.* XXIV, 359–61.

Bateson, E. ed. (1895), 'Chapel of St Waleric'. *History Northumberland* II, 489–95. Newcastle upon Tyne, London.

Battiscombe, C. F. ed. (1956), *The Relics of Saint Cuthbert...* Durham.

Beckwith, J. (1964), *Early Medieval Art*. London.

Bede, ed. J. Smith (1722), *Historiæ Ecclesiasticæ Gentis Anglorum Libri Quinque...* Cambridge.

Bede, ed. C. Plummer (1896), *Opera Historica: Historiam Ecclesiasticam Gentis Anglorum...* 2 vols. Oxford.

Bede, ed. B. Colgrave (1940), *Vita Sancti Cuthberti* in B. Colgrave ed. *Two Lives of St Cuthbert*. Cambridge.

Bede, edd. B. Colgrave and R. A. B. Mynors (1969), *Bede's Ecclesiastical History of the English People*. Oxford.

Beevor, T. (1851), in *Memoirs illustrative of the History and Antiquities of Norfolk and the city of Norwich...* Royal Arch. Inst. London.

Bennett, J. A. W. (1946–53), 'The Beginnings of Runic Studies in England'. *Saga-Book* XIII, 269–83.

Bentham, J. (1771), *The History and Antiquities of the Conventual and Cathedral Church of Ely...* Cambridge.

Biddle, M. (1965), 'Excavations at Winchester, 1964'. *Antiq. J.* XLV, 230–61.

Biddle, M. (1966), 'Excavations at Winchester, 1965'. *Antiq. J.* XLVI, 308–32.

Biddle, M. (1968), *Excavations near Winchester Cathedral 1961–7*. Winchester.

Binns, A. L. (1966), *East Yorkshire in the Sagas*. East Yorkshire Local History Series 22. York.

Birch, W. de G. (1879), 'Notes on an Inscribed Stone preserved in Ely Cathedral'. *JBAA* XXXV, 388–96.

Birch, W. de G. ed. (1881), *Memorials of St Guthlac of Crowland...* Wisbech.

Birch, W. de G. (1883–93), *Cartularium Saxonicum*. 3 vols. London.

Birch, W. de G. (1887), *Catalogue of Seals in the Department of Manuscripts in the British Museum* I. London.

Birch, W. de G. ed. (1892), *Liber Vitae: Register and Martyrology of New Minster and Hyde Abbey, Winchester*. London, Winchester.

Bjørkman, E. (1910), *Nordische Personennamen in England...* Studien zur englischen Philologie XXXVII. Halle.

Black, G. F. (1888–9), 'Notice of Two Sculptured Stones at Kirk Andreas, Isle of Man...'. *Proc. Soc. Ant. Scot.* NS XI, 332–43.

Blight, J. T. (1858), *Ancient Crosses and other Antiquities in the East of Cornwall*. London.

Blouet, L. (?1954), *Le Chrismale de Mortain, sa Vie et son Mystère*. Coutances.

Bloxam, M. H. (1877), 'On an Ancient Inscribed Sepulchral Slab, found at Monkwearmouth, in the County of Durham'. *Arch. J.* XXXIV, 298–300.

Bond, F. (1908), *Fonts and Font Covers*. London.

Bond, F. (1919), *Ely Cathedral*. Ely.

Booth, J. (?1936), *The Story of the Old Church and Monastery of Jarrow, A.D. 685* 2nd ed. Gloucester.

Boutell, C. (1849), *Christian Monuments in England and Wales...* London.

Bowen, M. (1967), 'Saxon Sundial in the Parish Church of All Saints, Orpington' in 'Researches and Discoveries in Kent'. *Arch. Cant.* LXXXII, 287–9.

Boyle, J. R. (?1822), *Comprehensive Guide to the County of Durham*. London.

Boyle, J. R. (1885), 'On the Monastery and Church of St Paul, Jarrow'. *Arch. Ael.* NS X, 195–216.

Boyle, J. R. (1886), 'On the Monastery and Church of St Peter, Monkwearmouth'. *Arch. Ael.* NS XI, 33–51.

Boyle, J. R. (1887–8), in 'Proceedings' 26 May 1888. *Proc. Soc. Ant. Newc.* NS III, 297–9.

Bradley, H., ed. S. Potter (1968), *The Making of English* rev. ed. London.

Brand, J. (1789), *The History and Antiquities...of Newcastle upon Tyne...* II. London.

Brand, J. (1792), in 'Appendix' 17 June 1790. *Arch.* X, 472.

Brandl, A. (1917), 'Zur Zeitbestimmung des Kreuzes von Ruthwell'. *Archiv* CXXXVI, 150–1.

Brassington, W. S. (?1895), *Historic Worcestershire...* London.

Braun, J. (1924), *Der christliche Altar in seiner geschichtlichen Entwicklung* I. Munich.

Neville, R. C., Baron Braybrooke (n.d.), *Catalogue of Rings in the Collection of the Right Hon. Lord Braybrooke, Audley End*. (No place or date of publication, but pre May 1859.)

Neville, R. C., Baron Braybrooke (1856), *The Romance of the Ring or the History and Antiquity of Finger Rings...* Saffron Walden.

Neville, R. C., Baron Braybrooke (1860), *A Catalogue of Rings in the Collection of the Right Hon. Lord Braybrooke, Audley End*. Saffron Walden.

Neville, R. C., Baron Braybrooke (1863), 'Ancient and Mediæval Finger Rings discovered in the County of Essex'. *Essex Arch. Soc.* II, 61–8.

Brayley, E. W. (1834), 'King Alfred's Jewel' in E. W. Brayley ed. *The Graphic and Historical Illustrator...* London.

Brøndsted, J. (1924), trans. A. J. Major, *Early English Ornament...* London, Copenhagen.

Brooke, J. C. (1779), 'An Illustration of a *Saxon* Inscription on the Church of *Kirkdale* in *Ryedale* in the *North-Riding* of the County of *York*'. *Arch.* V, 188–205.

Brooke, J. C. (1782), 'An Illustration of a *Saxon* Inscription remaining in the Church of *Aldbrough*, in *Holdernesse*, in the *East-Riding* of the County of *York*'. *Arch.* VI, 39–53.

Brown, G. B. (1915), *Saxon Art and Industry in the Pagan Period*. The Arts in Early England III. London.

Brown, G. B. (1916), 'Was the Anglo-Saxon an Artist?'. *Arch. J.* LXXIII, 171–94.

Brown, G. B. (1918–19), 'The Hartlepool Tombstones...'. *Proc. Soc. Ant. Scot.* 5S V, 195–228.

Brown, G. B. (1921), *The Ruthwell and Bewcastle Crosses...* The Arts in Early England V. London.

Brown, G. B. (1925), *Anglo-Saxon Architecture*. The Arts in Early England II 2nd ed. London.

Brown, G. B. (1926), *The Life of Saxon England in its Relation to the Arts*. The Arts in Early England I 2nd ed. London.

Brown, G. B. (1930), *Completion of the Study of the Monuments of the Great Period of the Art of Anglian Northumbria*. The Arts in Early England VI i. London.

Brown, G. B., ed. E. H. L. Sexton (1937), *Anglo-Saxon Sculpture*. The Arts in Early England VI ii. London.

Brown, G. B. and Lethaby, W. R. (1913), 'The Bewcastle and Ruthwell Crosses'. *Burl. Mag.* XXIII, 43–9.

Brown, W. (1899), 'St Cuthbert's Grave and Coffin'. *Ushaw Magazine* IX, 74–88, 117–32, 256–60.

Browne, G. F. (1880–4), in 'Proceedings' 26 May 1884. *Camb. Antiq. Comms.* V, cxxxii–cxxxv.

Browne, G. F. (1883), 'Description and Explanations of Saxon Stones...' in W. O. Blunt, *A Thousand Years of The Church in Chester-le-Street*, 182–8. London.

Browne, G. F. (1884–8), 'On various Inscriptions and supposed Inscriptions'. *Camb. Antiq. Comms.* VI, 1–16.

Browne, G. F. (1885a), 'Early Sculptured Stones in England.—I'. *Mag. Art* VIII, 78–82.

Browne, G. F. (1885b), 'Early Sculptured Stones in England.–II'. *Mag. Art* VIII, 154–9.

Browne, G. F. (1886), 'On Inscriptions at Jarrow and Monkwearmouth'. *Arch. Ael.* NS XI, 27–32.

Browne, G. F. (?1886), *Notes on the Remains of the Original Church of St Peter, Monkwearmouth...* Cambridge.

Browne, G. F. (1890), 'The Date of the Ruthwell Cross'. *Acad.* XXXVII, 170–1.

Browne, G. F. (1896), *The Conversion of the Heptarchy* rev. ed. London.

Browne, G. F. (1897), *Theodore and Wilfrith...* London.

Browne, G. F. (1899–1901), 'Runic and Ogam Characters and Inscriptions in the British Isles'. *Notices Proc. Royal Inst. G.B.* XVI, 164–87.

Browne, G. F. (1903), *St Aldhelm: his Life and Times.* London.

Browne, G. F. (1915), *The Recollections of a Bishop.* London.

Browne, G. F. (1916), *The Ancient Cross Shafts at Bewcastle and Ruthwell.* Cambridge.

Bruce, J. C. ed. (1880), *A Descriptive Catalogue of Antiquities, chiefly British, at Alnwick Castle.* Newcastle upon Tyne.

Bruce-Mitford, R. L. S. (1952), 'A Late-Saxon Silver Disk-Brooch from the Isle of Ely'. *BMQ* XVII, 15–16.

Bruce-Mitford, R. L. S. (1956), 'Late Saxon Disc-Brooches' in D. B. Harden ed. *Dark-Age Britain...*, 171–201. London.

Bruce-Mitford, R. L. S. (1969), 'The Art of the Codex Amiatinus'. *JBAA* 3 s XXXII, 1–25.

Bütow, H. (1935), *Das altenglische 'Traumgesicht vom Kreuz'.* Heidelberg.

Bugge, E. S. (1891–1903), *Norges Indskrifter med de Ældre Runer.* I *Det Norske Historiske Kildeskriftfond.* Christiania.

Bugge, E. S. (1908), 'Das Runendenkmal von Britsum in Friesland'. *Zeitschrift für Deutsche Philologie* XL, 174–84.

Burlin, R. B. (1968), 'The Ruthwell Cross, *The Dream of the Rood* and the Vita Contemplativa'. *Stud. Phil.* LXV, 23–43.

Butterworth, G. (1876), 'On the Priory and Church of Deerhurst'. *TBGAS* I, 96–104.

Butterworth, G. (1878), *Notes on The Priory and Church of Deerhurst, Gloucestershire.* Tewkesbury.

Butterworth, G. (1885), 'Newly Discovered Saxon Chapel at Deerhurst, Gloucestershire'. *JBAA* XLI, 413–18.

Butterworth, G. (1886–7), 'The Saxon Chapel at Deerhurst'. *TBGAS* XI, 105–16.

Butterworth, G. (1888), *Deerhurst, A Parish of the Vale of Gloucester.* Tewkesbury, London.

Cahen, M. and Olsen, M. (1930), *L'Inscription runique du Coffret de Mortain.* La Société de linguistique de Paris XXXII. Paris.

Calverley, W. S., ed. W. G. Collingwood (1899), *Notes on the Early Sculptured Crosses, Shrines and Monuments in the present Diocese of Carlisle.* CWAAS Extra Series XI. Kendal.

Camden, W. (1607), *Britannia*... London.

Cameron, C. L. (1901), 'Mortimer in Olden Time'. *Bucks. Berks. Oxon. Arch. J.* NS VII, 71–3.

Canham, A. S. (1890), 'Notes on the History of Crowland; its Charters and ancient Crosses'. *JBAA* XLVI, 116–29.

Canham, A. S. (1894), 'Notes on the History, Charters, and Ancient Crosses of Crowland'. *Fenland N & Q* II, 236–52.

Casson, S. (1931), 'Byzantinism'. *Burl. Mag.* LIX, 208–13.

Casson, S. (1933), 'Byzantium and Anglo-Saxon Sculpture'. *Burl. Mag.* LXII 26–36.

Cautley, H. M. (1937), *Suffolk Churches and their Treasures*. Ipswich.

Chadwick, H. M. (1901), 'Early Inscriptions in the North of England'. *Trans. Yorks. Dial. Soc.* I iii, 79–85.

Chamot, M. (1930), *English Mediæval Enamels*. University College (London) Monographs on English Mediæval Art II. London.

Chandler, R. (1763), *Marmora Oxoniensia*. Oxford.

Charlton, E. (1855–7), 'Runic Inscriptions'. *Proc. Soc. Ant. Newc.* I, 70–2.

Clapham, A. W. (1930), *English Romanesque Architecture before the Conquest*. Oxford.

Clapham, A. W. (1934a), *English Romanesque Architecture after the Conquest*. Oxford.

Clapham, A. W. (1934b), 'English Romanesque Sculpture'. *Listener* XII no. 302, 24 October 1934, 689–91.

Clapham, A. W. (1936), *Romanesque Architecture in Western Europe*. Oxford.

Clapham, A. W. (1947), 'Breamore Church'. *Arch. J.* CIV, 160.

Clapham, A. W. (1948a), 'The York Virgin and its Date'. *Arch. J.* CV, 6–13.

Clapham, A. W. (1948b), 'Churches seen in the East, North-East, and South of Yorkshire'. *Arch. J.* CV, 80–4.

Clarke, G. R. (1830), *The History and Description of the Town and Borough of Ipswich*... Ipswich.

Clarke, J. R. (1961), *The Alfred and Minster Lovell Jewels* 2nd ed. Oxford.

Clayton, P. T. B. (?1960), *Saxon Discoveries in London*. London.

Clifford, Bishop (1877), 'President's Inaugural Address'. *Proc. Som. Arch. Nat. Hist. Soc.* XXIII, 9–27.

Clutton-Brock, A. (1899), *The Cathedral Church of York*... Bell's Cathedral Series. London.

Cole, T. W., ed. A. J. Hatley (1945–7), 'Church Sundials'. *JBAA* 3 S X, 77–80.

Colgrave, B. ed. (1956), *Felix's Life of Saint Guthlac*. Cambridge.

Colgrave, B. and Cramp, R. (1965), *St Peter's Church, Wearmouth*. Gloucester.

Colgrave, B. and Romans, T. (1962), *A Guide to St Paul's Church Jarrow and its Monastic Buildings*. Gloucester.

Colgrave, H. (1955), *Saint Cuthbert of Durham* 3rd ed. Gateshead on Tyne.

Collingwood, R. G. and Wright, R. P. (1965), *The Roman Inscriptions of Britain*. I *Inscriptions on Stone*. Oxford.

Collingwood, W. G. (1901), 'Pre-Norman Remains'. *VCH Cumberland* I, 253–93. London.

Collingwood, W. G. (1903), 'Some Pre-Norman Finds at Lancaster'. *Reliq.* NS IX, 257–66.

Collingwood, W. G. (1903–4), in 'Proceedings' 9 September 1904. *Proc. Soc. Ant. Newc.* 3 S I, 219–26.

Collingwood, W. G. (1904), 'Some Crosses at Hornby and Melling in Lonsdale'. *Reliq.* NS X, 35–42.

Collingwood, W. G. (1907), 'Anglian and Anglo-Danish Sculpture in the North Riding of Yorkshire'. *YAJ* XIX, 267–413.

Collingwood, W. G. (1909), 'Anglian and Anglo-Danish Sculpture at York'. *YAJ* XX, 149–213.

Collingwood, W. G. (1911), 'Anglian and Anglo-Danish Sculpture in the East Riding...'. *YAJ* XXI, 254–302.

Collingwood, W. G. (1912), 'Anglo-Saxon Sculptured Stone'. *VCH Yorkshire* II, 109–31. London.

Collingwood, W. G. (1915a), 'Anglian and Anglo-Danish Sculpture in the West Riding...'. *YAJ* XXIII, 129–299.

Collingwood, W. G. (1915b), 'Notes on Early Crosses at Carlisle, Bewcastle and Beckermet'. *TCWAAS* NS XV, 125–31.

Collingwood, W. G. (1916), 'An Anglian Cross at Tullie House'. *TCWAAS* NS XVI, 279–81.

Collingwood, W. G. (1916–18), 'The Ruthwell Cross in its Relation to other Monuments of the Early Christian Age'. *Trans. Dumfr. Galloway Nat. Hist. Ant. Soc.* 3 S V, 34–84.

Collingwood, W. G. (1923), 'An Inventory of the Ancient Monuments of Cumberland'. *TCWAAS* NS XXIII, 206–76.

Collingwood, W. G. (1925), 'Early carved stones at Hexham'. *Arch. Ael.* 4 S I, 65–92.

Collingwood, W. G. (1927), *Northumbrian Crosses of the Pre-Norman Age*. London.

Collingwood, W. G. (1929), *Angles, Danes and Norse in the District of Huddersfield*. The Tolson Memorial Museum Publications Handbook 2. 2nd ed. Huddersfield.

Collingwood, W. G. (1932), 'A Pedigree of Anglian Crosses'. *Antiq.* VI, 35–54.

Collingwood, W. G. *et al.* (1911), in 'Proceedings' 27 April 1911. *TCWAAS* NS XI, 482–3.

Collinson, J. (1791), *The History and Antiquities of the County of Somerset...* I. Bath.

Condor, E. *et al.* (1911–12), in 'Proceedings' 13 June 1912. *Proc. Soc. Ant. Lon.* 2 S XXIV, 323–6.

Consitt, E. (1887), *Life of Saint Cuthbert*. London, New York.

Conway, M. (1912), 'The Bewcastle and Ruthwell Crosses'. *Burl. Mag.* XXI, 193–4.

Conybeare, E. (1906), *A History of Cambridgeshire*. Popular County Histories. London.

Cook, A. S. (1902), 'Notes on the Ruthwell Cross'. *PMLA* NS X, 367–90.

Cook, A. S. ed. (1905), *The Dream of the Rood. An Old English Poem attributed to Cynewulf*. Oxford.

Cook, A. S. (1912), *The Date of the Ruthwell and Bewcastle Crosses*. Trans. Connecticut Acad. Arts Sciences XVII, 213–361. New Haven, Connecticut.

Cook, A. S. (1915), 'The Date of the Old English Inscription on the Brussels Cross'. *MLR* X, 157–61.

Cooper, H. C. D. (?1964), *Notes on Old Byland Church*. (No place of publication.)

Cottrill, F. (1947), *Treasures of Winchester in the City Museums*. Winchester.

Cowen, J. D. and Barty, E. (1966), 'A lost Anglo-Saxon inscription recovered'. *Arch. Ael.* 4 S XLIV, 61–70.

Craig, J., in J. Sinclair ed. (1794), *Statistical Account of Scotland* X. Edinburgh.

Cramp, R. J. (1964), 'A name-stone from Monkwearmouth'. *Arch. Ael.* 4 S XLII, 294–8.

Cramp, R. J. (1965a), *Durham Cathedral: A Short Guide to the Pre-Conquest Sculptured Stones in the Dormitory*. Privately printed.

Cramp, R. J. (1965b), *Early Northumbrian Sculpture*. Jarrow Lecture 1965. Jarrow.

Craster, H. H. E. ed. (1914), 'Corbridge Township'. *History Northumberland* X, 3–233. Newcastle upon Tyne, London.

Crossley-Holland, K. trans., ed. B. Mitchell (1965), *The Battle of Maldon and other Old English Poems*. London.

Crossman, W. (1887–9), in 'Proceedings' 23 May 1889. *Proc. Soc. Ant. Lon.* 2S XII, 412–14.

Crowther, J. S. (1893), *An Architectural History of the Cathedral Church of Manchester...* Manchester.

Cuming, H. S. (1863), 'On Ancient Nielli'. *JBAA* XIX, 213–18.

Cuming, H. S. (1873), 'On Sun-Dials'. *JBAA* XXIX, 279–88.

Curtis, M. (1923), 'Old Byland'. *VCH NR Yorkshire* II, 3–5. London.

Dahl, I. (1938), 'Substantival Inflexion in Early Old English. Vocalic Stems'. *Lund Stud. Eng.* VII. Lund.

Dalton, O. M. (1903–5), 'A Note on the Alfred Jewel'. *Proc. Soc. Ant. Lon.* 2S XX, 71–7.

Dalton, O. M. (1909), *Catalogue of the Ivory Carvings of the Christian Era...of the British Museum*. London.

Dalton, O. M. (1911), *Byzantine Art and Archaeology*. Oxford.

Dalton, O. M. (1912), *British Museum: Franks Bequest: Catalogue of the Finger Rings...* London.

Dalton, O. M. (1925), *East Christian Art: A Survey of the Monuments*. Oxford.

Dalton, O. M. (1926–7), 'Early Chessmen from Dorsetshire'. *BMQ* I, 90–1.

Dalton, O. M. (1928), 'Early Chessmen of Whale's Bone excavated in Dorset'. *Arch.* LXXVII, 77–86.

Davidson, H. R. E. (1962), *The Sword in Anglo-Saxon England...* Oxford.

Davies, D. S. and Clapham, A. W. (1926), 'Pre-Conquest carved stones in Lincolnshire'. *Arch. J.* LXXXIII, 1–20.

Davis, C. E. (?1898), *The Saxon Cross found in Bath, July, 1898* 2nd ed. Bath.

Day, G. (?1904), *Seaford and Newhaven with their surroundings*. London.

Deanesly, M. (1961), *The Pre-Conquest Church in England*. An Ecclesiastical History of England I. London.

Dickens, A. G. (1961), 'Anglo-Scandinavian Antiquities'. *VCH York*, 332–6. London.

Dickins, B. (1946), 'The Dedication Stone of St Mary-le-Wigford, Lincoln'. *Arch. J.* CIII, 163–5.

Dickins, B. (1956), 'The Inscriptions upon the Coffin' in C. F. Battiscombe ed. *The Relics of Saint Cuthbert...*, 305–7. Durham.

Dickins, B. and Ross, A. S. C. (1940), 'The Alnmouth Cross'. *JEGP* XXXIX, 169–78.

Dickins, B. and Ross, A. S. C. edd. (1954), *The Dream of the Rood* 4th ed. London.

Dickson, W. (1852), *Four Chapters from the History of Alnmouth*. Newcastle upon Tyne.

Diehl, E. ed. (1925), *Inscriptiones Latinae Christianae Veteres* I. Berlin.

Dietrich, F. E. C. (1865), *De Cruce Ruthwellensi*. Marburg.

Dinwiddie, J. L. (1927), *The Ruthwell Cross and its Story*. Dumfries.

Dobbie, E. v. K. ed. (1942), *The Anglo-Saxon Minor Poems*. The Anglo-Saxon Poetic Records VI. New York.

Dobson, D. P. (1933), 'Anglo-Saxon Buildings and Sculpture in Gloucestershire'. *TBGAS* LV, 261–76.

Dodds, M. H. ed. (1940), 'Falstone Parish'. *History Northumberland* XV, 256–68. Newcastle upon Tyne.

Drummond, H. P. (1848), 'Church of St Nicholas, Ipswich'. *Suff. Arch. Assoc. Orig. Papers* Pt III November 1848, 21–8.

Dufty, A. R. (1951), 'St Nicholas' Church, Ipswich'. *Arch. J.* cviii, 136–7.

Dugdale, W. (1716), *A Brief Historical Account of the Cathedrals of York, Durham, and Carlisle...* (London 1715) in W. Dugdale, *The History of St Paul's Cathedral in London...* 2nd ed. Pt. iii. London.

Dugdale, W. (1817), *Monasticon Anglicanum* 2nd ed. i. London.

Duncan, H. (1857), 'An Account of the remarkable Monument...preserved in the Garden of Ruthwell Manse, Dumfriesshire'. *Arch. Scot.* iv, 313–26.

Duncan, P. B. (1836), *A Catalogue of the Ashmolean Museum...* Oxford.

Earle, J. (1901), *The Alfred Jewel: An Historical Essay*. Oxford.

Edwards, B. J. N. *et al.* (1966), 'A portion of an inscribed pre-conquest cross-shaft from Lancaster'. *Med. Arch.* x, 146–9.

Ekwall, B. O. E. (1924), 'The Scandinavian Element' in A. Mawer and F. M. Stenton edd. *Introduction to the Survey of English Place-names* i. EPNS i, 55–92. Cambridge.

Ekwall, B. O. E. (1930), 'How Long did the Scandinavian Language Survive in England?'. *A Grammatical Miscellany offered to Otto Jespersen on his Seventieth Birthday*, 17–30. London, Copenhagen.

Elgee, F. and Elgee, H. W. (1933), *The Archaeology of Yorkshire*. London.

Elliott, R. W. V. (1959), *Runes: An Introduction*. Manchester.

Ellis, H. (1849–53), in 'Proceedings' 20 June 1850. *Proc. Soc. Ant. Lon.* ii, 94.

Ellis, H. (1852), 'Portion of a Saxon Inscription'. *Arch.* xxxiv ii, 437.

Ellison, R. C. (1876), 'The Anglo-Saxon Monumental Stone found at Falstone in 1813'. *Arch. Ael.* NS vii, 272–3.

Eusebius, ed. J.-P. Migne (1875), *Commentaria in Psalmos* in *Patrologiæ Cursus Completus...Series Græca* xxiii. Paris.

Evans, J. (1873), 'Note on an Anglo-Saxon Knife, found in Kent, bearing an Inscription'. *Arch.* xliv ii, 331–4.

Evison, V. I. (1965), Review of Wilson, D. M. (1964). *Antiq. J.* xlv, 288–90.

Evison, V. I. (1967), 'A Sword from the Thames at Wallingford Bridge'. *Arch. J.* cxxiv, 160–89.

Eyre, C. (1887), *The History of S. Cuthbert...* 3rd ed. London, New York.

Fair, M. C. (1950), 'The West Cumberland group of pre-Norman crosses'. *TCWAAS* NS L, 91–8.

Fairholt, F. W. (1871), *Rambles of an Archaeologist among old books and in old places...* London.

Fallow, T. M. (1892), 'On a Portion of an Early Dial bearing runes, recently found'. *Reliq.* NS vi, 65–7.

Farrer, W. *et al.* (1914), 'Hornby'. *VCH Lancashire* viii, 191–201. London.

Feilitzen, O. v. (1937), *The Pre-Conquest Personal Names of Domesday Book*. Nomina Germanica. Uppsala.

Feilitzen, O. v. (1945), 'Some unrecorded old and middle english personal names'. *Namn och Bygd* xxxiii, 69–98.

Ferguson, R. S. (1893), 'An Archaeological Survey of Cumberland and Westmoreland'. *Arch.* liii ii, 485–531.

Figg, W. (1849), 'On Bishopston Church, with some General Remarks on the Churches of East Sussex'. *Sussex Arch. Colls.* ii, 272–84.

Figg, W. (1854), in 'Proceedings' 2 December 1853. *Arch. J.* xi, 60–1.

Figg, W. (1856), in 'Catalogue of Antiquities exhibited...at Chichester in July 1853'. *Sussex Arch. Colls.* VIII, 281–344.

Fisher, E. A. (1959), *An Introduction to Anglo-Saxon Architecture & Sculpture.* London.

Fisher, E. A. (1962), *The Greater Anglo-Saxon Churches...* London.

Fitch, Mr (1848), in 'Archaeological Intelligence'. *Arch. J.* V, 64–5.

de Fleury, C. Rohault (1870), *Mémoire sur les Instruments de la Passion de N.-S. J.-C.* Paris.

Flom, G. T. (1930), *Introductory Old English Grammar and Reader.* Boston, Massachusetts.

Förstemann, E. W. (1913), *Altdeutsches Namenbuch* II i 2nd ed. Bonn.

Förstemann, E. W. (1916), *Altdeutsches Namenbuch* II ii 2nd ed. Bonn.

Förster, M. (1906), 'Zwei altenglische Steininschriften'. *Englische Studien* XXXVI, 446–9.

Fowler, J. T. (1869–70), 'An Account of the Anglo Saxon Ring discovered near Driffield, in Yorkshire...'. *Proc. Geol. Polyt. Soc. WR Yorks.* V, 157–62.

Fowler, J. T. (1870), 'On some Ancient Inscribed Stones at Dewsbury'. *YAJ* I, 221–5.

Fowler, J. T. (1895), 'Runic Dial found at Skelton'. *YAJ* XIII, 189–90.

Fox, C. F. (1923), *The Archaeology of the Cambridge Region...* Cambridge.

Frank, G. (1888), *Ryedale and North Yorkshire Antiquities.* York, London.

Franks, A. W. (1873–6), in 'Proceedings' 14 January 1875. *Proc. Soc. Ant. Lon.* 2S VI, 305–7.

Franks, A. W. (1879–81), in 'Proceedings' 17 March 1881. *Proc. Soc. Ant. Lon.* 2S VIII, 468–70.

French, G. R. ed. (1863), *A Catalogue of the Antiquities and Works of Art exhibited at Ironmongers' Hall, London, in the month of May, 1861.* London.

Friesen, O. v. (1933), *Runorna.* Nordisk Kultur VI. Stockholm.

Fyson, D. R. (1960), 'Some late Anglian sculpture'. *Arch. Ael.* 4S XXXVIII, 149–52.

Gage, J. (1836), 'Sepulchral Stones found at Hartlepool in 1833'. *Arch.* XXVI, 479–82.

Galbraith, K. J. (1968), 'Early Sculpture at St Nicholas' Church, Ipswich'. *Proc. Suff. Inst. Arch.* XXXI ii, 172–84.

Garstang, J. (1906), 'Anglo-Saxon Remains'. *VCH Lancashire* I, 257–68. London.

Gatty, A., ed. H. K. F. Eden and E. Lloyd (1900), *The Book of Sun-Dials* 4th ed. London.

Gaye, L. L. W. and Galpin, A. (1912), 'Saxon Sun-dials, Masons' Marks and Consecration Crosses'. *Knowledge* XXXV, No. 525 (April 1912), 127–32.

Gibbs, M. ed. (1939), *Early Charters of the Cathedral Church of St Paul, London.* Royal Historical Society. London.

Gibson, E. ed. (1695), *Camden's Britannia.* London.

Gibson, J. P. (1911–12), in 'Proceedings' 25 January 1911. *Proc. Soc. Ant. Newc.* 3S V 1–2.

Gilbert, E. (1951–6), 'The Anglian remains in Jarrow Church'. *Proc. Soc. Ant. Newc.* 5S I, 311–33.

Gilbert, E. (1954), 'Deerhurst reconsidered'. *TBGAS* LXXIII, 73–114.

Gilbert, E. (1964), *Guide to the Priory Church & Saxon Chapel, Deerhurst* rev. ed. Tewkesbury.

Giles, J. A. (1848), *The Life and Times of Alfred the Great.* London.

Giles, J. A. (1858), 'Description of King Alfred's Jewel, with some observations on the art of working in gold and silver amongst the Anglo-Saxons' in J. A. Giles *et al.* edd., *The Whole Works of King Alfred the Great...* I. London.

Godfrey, J. (1962), *The Church in Anglo-Saxon England.* Cambridge.

Godfrey, W. H. (1948), 'The Parish Church of St Andrew, Bishopstone'. *Sussex Arch. Colls.* LXXXVII, 164–83.

Godfrey, W. H. ed. (1957), *Guide to the Church of St Andrew Bishopstone*. Oxford.

Goldschmidt, A. (1914), *Die Elfenbeinskulpturen*... I. Berlin.

Goldschmidt, A. (1918), *Die Elfenbeinskulpturen*... II. Berlin.

Goldschmidt, A. (1926), *Die Elfenbeinskulpturen*... IV. Berlin.

Gordon, A. (1726), *Itinerarium Septentrionale*... London.

Gorham, G. C. (1820), *The History and Antiquities of Eynesbury and St Neot's in Huntingdonshire; and of St Neot's in the County of Cornwall*... London.

Gorham, G. C. (1826), 'Anglo-Saxon Jewel, representing St Neot'. *Gents. Mag.* XCVI i, 497–9.

Goscelinus, ed. J.-P. Migne (1854), *S. Augustini Anglorum Apostoli Vita Minor* in *Patrologiæ Cursus Completus*... *Series Secunda* CL, cols. 743–64. Paris.

Gough, R. (1780), *British Topography*... I. London.

Gough, R. ed. (1806), W. Camden, *Britannia: or a Chorographical Description of the Flourishing Kingdoms of England, Scotland, and Ireland*... 2nd ed. 4 vols. London.

Gough, R. (1838), 'Sculptures from Various Parts of Yorkshire' in J. Carter, *Specimens of the Ancient Sculpture and Painting now remaining in England*..., 144–5. London.

Graham, P. A. (1920), *Highways and Byways in Northumbria*. London.

Gray, I. E. (1962), *The Church of St Mary the Virgin Newent*. Gloucester.

Green, A. R. (1926), *Sundials, Incised Dials or Mass-Clocks*... London.

Green, A. R. (1928), 'Anglo-Saxon Sundials'. *Antiq. J.* VIII, 489–516.

Green, A. R. (?1942), *The Saxon Church at Breamore*. Salisbury.

Green, A. R. and Green, P. M. (1951), *Saxon Architecture and Sculpture in Hampshire*. Winchester.

Green, V. H. H. (19), *Hauxwell Church*. Barnard Castle.

Greenwell, W. *et al.* (1862–8), 'Church Reports. III. S. Peter, Monkwearmouth'. *Trans. A.A. Soc. Durh. North.* I, Appendix, 3–8.

Greenwell, W. and Westwood, J. O. (1869), in 'Proceedings' 5 March 1869. *Arch. J.* XXVI, 282–3.

Grein, C. W. M., ed. R. P. Wülker (1894), *Bibliothek der angelsächsischen Poesie* II. Der Verceller Handschrift... Leipzig.

Greswell, W. H. P. (1922), *Dumnonia and the Valley of the Parret. A historical Retrospect*. Taunton.

Grienberger, T. v. (1900), 'Neue Beiträge zur Runenlehre'. *Zeitschrift für Deutsche Philologie* XXXII, 289–304.

Grose, F. (1784), *The Antiquities of England & Wales* II new ed. London.

Grosjean, P. (1961), 'Un fragment d'obituaire anglo-saxon du viiie siècle, naguère conservé à Munich'. Appendix 1. 'L'inscription latine de Hackness'. *Anal. Bolland.* LXXIX, 340–3.

Grueber, H. A. (1908), 'An Anglo-Saxon Brooch'. *Num. Chr.* 4S VIII, 83–4.

Grueber, H. A. and Keary, C. F. (1893), *A Catalogue of English Coins in the British Museum. Anglo-Saxon-Series* II. London.

Gurney, H. (1824), 'Observations on the Seal of Ethilwald Bishop of Dunwich, lately discovered at Eye, in Suffolk'. *Arch.* XX, 479–83.

Hackenbroch, Y. (1938), *Italienisches Email des frühen Mittelalters*. Basle, Leipzig.

Haigh, D. H. (1846a), 'Notes on Monumental Stones discovered at Hartlepool'. *JBAA* I, 185–96.

Haigh, D. H. (1846b), 'Deerhurst Church, Gloucestershire'. *JBAA* I, 9–19.

Haigh, D. H. (1852), in 'Proceedings' 15 January 1851. *JBAA* VII, 75–6.

Haigh, D. H. (1855–7), 'The Hackness Monument'. *Proc. Soc. Ant. Newc.* I, 176–8.

Haigh, D. H. (1856–7), 'On the Fragments of Crosses discovered at Leeds, in 1838'. *Proc. Geol. Polyt. Soc. WR Yorks.* III, 502–33.

Haigh, D. H. (1857), 'The Saxon Cross at Bewcastle'. *Arch. Ael.* NS I, 149–95.

Haigh, D. H. (?1858), *Notes on the History of S. Begu & S. Hild*... Hartlepool.

Haigh, D. H. (1861), *The Conquest of Britain by the Saxons*... London.

Haigh, D. H. (1869–70), 'The Runic Monuments of Northumbria'. *Proc. Geol. Polyt. Soc. WR Yorks.* V, 178–217.

Haigh, D. H. (1870), 'The Castlegate Inscription'. *Ann. Rpt. Council Yorks. Philos. Soc.* 50–6.

Haigh, D. H. (1875), 'On the Monasteries of S. Heiu and S. Hild'. *YAJ* III, 349–91.

Haigh, D. H. (1876), 'The Coins of the Danish Kings of Northumberland'. *Arch. Ael.* NS VII, 20–77.

Haigh, D. H. (1877), 'On Runic Inscription discovered at Thornhill'. *YAJ* IV, 416–55.

Haigh, D. H. (1879), 'On Yorkshire Dials'. *YAJ* V, 134–222.

Haigh, D. H. (1881), 'Note on an Inscribed Stone at Wensley'. *YAJ* VI, 45–6.

Haigh, D. H. *et al.* (1859), 'On the Fragments of Crosses discovered at Leeds, in 1838' in J. B. Greenwood, *The Early Ecclesiastical History of Dewsbury*..., 224–9. London, Dewsbury.

Haigh, D. H. *et al.*, ed J. T. Fowler (1881), 'On an Inscribed Stone found at Yarm'. *YAJ* VI, 47–52.

Hall, G. R. (1889), 'Notes on a Pre-Conquest Memorial Stone from Birtley...'. *Arch. Ael.* NS XIII, 252–77.

Hall, S. C. and Hall, A. M. (1859), *The Book of the Thames from Its Rise to its Fall*. London.

Hamper, W. (1821), 'The Runic Inscription on the Font at Bridekirk considered, and a new Interpretation proposed'. *Arch.* XIX, 379–82.

Hampson, E. M. and Atkinson, T. D. (1953), 'City of Ely'. *VCH Cambridgeshire* IV, 28–89. London.

Hanshall, J. H. (1823), 'The Ring of Alhstan, Bishop of Sherbourne, found at Llysfaen, Carnarvonshire'. *Gents. Mag.* XCIII ii, 483–4.

Harcourt, Rev. Canon (1848), in J. Fawcett, *Church Rides in the Neighbourhood of Scarborough, Yorkshire.* London, Scarborough.

Harder, H. (1932), 'Eine angelsächsische Ring-Inschrift'. *Archiv* CLXI, 37–9.

Hauttman, M. (1929), *Die Kunst des frühen Mittelalters.* Propyläen-Kunstgeschichte VI. Berlin.

Haverfield, F. J. and Greenwell, W. (1899), *A Catalogue of the Sculptured and Inscribed Stones in the Cathedral Library, Durham.* Durham.

Hayward, F. H. (1935), *Alfred the Great.* Great Lives No. 62. London.

Hedges, J. R. (1881), *The History of Wallingford in the County of Berks*... I. London.

Hencken, H. O'N. (1932), *The Archaeology of Cornwall and Scilly.* London.

Henry, F. (1940), *Irish Art in the Early Christian Period.* London.

Hensen, A. (1925), 'Het Egmonder Kruis'. *Het Gildeboek* VIII, 92–7.

Hewison, J. K. (1914), *The Runic Roods of Ruthwell and Bewcastle*... Glasgow.

Hewitt, J. (1874), 'Inscription recording the Building of St Chad's Church, Stafford'. *Arch. J.* XXXI, 216–20.

Hickes, G. (1700–1), in a letter. *Philos. Trans.* XXII, 464–9.

Hickes, G. (1705), *Linguarum Vett. Septentrionalium Thesaurus*... 2 vols. Oxford.

Hill, A. du Boulay (1897a), in Account of a Meeting of the *Royal Archaeological Institute* 9 August 1897. *Athenæum* No. 3642, 233.

Hill, A. du Boulay (1897b), in 'Proceedings' 9 August 1897. *Arch. J.* LIV, 408–9.

Hill, A. du Boulay (1898), 'A Saxon Church at Breamore, Hants.'. *Arch. J.* LV, 84–7.

Hill, A. du Boulay (1916), 'Pre-Norman Churches and Sepulchral Monuments of Nottinghamshire'. *Arch. J.* LXXIII, 195–206.

Hill, J. W. F. (1948), *Medieval Lincoln*. Cambridge.

Himsworth, J. B. (1953), *The Story of Cutlery from Flint to Stainless Steel*. London.

Hinds A. B. ed. (1896), 'Hexham Borough'. *History Northumberland* III, 105–308. Newcastle upon Tyne, London.

Hodges, C. C. (1893), 'The Pre-Conquest Churches of Northumbria'. *Reliq.* NS VII, 1–18, 65–85, 140–56.

Hodges, C. C. (1894), 'The Pre-Conquest Churches of Northumbria'. *Reliq.* NS VIII, 1–12, 65–83, 193–205.

Hodges, C. C. (1905), 'Anglo-Saxon Remains'. *VCH Durham* I, 211–40. London.

Hodges, C. C., rev. J. Gibson (1921), *Guide to the Priory Church of St Andrew, Hexham*... 2nd ed. Hexham.

Hodges, C. C. (1921–2), in 'Proceedings' 29 August 1922. *Proc. Soc. Ant. Newc.* 3S X, 292–5.

Hodges, C. C. and Gibson, J. (1919), *Hexham and its Abbey*. Hexham.

Hodgkin, J. E. (1913), *Durham*. London.

Hodgkin, R. H. (1952), *A History of the Anglo-Saxons* 3rd ed. 2 vols. Oxford.

Hodgson, J. C. ed. (1897), 'Birtley Church'. *History Northumberland* IV, 357–62. Newcastle upon Tyne, London.

Hodgson, J. F. (1895), 'Darlington and Hartlepool Churches'. *Arch. Ael.* NS XVII, 145–243.

Hodgson, J. F. (1899), 'The Church of St Andrew Auckland...'. *Arch. Ael.* NS XX, 28–206.

Hodgson, J. F. (1902), 'On "Low Side Windows"'. *Arch. Ael.* NS XXIII, 42–235.

Hodgson, J. F. (1906–11), 'The Churches of Escomb, Jarrow, and Monkwearmouth. The monastical choir, or church of S. Paul, Jarrow'. *Trans. A. A. Soc. Durh. North.* VI, 131–62.

Hofmann, D. (1955), 'Die Inschriften von Kirkdale und Aldbrough'. *Bibliotheca Arnamagnæana* XIV, 211–13.

Hollings, M. (1923), 'Stratfield Mortimer'. *VCH Berkshire* III, 422–8. London.

Home, G. (1915), *The Evolution of an English Town. Being the story of the ancient town of Pickering in Yorkshire*... 2nd ed. London.

Horsfield, T. W. (1835), *The History, Antiquities, and Topography of the County of Sussex* I. Lewes.

Horsley, J. (1732), *Britannia Romana*... London.

Howorth, H. H. (1914), 'The great Crosses of the seventh century in Northern England'. *Arch. J.* XXI, 45–64.

Howorth, H. H. (1917), *The Golden Days of the Early English Church*... 3 vols. London.

Hübner, Ae. (1876), *Inscriptiones Britanniae Christianae*. Berlin, London.

Hughes, H. D. and Falkner, J. M. (1925), *A History of Durham Cathedral Library*. Durham.

Hunter Blair, P. (1956), *An Introduction to Anglo-Saxon England*. Cambridge.

Hutchinson, W. (1778), *A View of Northumberland*... II. Newcastle upon Tyne.

Hutchinson, W. (1787), *The History and Antiquities of the County Palatine of Durham* II. Newcastle upon Tyne.

Hyslop, R. (1960), *St Peter's Church Monkwearmouth*. Gloucester.

Iago, W. (1890–1), 'Recent Archaeological Discoveries in Cornwall...'. *J. Royal Inst. Cornwall* x, 185–262.

Iago, W. (1896), in 'Report of the Forty-Ninth Annual Meeting held at Launceston' 13 August 1895. *Arch. Camb.* 5 S XIII, 145–75.

Jackson, C. J. (1911), *An Illustrated History of English Plate...* I. London.

Jackson, E. D. C. and Fletcher, E. G. M. (1956), 'Porch and Porticus in Saxon Churches'. *JBAA* 3 S XIX, 1–13.

Jackson, F. H. and Appleton, C. R. (?1964), *Chester-le-Street Urban District Council: Official Guide*. London.

Jefferson, S. (1842), *The History and Antiquities of Cumberland...* II. Carlisle.

Jerome, ed. J.-P. Migne (1845), *Vita S. Pauli Primi Eremitae* in *Patrologiæ Cursus Completus... Series (Latina) Prima* XXIII. Paris.

Jessup, R. F. (1930), *The Archaeology of Kent*. London.

Jessup, R. F. (1950), *Anglo-Saxon Jewellery*. London.

Jewitt, L. (1879–80), 'A Note on King Alfred's Jewel'. *Reliq.* XX, 65–6.

Johnson, M. (1781), in a letter 2 May 1737. *Bibliotheca Topographica Britannica* II ii, 67–70. London.[1]

Johnson, R. J. (1866), 'S. Peter's, Monkwearmouth'. *Ecclesiologist* XXVII, 361–4.

Jones, W. (1877), *Finger-Ring Lore...* London.

Kaske, R. E. (1967), 'The Silver Spoons of Sutton Hoo'. *Speculum* XLII, 670–2.

Kemble, J. M. (1840), 'On Anglo-Saxon Runes'. *Arch.* XXVIII, 327–72.

Kendrick, T. D. (1934), 'Some Types of Ornamentation on Late Saxon and Viking Period Weapons in England'. *Eurasia Sept. Antiq.* IX, 392–8.

Kendrick, T. D. (1938), *Anglo-Saxon Art to A.D. 900*. London.

Kendrick, T. D. (1941), 'Late Saxon Sculpture in Northern England'. *JBAA* 3 S VI, 1–19.

Kendrick, T. D. (1949), *Late Saxon and Viking Art*. London.

Kendrick, T. D. and Hawkes, C. F. C. (1932), *Archaeology in England and Wales 1914–1931*. London.

Kendrick, T. D. and Radford, C. A. R. (1943), 'Recent Discoveries at All Hallows, Barking'. *Antiq. J.* XXIII, 14–18.

Kent, W. R. G. (1947), *The Lost Treasures of London*. London.

Keyser, C. E. (1905), 'Notes on a Sculptured Tympanum at Kingswinford Church, Staffordshire...'. *Arch. J.* LXII, 137–46.

Keyser, C. E. (1921), 'An Architectural Account of the Churches of Great and Little Coxwell, Coleshill, Inglesham, Buscot and Eaton Hastings' cont. *Bucks. Berks. Oxon. Arch. J.* XXVI, 33–44.

Keyser, C. E. (1927), *A List of Norman Tympana and Lintels...* 2nd ed. London.

King, E. (1964), *The Church of Saint Peter Hackness* rev. ed. London.

Kirby, J. (1764), *The Suffolk Traveller...* 2nd ed. London.

Kitchin, G. W. (1905), 'The Contents of St Cuthbert's Shrine'. *VCH Durham* I, 241–58. London.

Kitzinger, E. (1956), 'The Coffin-Reliquary' in C. F. Battiscombe ed. *The Relics of Saint Cuthbert...*, 202–304. Durham.

Knowles, W. H. (1931), 'The Church of S. John Baptist, Inglesham, Wilts.'. *TBGAS* LIII, 191–206.

Kurth, B. (1943), 'Ecclesia and an Angel on the Andrew Auckland Cross'. *J. Warburg Courtauld Insts.* VI, 213–14.

[1] Bound in vol. III.

Labarte, J. (1855), *Handbook of the Arts of the Middle Ages and Renaissance*... London.

Labarte, J. (1875), *Histoire des Arts Industriels au Moyen Âge et à l'Époque de la Renaissance* 2nd ed. III. Paris.

de Laborde, L. E. S. J. (1852), *Notice des Émaux exposés dans les Galeries du Musée du Louvre* I. Paris.

Lambe, R. (1774), *An Exact and Circumstantial History of the Battle of Floddon. In verse*... Berwick upon Tweed.

Lambert, M. R. and Sprague, M. S. (1933), *Lincoln*. Oxford.

Langdon, A. G. (1906), 'Early Christian Monuments'. *VCH Cornwall* I, 407–49. London.

Langdon, A. G. and Allen, J. R. (1888), 'The Early Christian Monuments of Cornwall'. *JBAA* XLIV, 301–25.

Langdon, A. G. and Allen, J. R. (1895), 'Catalogue of the Early Christian Inscribed Monuments in Cornwall'. *Arch. Camb.* 5 S XII, 50–60.

Langlands, J. C. (1856–62), 'Annual Address'. *Proc. Berw. Nat. Club* IV, 119–39.

Laveille, A. (1899), 'L'Église de Mortain' in l'Abbé Adam *et al.*, *La Normandie Monumentale*... *Manche* II. Le Havre.

Leclercq, H. (1907 *a*), 'Autel' in F. Cabrol and H. Leclercq edd., *Dictionnaire d'Archéologie Chrétienne et de Liturgie* I ii, cols. 3155–89. Paris.

Leclercq, H. (1907 *b*), 'Anneaux' in F. Cabrol and H. Leclercq edd., *Dictionnaire d'Archéologie Chrétienne et de Liturgie* I ii, cols. 2174–223. Paris.

Leclercq, H. (1910 *a*), 'Cercueils' in F. Cabrol and H. Leclercq edd., *Dictionnaire d'Archéologie Chrétienne et de Liturgie* II ii, cols. 3274–96. Paris.

Leclercq, H. (1910 *b*), 'Cadrans Solaires' in F. Cabrol and H. Leclercq edd., *Dictionnaire d'Archéologie Chrétienne et de Liturgie* II ii, cols. 1541–6. Paris.

Leclercq, H. (1930), 'Londres' in F. Cabrol and H. Leclercq edd., *Dictionnaire d'Archéologie Chrétienne et de Liturgie* IX ii, cols. 2336–407. Paris.

Leclercq, H. (1935), 'Mortain' in F. Cabrol and H. Leclercq edd., *Dictionnaire d'Archéologie Chrétienne et de Liturgie* XII i, cols. 52–6. Paris.

Le Cordier (1865), 'Coffret de l'ancienne collégiale de Mortain'. *Bulletin Monumental* 4 S I, 182–4.

Leeney, F., ed. W. Rye (1909), *Norwich City Museum: Catalogue of Antiquities*. Norwich.

Leeney, O. H. (1911), 'The Church of Bishopstone, Sussex'. *Antiq.* XLVII, 369–74.

Legge, W. H. (1903), 'The Ancient Church of Bishopston, in Sussex'. *Reliq.* NS IX, 173–85.

Leland, J., ed. T. Hearne (1744), *The Itinerary of John Leland the Antiquary* 2nd ed. 9 vols. Oxford.

Leland, J., ed. T. Hearne (1770), *Antiquarii de Rebus Britannicis Collectanea* rev. ed. 6 vols. London.

Lethaby, W. R. (1912), 'The Ruthwell Cross'. *Burl. Mag.* XXI, 145–6.

Lethaby, W. R. (1913), 'Is Ruthwell Cross an Anglo-Celtic Work?'. *Arch. J.* LXX, 145–61.

Lethbridge, T. C. (1938), 'Anglo-Saxon Remains'. *VCH Cambridgeshire* I, 305–33. London.

Levison, W. (1943), 'The inscription on the Jarrow cross'. *Arch. Ael.* 4 S XXI, 121–6.

Levison, W. (1946), *England and the Continent in the Eighth Century*. Oxford.

Lewis, S. (1842), *A Topographical Dictionary of England*... 5th ed. IV. London.

Lind, E. H. (1905–15), *Norsk-Isländska Dopnamn ock Fingerade Namn från Medeltiden*. Uppsala.

Lingard, J. (1845), *The History and Antiquities of the Anglo-Saxon Church*. London.

Logeman, H. (1891), *L'Inscription anglo-saxonne du Reliquaire de la Vraie Croix au Trésor de l'Église des SS.-Michel-et-Gudule à Bruxelles*. Mémoires couronnés et autres Mémoires XLV. Gand, Leipzig.

27

Longhurst, M. H. ed. (1923), *Burlington Fine Arts Club. Catalogue of an Exhibition of Carvings in Ivory*. London.

Longhurst, M. H. (1926), *English Ivories*. London.

Longstaffe, W. H. D. (1861), 'Hexham Church'. *Arch. Ael.* NS V, 150–8.

Lower, M. A. (1840), in a letter 29 January 1840. *Gents. Mag.* NS XIV, 496.

Lundström, P. (1960), 'The Man with the Captive Birds'. *Acta Arch.* XXXI, 190–8.

Lysons, D. and Lysons, S. (1816), *Magna Britannia...* London.

Macalister, R. A. S. (1929), 'The Ancient Inscriptions of the South of England'. *Arch. Camb.* LXXXIV, 179–96.

Mackay, M. L. (1923), 'Skelton'. *VCH NR Yorkshire* II, 405–10. London.

Maclagan, E. (1923), 'A Romanesque Relief in York Minster'. *Proc. Brit. Acad.* X, 479–85.

MacLean, G. E. (1893), *An Old and Middle English Reader...* New York, London.

Maclean, J. (1876), *The Parochial and Family History of the Deanery of Trigg Minor, in the County of Cornwall* II. London, Bodwin.

Macray, J. (1862), 'King Alfred's Jewel'. *N & Q* 3 S II, 493.

Madden, F. (1856), 'Anglo-Saxon Charters of Eadgar and Offa, granted to the Abbey of St Denis'. *Arch. J.* XIII, 355–71.

Magnuson, F. (1820), 'Forsøg til Forklaring...'. *Antiq. Annaler* III, 339–51.

Magnuson, F. (1822), 'De Annulo aureo...'. *Arch. Ael.* I, 136–41.

Maryon, H. (1950), 'A Sword of the Viking Period from the River Witham'. *Antiq. J.* XXX, 175–9.

Maskell, W. (1872), *A Description of the Ivories Ancient & Mediæval in the South Kensington Museum*. London.

Maskell, W. (1875), *Ivories: Ancient and Mediæval*. South Kensington Museum Art Handbooks No. 2. London.

Mason, J. R. and Valentine, H. (1928), 'Find of pre-Norman Stones at St Michael's Church, Workington'. *TCWAAS* NS XXVIII, 59–62.

Meaney, A. (1964), *A Gazetteer of Early Anglo-Saxon Burial Sites*. London.

Mee, A., ed. E. T. Long (1966), *The King's England. Gloucestershire* rev. ed. London.

Michel, A. ed. (1905), *Histoire de l'Art depuis les Premiers Temps Chrétiens jusqu'à nos Jours* I ii. Paris.

Micklethwaite, J. T. (1896), 'Something about Saxon Church Building'. *Arch. J.* LIII, 293–351.

Middleton, J. H. (1885–7), in 'Proceedings' 26 November 1885. *Proc. Soc. Ant. Lon.* 2 S XI, 15–19.

Middleton, J. H. (1887), 'On a Saxon Chapel at Deerhurst, Gloucestershire'. *Arch.* L i, 66–71.

Millers, G. (1808), *A Description of the Cathedral Church of Ely...* London.

Milles, Dr (1773), 'Observations on the *Aestel*'. *Arch.* II, 75–9.

Milner, J. (1812), 'Account of an Ancient Manuscript of St John's Gospel'. *Arch.* XVI, 17–21.

Minns, G. W. (1899–1900), 'On a Saxon Sepulchral Monument at Whitchurch'. *Papers Proc. Hamps. Field Club Arch. Soc.* IV, 171–4.

Mitchell, H. P. (1925), 'English or German? A Pre-Conquest Gold Cross'. *Burl. Mag.* XLVII, 324–30.

Moger, O. M. (1911), 'Breamore Liberty'. *VCH Hampshire* IV, 596–602. London.

Molinier, E. C. L. M. (1902), *Histoire générale des arts appliqués à l'industrie du Ve à la fin du XVIIIe siècle* IV. Paris.

Morewood, C. C. (1914), 'Great Edston'. *VCH NR Yorkshire* I, 476–8. London.

Morris, J. E. (1931), *The North Riding of Yorkshire* 3rd ed. London.

Morris, J. E. (1932), *The East Riding of Yorkshire* 3rd ed. London.

Moss, A. A. (1952–4), 'Niello'. *Stud. Conserv.* I, 49–62.

Moss, A. A. (1953), 'Niello'. *Antiq. J.* XXXIII, 75–7.

Moulin, H. (1865), *Dissertation historique et archéologique sur l'église collégiale de Mortain.* Mortain.

Moulin, H. (1923), *La petite Suisse normande* 2nd ed. Mortain.

Musgrave, W. (1698), in a letter. *Philos. Trans.* XX, 441.

Musgrave, W. (1715), *Dissertatio de Icuncula quondam M. Regis Aelfredi.* Exeter.

Musgrave, W. (1716), *Dissertatio de Icuncula Quondam M. Regis Aelfredi* (Exeter 1715) in *Belgium Britannicum...* II. Exeter.

Nairn, I. and Pevsner, N. (1965), *The Buildings of England. Sussex.* Harmondsworth.

Napier, A. S. (1901), 'Contributions to Old English Literature: 2. The Franks Casket'. *An English Miscellany presented to Dr Furnivall in honour of his seventy-fifth birthday*, 362–81. Oxford.

Napier, A. S. (1903–6), 'Contributions to Old English Lexicography'. *Trans. Phil. Soc.*, 265–358.

Nelson, P. (1939), 'An Anglo-Saxon Gold Finger-ring'. *Antiq. J.* XIX, 182–4.

Nicolson, W., ed. Bishop of Barrow-in-Furness (1902), 'Diaries' Part II. *TCWAAS* NS II, 155–230.

Norman, F. (1936), Review of Bütow (1935). *Angl. Beib.* XLVII, 6–10.

Nuttall, B. H. (?1963), *West Riding Village: A History of Thornhill.* Thornhill.

Okasha, E. (1967), 'An Anglo-Saxon inscription from All Hallows, Barking-by-the-Tower'. *Med. Arch.* XI, 249–51.

Okasha, E. (1968), 'The Non-Runic Scripts of Anglo-Saxon Inscriptions'. *Trans. Camb. Bibl. Soc.* IV, 321–38.

Okasha, E. (1969), 'Notes on some Anglo-Saxon Architectural Sculpture'. *JBAA* 3 s XXXII, 26–9.

Okasha, E. and Webster, L. (1970), 'An Anglo-Saxon Ring from Bodsham, Kent'. *Antiq. J.* L i, 102–4.

Oliver, G. (1829), 'Account of the Town of Castor, co. Lincoln'. *Gents. Mag.* XCIX ii, 221–4.

Oliver, G. (1831), 'Some Account of Castor, co. Lincoln'. *Gents. Mag.* XCXI ii, 203–5.

Olsen, M. (1930), 'Notes on the Urswick inscription'. *Norsk Tidsskrift* IV, 282–6.

Oman, C. C. (1930), *Victoria and Albert Museum. Department of Metalwork. Catalogue of Rings.* London.

Oman, C. C. (1931), 'Anglo-Saxon Finger Rings'. *Apollo* XIV, 104–9.

Oman, C. C. (1957), *English Church Plate 597–1830.* London.

Page, R. I. (1958), 'Northumbrian *æfter* (= in memory of)+accusative'. *Stud. Neophil.* XXX, 145–52.

Page, R. I. (1959 a), 'Language and Dating in OE Inscriptions'. *Angl.* LXXVII, 385–406.

Page, R. I. (1959 b), 'An early drawing of the Ruthwell Cross'. *Med. Arch.* III, 285–8.

Page, R. I. (1961), 'The Old English Rune *ear*'. *Med. Aev.* XXX, 65–79.

Page, R. I. (1962), 'The Use of Double Runes in Old English Inscriptions'. *JEGP* LXI, 897–907.

Page, R. I. (1964), 'The Inscriptions' in D. M. Wilson, *Anglo-Saxon Ornamental Metalwork 700–1100 in the British Museum.* Catalogue of Antiquities of the Later Saxon Period I, 67–90. London.

Page, R. I. (1967), 'Note on the Inscription', in M. Bowen, 'Saxon Sundial in the Parish Church of All Saints, Orpington', in 'Researches and Discoveries in Kent'. *Arch. Cant.* LXXXII, 289–91.

Page, R. I. (1968), 'The runic solidus of Schweindorf, Ostfriesland, and related runic solidi'. *Med. Arch.* XII, 12–25.

Page, R. I. (1969), 'Runes and Non-Runes' in D. A. Pearsall and R. A. Waldron edd., *Medieval Literature and Civilisation. Studies in memory of G. N. Garmonsway*. London.

Page, W. *et al.* (1937), 'Little Billing'. *VCH Northamptonshire* IV, 74–6. London.

Paley, F. A. (1844), in T. Combe ed., *Illustrations of Baptismal Fonts*. London.

Parker, C. A., rev. W. G. Collingwood (1926), *The Gosforth District: its Antiquities and Places of Interest. CWAAS* Extra Series XV. Kendal.

Parker, J. H. (1846), *A Companion to the Fourth Edition of a Glossary of Terms used in...Gothic Architecture*. Oxford.

Pauli, R., ed. T. Wright (1852), *The Life of King Alfred*. London.

Payne, G. (1893), *Collectanea Cantiana: or Archaeological Researches in the Neighbourhood of Sittingbourne, and other parts of Kent*. London.

Peers, C. R. (1901), 'Saxon Churches of the St Pancras type'. *Arch. J.* LVIII, 402–34.

Peers, C. R. (1915–16), in 'Proceedings' 26 May 1915. *Proc. Soc. Ant. Newc.* 3 S VII, 53.

Peers, C. R. (1925), 'The Inscribed and Sculptured Stones of Lindisfarne'. *Arch.* LXXIV, 255–70.

Peers, C. R. *et al.* (1906–7), in 'Proceedings' 1 February 1906. *Proc. Soc. Ant. Lon.* 2 S XXI, 52–9.

Peers, C. R. *et al.* (1914–15), in 'Proceedings' 11 March 1915. *Proc. Soc. Ant. Lon.* 2 S XXVII, 132–7.

Peers, C. R. and Radford, C. A. R. (1943), 'The Saxon Monastery of Whitby'. *Arch.* LXXXIX, 27–88.

Pegge, S. (1773), 'Observations on the Mistakes of Mr *Lisle* and Mr *Hearne*...'. *Arch.* II, 68–74.

Pegge, S. (1777), 'Illustration of a gold enamelled Ring supposed to have been the Property of *Alhstan*, Bishop of *Sherbourne*...'. *Arch.* IV, 47–68.

Pegge, S. (1779), 'Remarks on Governor *Pownall's* Conjecture concerning the *Croyland* Boundary Stone'. *Arch.* V, 101–5.

Pegge, S. (1780), under pseudonym T. Row, in a letter. *Gents. Mag.* L, 74–5.

Pegge, S. (1785), 'Observations on the present *Aldbrough* Church at *Holderness*...'. *Arch.* VII, 86–9.

Pegge, S. (1787), *A Sylloge of the remaining Authentic Inscriptions relative to the Erection of our English Churches*... Bibliotheca Topographica Britannica VI, No. XLI. London.

Penn, A. W. *et al.* (1961), *St Gregory's Minster, Kirkdale* rev. ed. Kirkdale.

Pennant, T. (1774), *A Tour in Scotland and Voyage to the Hebrides MDCCLXXII*. Chester.

Pettigrew, T. J. (1888), *Chronicles of the Tombs*... London.

Pevsner, N. (1951), *The Buildings of England. Cornwall*. Harmondsworth.

Pevsner, N. (1953), *The Buildings of England. County Durham*. Harmondsworth.

Pevsner, N. (1954), *The Buildings of England. Cambridgeshire*. Harmondsworth.

Pevsner, N. (1957), *The Buildings of England. Northumberland*. Harmondsworth.

Pevsner, N. (1961a), *The Buildings of England. Northamptonshire*. Harmondsworth.

Pevsner, N. (1961b), *The Buildings of England. Suffolk*. Harmondsworth.

Pevsner, N. (1962), *The Buildings of England. London. 2. The Cities of London and Westminster* 2nd ed. Harmondsworth.

Pevsner, N. (1963), *The Buildings of England. Wiltshire*. Harmondsworth.

Pevsner, N. (1966), *The Buildings of England. Berkshire*. Harmondsworth.

Pevsner, N. (1967a), *The Buildings of England. Cumberland and Westmoreland*. Harmondsworth.

Pevsner, N., rev. E. Radcliffe (1967b), *The Buildings of England. Yorkshire. The West Riding* 2nd ed. Harmondsworth.

Pevsner, N. (1969), *The Buildings of England. Lancashire. 2. The Rural North*. Harmondsworth.

Pevsner, N. and Harris, J. (1964), *The Buildings of England. Lincolnshire*. Harmondsworth.

Pevsner, N. and Lloyd, D. (1967), *The Buildings of England. Hampshire and the Isle of Wight*. Harmondsworth.

Pfeilstücker, S. (1936), *Spätantikes und germanisches Kunstgut in der frühangelsächsischen Kunst, nach lateinischen und altenglischen Schriftquellen*. Berlin.

Phelps, J. J. (1905), 'An Ancient Sculptured Stone in Manchester Cathedral'. *Trans. Lancs. Ches. Antiq. Soc.* XXIII, 172–98.

Phillips, E. M. (1939), 'Supplementary Notes on the Ancient Stone Crosses of Devon'. *Trans. Devon Assoc. Adv. Sc. Lit. Art* LXXI, 231–41.

Phillips, E. M. (1950), in A. Fox, 'Seventeenth Report on the Early History of Devon'. *Trans. Devon Assoc. Adv. Sc. Lit. Art* LXXXII, 105–6.

Phillips, E. M. (1954), 'Supplementary Notes on the Ancient Stone Crosses of Devon (4th paper)'. *Trans. Devon Assoc. Adv. Sc. Lit. Art* LXXXVI, 173–94.

Pigeon, E.-A. (1888), *Le Diocèse d'Avranches...* I. Coutances.

Pilkington, A. (1915), 'A Memorial of the Past'. *Country Life* 2 January 1915.

Plenderleith, H. J. (1956), 'The Methods used in the Preservation of the Relics' in C. F. Battiscombe ed., *The Relics of Saint Cuthbert...*, 531–44. Durham.

Ploss, E. (1958), 'Der Inschriftentypus "N.N. me fecit"...'. *Zeitschrift für Deutsche Philologie* LXXVII, 25–46.

Plummer, C. ed., ed. J. Earle (1899), *Two of the Saxon Chronicles Parallel...* II. Oxford.

Poole, G. A. and Hugall, J. W. (1848), *The Churches of Scarborough, Filey and the Neighbourhood*. Scarborough.

Poole, G. A. and Hugall, J. W. (?1850), *An Historical & Descriptive Guide to York Cathedral and its Antiquities*. York.

Porter, A. K. (1931), *The Crosses and Culture of Ireland*. New Haven, Connecticut.

Potts, R. U. (1924), 'An eleventh-century burial cross at St Augustine's, Canterbury'. *Antiq. J.* IV, 422–5.

Potts, R. U. (1926), 'The Tombs of the Kings and Archbishops in St Austin's Abbey'. *Arch. Cant.* XXXVIII, 97–112.

Poulson, G. (1841), *The History and Antiquities of the Seigniory of Holderness...* II. Hull.

Powell, F. W. (1909), *A Short Account of S. Gregory's Minster, Kirkdale*. Leeds.

Powell, W. R. *et al.* (1953), 'Potterne'. *VCH Wiltshire* VII, 207–17. London.

Pownall, T. (1775), 'On the Boundary Stone of *Croyland Abbey*'. *Arch.* III, 96–100.

Pownall, T. (1782), 'On *Roman* Earthen Ware, and the Boundary-Stone of *Croyland* Abbey'. *Arch.* VI, 392–9.

Prior, E. S. and Gardner, A. (1912), *An Account of Medieval Figure-Sculpture in England*. Cambridge.

Purday, C. H. (1858), in 'Proceedings' 4 December 1857. *Arch. J.* XV, 85–6.

Quentin, H. (1908), *Les martyrologes historiques du Moyen Âge...* 2nd ed. Paris.

Radford, C. A. R. (1946), 'A Lost Inscription of Pre-Danish Age from Caistor'. *Arch. J.* CIII, 95–9.

Radford, C. A. R. (1954a), 'Saint Paul's Church, Jarrow'. *Arch. J.* CXI, 203–5.

Radford, C. A. R. (1954b), 'St Peter's Church, Monkwearmouth'. *Arch. J.* CXI, 209–11.

Radford, C. A. R. (1956), 'The Portable Altar' in C. F. Battiscombe ed., *The Relics of Saint Cuthbert...*, 326–35. Durham.

Radford, C. A. R. (?1960), 'The Saxon Cross' in P. T. B. Clayton, *Saxon Discoveries in London*, 13–16. London.

Radford, C. A. R. (1966), 'Breamore Church'. *Arch. J.* CXXIII, 203.

Radnor, Lord (1785), in 'Appendix' 22 March 1781. *Arch.* VII, 421.

Raine, A. (1955), *Mediaeval York*. London.

Raine, James the elder (1828), *St Cuthbert: with an account of the state in which his remains were found upon the opening of his tomb in Durham Cathedral, in the year MDCCCXXVII*. Durham.

Raine, James the elder (1852), *The History and Antiquities of North Durham...* London.

Raine, James the younger, ed. (1854), *The Inventories and Account Rolls of...Jarrow & Monkwearmouth, in the County of Durham*. Surtees Soc. XXIX.

Raine, James the younger, ed. (1864), *Priory of Hexham*. Surtees Soc. XLIV.

Read, C. H. (1903), 'On a Morse Ivory Tau Cross Head of English work of the Eleventh Century'. *Arch.* LVIII ii, 407–12.

Redin, M. (1919), *Studies on Uncompounded Personal Names in Old English*. Uppsala.

Reginald (1835), *Reginaldi Monachi Dunelmensis Libellus de Admirandis Beati Cuthberti*. Surtees Soc. I.

Rice, D. T. (1947), *The Byzantine Element in Late Saxon Art*. W. H. Charlton Memorial Lecture. London.

Rice, D. T. (1952), *English Art 871–1100*. The Oxford History of English Art II. Oxford.

Rice, D. T. (1956), 'New light on the Alfred Jewel'. *Antiq. J.* XXXVI, 214–17.

Richardson, M. A. (1842), *The Local Historian's Table Book of Remarkable Occurrences, Historical Facts, Traditions, Legendary and Descriptive Ballads, etc. etc... Historical Division* II. London, Newcastle upon Tyne.

Rickman, T., ed. J. R. Parker (1862), *An Attempt to Discriminate the Styles of Architecture in England from the Conquest to the Reformation* 6th ed. Oxford, London.

Rivoira, G. T., trans. G. McN. Rushforth (1912), 'Antiquities of S. Andrews'. *Burl. Mag.* XXI, 15–25.

Rivoira, G. T., trans. G. McN. Rushforth (1933), *Lombardic Architecture...* II. Rev. ed. Oxford.

Rix, J. (1858a), 'King Alfred's Jewel'. *N & Q* 2s VI, 78.

Rix, J. (1858b), 'Alfred's Jewel'. *N & Q* 2s VI, 357–8.

Robertson, A. J. (1956), *Anglo-Saxon Charters* 2nd ed. Cambridge.

Robson, I. S. (1899), 'England's Oldest Handicrafts'. *Antiquary* XXXV, 200–4.

Rose, J. D. (1909), *Jarrow Church & Monastery...* Jarrow.

Ross, A. S. C. (1933), 'The Linguistic Evidence for the date of the "Ruthwell Cross"'. *MLR* XXVIII, 145–55.

Ross, A. S. C. (1935–6), 'Notes on the Runic Stones at Holy Island'. *Englische Studien* LXX, 36–9.

Rousseau, H. (1902), 'La Ruthwell Cross'. *Annales de la Soc. d'Arch. de Bruxelles*, 53–71.

Routledge, C. F. (1897), 'St Martin's Church, Canterbury'. *Arch. Cant.* XXII, 1–28.

Routledge, C. F. (1898), *The Church of St Martin Canterbury...* London.

Rowe, G. (1874), 'On the Churches of Lastingham and Kirkdale, in Yorkshire...'. *AASR* XII ii, 202–10.

Russell, A. (1914a), 'Kirkdale'. *VCH NR Yorkshire* I, 517–23. London.

Russell, A. (1914*b*), 'Hauxwell'. *VCH NR Yorkshire* I, 245–51. London.

Russell, A. and Clapham, A. W. (1923), 'Hackness'. *VCH NR Yorkshire* II, 528–32. London.

St Croix, W. de (1875), 'Sundials'. *Sussex Arch. Colls.* XXVI, 274–5.

Saunders, O. E. (1932), *A History of English Art in the Middle Ages*. Oxford.

Savage, H. E. (1900), 'Jarrow Church and Monastery'. *Arch. Ael.* NS XXII, 30–60.

Saxl, F. (1943), 'The Ruthwell Cross'. *J. Warburg Courtauld Insts.* VI, 1–19.

Saxl, F., ed. H. Swarzenski (1954), *English Sculptures of the Twelfth Century*. London.

Saxl, F. and Wittkower, R. (1948), *British Art and the Mediterranean*. London.

Scarth, H. M. (1860), 'Remarks on some Ancient Sculptured Stones'. *Proc. Som. Arch. Nat. Hist. Soc.* X, 113–30.

Schapiro, M. (1944), 'The Religious Meaning of the Ruthwell Cross'. *Art Bulletin* XXVI, 232–45.

Schneider, K. (1959), 'Zu den Inschriften und Bildern des Franks Casket und einer ae. Version von Balders Tod'. *Festschrift für Walther Fischer*, 4–20. Heidelberg.

Schneider, K. (1968), 'Six Old English Runic Inscriptions Reconsidered' in A. H. Orrick ed., *Nordica et Anglica, Studies in Honor of Stefán Einarsson*. The Hague, Paris.

Scott, F. S. (1956), 'The Hildithryth stone and the other Hartlepool name-stones'. *Arch. Ael.* 4S XXXIV, 196–212.

Searle, W. G. (1897), *Onomasticon Anglosaxonicum*... Cambridge.

Sharp, C. (1851), *History of Hartlepool...With a Supplemental History to 1851, inclusive*. Hartlepool.

Shaw, H. (1858), *Dresses and Decorations of the Middle Ages* rev. ed. I London.

Shaw, M. B. (1939), in 'Proceedings' 16 September 1938. *TCWAAS* NS XXXIX, 321–2.

Shelton, M. ed. (1737), *Wotton's Short View of George Hickes's...Treasury of the Ancient Northern Languages* 2nd ed. London.

Sheppard, T. (1923), 'Saxon Gold Ring found at Driffield, East Yorks.'. *Trans. ER Antiq. Soc.* XXIV, 43–50.

Shore, T. W. (1898), 'The History and Antiquities of Whitchurch' in 'Visit of Field Club'. *Hampshire N & Q* IX, 123–6.

Shortt, W. T. P. (1836), in a letter 24 June 1836. *Gents. Mag.* NS VI, 154–7.

Shortt, W. T. P. (?1841), *Sylva Antiqua Iscana, Numismatica, quinetiam Figulina, or Roman and other Antiquities of Exeter*... Exeter, London.

Silver, T. (1831), *The Coronation Service or Consecration of the Anglo-Saxon Kings, as it illustrates the Origin of the Constitution*. Oxford.

Smith, A. ed. (1929), *Roman Antiquities in the City and County Museum, Lincoln*. Lincoln.

Smith, C. R. (1846), in 'Proceedings of the Committee' 10 December 1845. *JBAA* I, 341.

Smith, C. R. (1871), 'Saxon Sepulchral Monuments in the Church at Whitchurch, Hants.'. *Builder* XXIX, No. 1501, 11 November 1871, 884.

Smith, H. C. (1908), *Jewellery*. London.

Smith, H. L. (1858), 'Alfred's Jewel'. *N & Q* 2S VI, 312–13.

Smith, R. A. (1900), 'Anglo-Saxon Remains'. *VCH Hampshire* I, 373–98. London.

Smith, R. A. (1901), 'Anglo-Saxon Remains'. *VCH Worcestershire* I, 223–33. London.

Smith, R. A. (1901–3), in 'Proceedings' 29 January 1903. *Proc. Soc. Ant. Lon.* 2S XIX, 210–12.

Smith, R. A. (1902), 'Anglo-Saxon Remains'. *VCH Hertfordshire* I, 251–61. London.

Smith, R. A. (1906*a*), 'Anglo-Saxon Remains'. *VCH Somerset* I, 373–81. London.

Smith, R. A. (1906*b*), 'Anglo-Saxon Remains'. *VCH Berkshire* I, 229–49. London.

Smith, R. A. (1906*c*), 'Anglo-Saxon Remains'. *VCH Devon* I, 373–4. London.

Smith, R. A. (1908), 'Anglo-Saxon Remains'. *VCH Kent* I, 339–87. London.

Smith, R. A. (1909–11), in 'Proceedings' 8 December 1910. *Proc. Soc. Ant. Lon.* 2 S XXIII, 302–7.

Smith, R. A. (1911), 'Anglo-Saxon Remains'. *VCH Suffolk* I, 325–55. London.

Smith, R. A. (1912), 'Anglo-Saxon Remains'. *VCH Yorkshire* II, 73–109. London.

Smith, R. A. (1923), *British Museum: A Guide to the Anglo-Saxon and Foreign Teutonic Antiquities in the Department of British and Mediaeval Antiquities.* London.

Smith, R. A. (1925), 'The Beeston Tor Hoard'. *Antiq. J.* V, 135–40.

Smith, W. and Cheetham, S. edd. (1875), *A Dictionary of Christian Antiquities...* I. London.

Smith, W. and Cheetham, S. edd. (1880), *A Dictionary of Christian Antiquities...* II. London.

Spiers, R. J. (1849), in 'Proceedings' 7 December 1849. *Arch. J.* VI, 412.

Spink, D. F. (1949–51), in 'Proceedings' 24 May 1950. *Brit. Num. J.* 3 S VI, 234.

Spurr, A. ed. (1964), *A Guide to the Parish Church of St Mary and St Cuthbert Chester-le-Street.* Gloucester.

Stephens, G. (1865), 'The Beckermont Inscription'. *Arch. Ael.* NS VI, 191–2.

Stephens, G. (1866–7), *The Old-Northern Runic Monuments of Scandinavia and England...* I. Copenhagen.

Stephens, G. (1867–8), *The Old-Northern Runic Monuments of Scandinavia and England...* II. Copenhagen.

Stephens, G. (1882), 'Further Remarks on an Inscribed Stone found at Yarm'. *YAJ* VII, 112–18.

Stephens, G. (1884*a*), *The Old-Northern Runic Monuments of Scandinavia and England...* III. Copenhagen.

Stephens, G. (1884*b*), *Handbook of the Old-Northern Runic Monuments of Scandinavia and England.* London, Edinburgh, Copenhagen.

Stephens, G. (1885), 'On the Shaft of an Anglic Cross discovered in the Church at Chester-le-Street'. *Arch. Ael.* NS X, 88–92.

Stephens, G. (1891–2), in 'Proceedings' 29 June 1892. *Proc. Soc. Ant. Newc.* NS V, 189–90.

Stephens, G. (1894), *The Runes, Whence Came They.* London, Copenhagen.

Stephens, G., ed. S. O. M. Söderberg (1901), *The Old-Northern Runic Monuments of Scandinavia and England...* IV. Edinburgh, Lund.

Stevens, W. O. (1904), *The Cross in the Life and Literature of the Anglo-Saxons.* Yale Stud. Eng. XXIII. New York.

Stevenson, W. H. (1912), 'Yorkshire Surveys and other Eleventh-Century Documents in the York Gospels'. *Eng. Hist. Review* XXVII, 1–25.

Stoll, R. R., trans. J. Maxwell Brownjohn (1967), *Architecture and Sculpture in Early Britain...* London.

Stone, L. (1955*a*), 'Anglo-Saxon Art'. *VCH Wiltshire* II, 35–41. London.

Stone, L. (1955*b*), *Sculpture in Britain. The Middle Ages.* The Pelican History of Art. Harmondsworth.

Stothard, H. (1846), in 'Proceedings of the Committee' 22 October 1845. *JBAA* I, 327.

Stuart, J. (1867), *Sculptured Stones of Scotland* 2nd ed. II. Edinburgh.

Stukeley, W. (1724), *Itinerarium Curiosum. Or, an Account of the Antiquitys and Remarkable Curiositys In Nature or Art, Observ'd in Travels thro' Great Brittan.* London.

Stukeley, W. (1776), *Itinerarium Curiosum: or, an Account of the Antiquities and Remarkable Curiosities in Nature or Art, observed in travels through Great Britain* 2nd ed. London.

Surtees, R. (1820), *The History and Antiquities of the County Palatine of Durham...* II. London.

Swanton, M. J. (1969), 'Ambiguity and Anticipation in "The Dream of the Rood"'. *Neuphil. Mitteil.* 3 S LXX, 407–25.

Swanton, M. J. ed. (1970), *The Dream of the Rood.* Manchester.

Swarzenski, H. (1967), *Monuments of Romanesque Art...* 2nd ed. London.

Sweet, H. ed. (1885), *The Oldest English Texts.* EETS LXXXIII. London.

Sweet, H. (1887), *A Second Anglo-Saxon Reader. Archaic and Dialectal.* Oxford.

Symeon, ed. H. Hinde (1867), *Symeon Dunelmensis. Opera et Collectanea.* Surtees Soc. LI.

Sympson, E. M. (1906), *Lincoln, a historical and topographical account of the City.* London.

Taralon, J. (1958), 'Note technique sur le coffret de Mortain'. *Les monuments historiques de la France* IV, 83–93.

Tate, G. (1866), *The History of the Borough, Castle, and Baronry of Alnwick...* I. Alnwick.

Taylor, C. S. (1902), 'Deerhurst, Pershore, and Westminster'. *TBGAS* XXV, 230–84.

Taylor, H. (1903), 'The Ancient Crosses of Lancashire: The Hundred of Lonsdale'. *Trans. Lancs. Ches. Antiq. Soc.* XXI, 1–110.

Taylor, H. (1904), 'The Ancient Crosses of Lancashire: The Hundred of Salford'. *Trans. Lancs. Ches. Antiq. Soc.* XXII, 73–153.

Taylor, H. (1906), *The Ancient Crosses and Holy Wells of Lancashire.* Manchester.

Taylor, H. M. and Taylor, J. (1961), 'The seventh-century church at Hexham: A new appreciation'. *Arch. Ael.* 4 S XXXIX, 103–34.

Taylor, H. M. and Taylor, J. (1965), *Anglo-Saxon Architecture.* 2 vols. Cambridge.

Taylor, J. and Taylor, H. M. (1966), 'Architectural sculpture in pre-Norman England'. *JBAA* 3 S XXIX, 3–51.

Taylor, R. V. (1881), 'Yorkshire Sun Dials' in W. Smith ed., *Old Yorkshire* I, 144–50. London.

Thomas, A. C. (1964), 'Ardwall Island, Gatehouse-of-Fleet'. *Discovery and Excavation*, 34–5.

Thomas, A. C. (1965), 'The Coveted Isles' in D. T. Rice ed., *The Dark Ages...*, 241–68. London.

Thomas, A. C. (1966), 'Ardwall Isle: The Excavation of an early Christian site of Irish Type'. *Trans. Dumfr. Galloway Nat. Hist. Ant. Soc.* 3 S XLIII, 84–116.

Thomas, A. C. (1967), 'An Early Christian cemetery and chapel on Ardwall Isle, Kirkcudbright'. *Med. Arch.* XI, 127–88.

Thompson, A. H. (1913), 'Leake. Church of St Mary'. *YAJ* XXII, 231–5.

Thompson, J. D. A. (1956), *Inventory of British Coin Hoards A.D. 600–1500.* Royal Num. Soc. Special Publications I. Oxford.

Thompson, J. D. A. (1959), 'Some additions and corrections to J. D. A. Thompson, *Inventory of British Coin Hoards*: a recension'. *Med. Arch.* III, 280–2.

Tillott, P. M. (1961), 'The Parish Churches'. *VCH York*, 365–404. London.

Todd, J., ed. J. E. Soulsby (1969), *Waterperry Church* 2nd imp. Oxford.

Tolkien, J. R. R. (1929), 'Ancrene Wisse & Hali Meiðhad'. *Essays & Studies* XIV, 104–26.

Tonnochy, A. B. (1932), 'A Romanesque censer-cover in the British Museum'. *Arch. J.* LXXXIX, 1–16.

Tonnochy, A. B. (1937), 'The Censer in the Middle Ages'. *JBAA* 3 S II, 47–62.

Tonnochy, A. B. (1952), *Catalogue of British Seal-Dies in the British Museum*. London.

Trollope, E. (1862), 'Notes on Market Rasen, and places in its vicinity'. *AASR* VI ii, 139–75.

Trollope, E. and Trollope, A. (1860), 'Contributions to the History of Britain under the Romans. Roman Inscriptions and Sepulchral Remains at Lincoln'. *Arch. J.* XVII, 1–21.

Tudor, C. L. R. (1876), *A Brief Account of Kirkdale Church...* London.

Turner, J. and Bradley, J. (1784), in letters. *Antiq. Rep.* IV, 161–2.

Twycross-Raines, G. F. (1920), 'Aldbrough Church, Holderness'. *Trans. ER Antiq. Soc.* XXIII, 28–33.

Tyrrell-Green, E. (1928), *Baptismal Fonts Classified and Illustrated*. London.

Upcott, K. M. (1911), 'Whitchurch'. *VCH Hampshire* IV, 299–305. London.

Vaughan, J. (1914), *Winchester Cathedral Close. Its Historical and Literary Associations*. London.

Velge, H. (?1925), *La Collégiale des saints Michel & Gudule à Bruxelles*. Brussels.

Viëtor, W. (1895), *Die Northumbrischen Runensteine*. Marburg-in-Hessen.

Viëtor, W. (1901), *The Anglo-Saxon Runic Casket. (The Franks Casket)*. Marburg-in-Hessen.[1]

Wadstein, N. E. (1900), *The Clermont Runic Casket...* Skrifter utgifna af K. Humanistiska Vetenskaps-Samfundet i Upsala VI, 7. Uppsala.

Waller, J. G. (1846), in 'Proceedings of the Committee' 14 May 1845. *JBAA* I, 146–7.

Ward, F. A. B. (1966), *Science Museum. Descriptive Catalogue of the Collection Illustrating Time Measurement*. London.

Waring, J. B. ed. (1858), *Art Treasures of the United Kingdom from the Art Treasures Exhibition, Manchester* I. London.

Warren, J. (1851), in 'Proceedings' 1 May 1850. *JBAA* VI, 153–4.

Warren, J. (1853), in 'Proceedings' 25 September 1850. *Proc. Bury W. Suffolk Arch. Inst.* I, 223.

Waterton, E. (1859), in 'Proceedings' 7 January 1859. *Arch. J.* XVI, 192–4.

Waterton, E. (1859–61 a), in 'Proceedings' 8 March 1860. *Proc. Soc. Ant. Lon.* 2S I, 107.

Waterton, E. (1859–61 b), in 'Proceedings' 20 December 1860. *Proc. Soc. Ant. Lon.* 2S I, 276–8.

Waterton, E. (1862), 'On Niello: a Discourse delivered at the Special Exhibition of Works in Niello and Enamel, June, 1862'. *Arch. J.* XIX, 323–39.

Waterton, E. (1863), 'On Episcopal Rings'. *Arch. J.* XX, 224–38.

Watkin, W. T. (1874), 'On Some Forgotten or Neglected Roman Inscriptions found in Britain'. *Arch. J.* XXXI, 344–59.

Way, A. (1845), in 'Some Account of the Objects collected in the Museum formed at the Deanery at Winchester, during the week of the Meeting'. *Proc. Royal Arch. Inst.* xxxix–liv.

Way, A. (1846 a), 'Decorative Processes connected with the Arts during the Middle Ages. Enamel'. *Arch. J.* II, 155–72.

Way, A. (1846 b), in 'Proceedings of the Committee' 14 May 1845. *Arch. J.* II, 201.

Way, A. and du Noyer, G. V. (1868), 'Ancient Sun-dials'. *Arch. J.* XXV, 207–23.

Wellbeloved, C. (1881), *A Hand-Book to the Antiquities in the Grounds and Museum of the Yorkshire Philosophical Society* 7th ed. York.

Wells, H. B. (1953), 'Haddenham'. *VCH Cambridgeshire* IV, 140–9. London.

Westwood, J. O. (1846), in 'Proceedings of the Committee' 13 August 1845. *JBAA* I, 249–51.

1 Bilingual text: *Das angelsächsische Runenkästchen aus Auzon bei Clermont-Ferrand*.

Westwood, J. O. (1849), in 'Proceedings' 2 February 1849. *Arch. J.* VI, 76.

Westwood, J. O. (1855), in 'Proceedings' 13 April 1855. *Arch. J.* XII, 202.

Westwood, J. O. (1868), *Fac-similes of the Miniatures & Ornaments of Anglo-Saxon & Irish Manuscripts.* London.

Westwood, J. O. (1876), *A Descriptive Catalogue of the Fictile Ivories in the South Kensington Museum...* London.

Westwood, J. O. (1885–7), in 'Proceedings' 16 December 1886. *Proc. Soc. Ant. Lon.* 2 S XI, 224–6.

Westwood, J. O. (1886–93), 'On (I.) An Anglo- or Dano-Saxon Memorial preserved in Stratfield Mortimer Church, Berks.'. *Proc. Oxf. Hist. Soc.* NS V, 293–5.

Whellan, W. (1860), *The History & Topography of the Counties of Cumberland and Westmoreland...* Pontefract.

Whitaker, T. D. (1816), *Loidis & Elmete...* Leeds, Wakefield.

Whitaker, T. D. (1823), *An History of Richmondshire...* I. London.

Whitelock, D. ed. (1967), *Sweet's Anglo-Saxon Reader in Prose and Verse* rev. ed. Oxford.

Whitley, H. M. (1919), 'Primitive Sundials of West Sussex Churches'. *Sussex Arch. Colls.* LX, 126–40.

Willmore, H. H. (1939), 'Stone Coffins, Gloucestershire'. *TBGAS* LXI, 135–77.

Wilson, D. M. (1958), 'Some archaeological additions and corrections to J. D. A. Thompson, *Inventory of British Coin Hoards*'. *Med. Arch.* II, 169–71.

Wilson, D. M. (1960), *The Anglo-Saxons.* Ancient Peoples & Places XVI. London.

Wilson, D. M. (1964), *Anglo-Saxon Ornamental Metalwork 700–1100 in the British Museum.* Catalogue of Antiquities of the Later Saxon Period I. London.

Wilson, D. M. and Blunt, C. E. (1961), 'The Trewhiddle Hoard'. *Arch.* XCVIII, 75–122.

Wilson, D. M. and Hurst, D. G. (1965), 'Medieval Britain in 1964'. *Med. Arch.* IX, 170–220.

Wilson, D. M. and Hurst, D. G. (1968), 'Medieval Britain in 1967'. *Med. Arch.* XII, 155–211.

Wilson, D. M. and Klindt-Jensen, O. (1966), *Viking Art.* London.

Wilson, F. R. (1862–8), 'On Hexham Abbey Church'. *Trans. A.A. Soc. Durh. North.* I, 19–27.

Wise, F. ed. (1722), *Annales Rerum Gestarum Ælfredi Magni, auctore Asserio menevensi.* Oxford.

Wise, M. J. and Ross, A. S. C. (1953–4), 'Alnmouth Old Church'. *Durh. Univ. J.* NS XV, 25.

Wodderspoon, J. (1850), *Memorials of the Ancient Town of Ipswich in the County of Suffolk.* Ipswich, London.

Wood, J. (1822), 'Some Account of a Saxon Inscription, on a Stone found near Falstone...'. *Arch. Ael.* I, 103–4.

Wordsworth, J. (1879), 'Anglo-Saxon Dedicatory Inscription on the Tower of St Mary-le-Wigford Church in Lincoln...'. *AASR* XV i, 16–17.

Wotton, W. ed. (1708), *Linguarum vett. septentrionalium Thesauri grammaticocritici et archaeologici, auctore G. Hickesio...* London.

Wright, T. (1845), 'On Anglo-Saxon Architecture'. *Arch. J.* I, 24–35.

Wright, T. (1852), 'Letter...on a Leaden Tablet or Book Cover, with an Anglo-Saxon Inscription'. *Arch.* XXXIV ii, 438–40.

Young, G. (1817), *A History of Whitby...* 2 vols. Whitby.

Zarnecki, G. (1953), 'The Newent Funerary Tablet'. *TBGAS* LXXII, 49–55.

Zarnecki, G. (1966), '1066 and Architectural Sculpture'. *Proc. Brit. Acad.* LII, 87–104.

Zinner, E. (1964), *Alte Sonnenuhren an europäischen Gebäuden*. Wiesbaden.

Zupitza, J. (1891), review of Logeman (1891). *Archiv* LXXXVII, 462.

(—) (1779), initialled 'Y.Z.', in a letter. *Gents. Mag.* XLIX, 535–6.

(—) (1780), in a letter. *Gents. Mag.* L, 128.

(—) (1789), 'Description of a Cross at Ruthvell in Annandale'. *Vetusta Monumenta* II, pls. liv–lv and following pages 1–3.[1]

(—) (1822), in 'Donations to the Society'. *Arch. Ael.* I, 6.

(—) (1833), initialled 'XY', 'Runic Gravestones found at Hartlepool'. *Gents. Mag.* CIII ii, 218–20.

(—) (1836–68), *Ashmolean Museum Catalogue*. Oxford.

(—) (1838), 'Sepulchral Stones at Hartlepool'. *Gents. Mag.* NS X, 536.

(—) (1844), 'Sepulchral Stones found at Hartlepool' in 'Antiquarian Researches'. *Gents. Mag.* NS XXI, 187–8.

(—) (1845), *The New Statistical account of Scotland* IV. Edinburgh, London.

(—) (1846), in 'Archaeological Intelligence'. *Arch. J.* III, 259.

(—) (1850), (Rev. Precentor of Lincoln), in *Memoirs illustrative of the History and Antiquities of the County and City of Lincoln . . .* Royal Arch. Inst. xliv. London.

(—) (1855), in 'Donations to the Society'. *Arch. Ael.* IV, 5.

(—) (1858a), signed 'Eighty-Three', 'King Alfred's Jewel'. *N & Q* 2S VI, 46–7.

(—) (1858b), initialled 'L.B.L.', 'Alfred's Jewel'. *N & Q* 2S VI, 233.[2]

(—) (1859), *Catalogue of the Archaeological Museum formed at Carlisle*. Royal Arch. Inst.

(—) (1861), 'Hexham Church'. *Arch. Ael.* NS V, 150–8.

(—) (1862–8), 'St Peter's, Monkwearmouth'. *Trans. A.A. Soc. Durh. North.* I, 141–4.

(—) (1868), *Historia Translationum Sancti Cuthberti*. Surtees Soc. LI, 158–201.

(—) (1869–79), in 'Account of Meeting 1878'. *Trans. A.A. Soc. Durh. North.* II, lxxxi–lxxxiii.

(—) (1871), in account of a meeting of *L'Association Normande* 23 June 1870. *Annuaire des Cinq Départements de la Normandie* XXXVII, 227–33.

(—) (1872), *Ann. Rpt. Council Yorks. Phil. Soc.* 9.

(—) (1873), in 'Collectanea'. *Arch. Camb.* 4S IV, 304.

(—) (1877), 'Saxon Inscription at St Mary-le-Wigford, Lincoln' in 'Antiquarian Intelligence'. *JBAA* XXXIII, 132–3.

(—) (1886), 'Sculptured Stones from St Nicholas' Church, Ipswich'. *Builder* LI, No. 2278, 2 October 1886, 478–80.

(—) (1887–8), in 'Proceedings' 31 August 1888. *Proc. Soc. Ant. Newc.* NS III, 398–405.

(—) (1888), 'The Ruthwell Cross'. *Reliq.* NS II, 85–8.

(—) (1892), in 'Quarterly Notes'. *Reliq.* NS VI, 55–6.

(—) (1899a), 'Alfred the Great's Jewel'. *Bucks. Berks. Oxon. Arch. J.* V, 59–61.

(—) (1899b), in *Reliq.* NS V, 189–92.

(—) (1900a), review of Calverley (1889). *Arch. J.* LVII, 87–8.

(—) (1900b), review of Haverfield and Greenwell (1899). *Reliq.* NS VI, 65–9.

(—) (1901a), *British Museum: Alfred the Great Millenary Exhibition, 1901*. London.

(—) (1901b), 'The Alfred Jewel', review of Earle (1901). *Antiq.* XXXVII, 212–16.

[1] Possibly by R. Gough. R. I. Page, in a personal communication.
[2] Probably by Rev. L. B. Larking. B. Dickins, in a personal communication.

(—) (1901 c), 'Gossip of an Antiquary'. *Bucks. Berks. Oxon. Arch. J.* NS VII, 65–8.

(—) (1903), 'Early Inscriptions in Bilsdale Church'. *YAJ* XVII, 237–40.

(—) (1905), *English Church History Exhibition, at the Town Hall, St Albans, from 27th June to 15th July 1905.* London.

(—) (1913–14), in 'Proceedings' 15 July 1914. *Proc. Soc. Ant. Newc.* 3S VI, 197–9.

(—) (1920), *The Royal Commission on Ancient and Historical Monuments & Constructions of Scotland. Seventh Report. With Inventory of Monuments and Constructions in the County of Dumfries.* Edinburgh.

(—) (1924), in 'Excursions 1924'. *Proc. Suff. Inst. Arch.* XVIII, 241–51.

(—) (1930 a), *Victoria & Albert Museum. Exhibition of English Mediæval Art 1930.* London.

(—) (1930 b), *Burlington Fine Arts Club. Catalogue of an Exhibition of Art in the Dark Ages in Europe (circa 400–1000 A.D.).* London.

(—) (1930 c), *Victoria & Albert Museum. 100 Masterpieces, Early Christian and Mediaeval.* London.

(—) (1931), in 'Proceedings' 9 July 1931. *TBGAS* LIII, 55–63.

(—) (1934), in 'Proceedings' 11 July 1934. *TBGAS* LVI, 18–26.

(—) (? 1938), *Official Handbook and Guide to the County Borough of Ipswich.* Ipswich.

(—) (1944), *University of Oxford. Ashmolean Museum. Report of the Visitors.* Oxford.

(—) (1950), initialled 'T.S.M.', 'Saxon Pocket Watch'. *Country Life* 23 June 1950, 1890.

(—) (1951 a), *University of Oxford. Ashmolean Museum. Report of the Visitors.* Oxford.

(—) (1951 b), *Messrs. Sotheby & Co. Sale Catalogue 17 January 1951.*

(—) (1952 a), in *Country Life* 22 August 1952, 537.

(—) (1952 b), in *Toc H J.* XXX, 88.

(—) (? 1953), *The Parish Church of St Mary-le-Wigford Lincoln.* Gloucester.

(—) (1958), *The Parish Church of St Andrew Bishop Auckland.* Gloucester.

(—) (1960), *Catalogue of Mediaeval Works of Art...June 17th, 1960.* Messrs Sotheby and Co. London.

(—) (1962), *The Parish Church of All Saints Orpington.* Gloucester.

(—) (1968), *Treasures of Britain and Treasures of Ireland.* Drive Publications Ltd. London.

(—) (19   a), *The Churches of St Benedict and St Mary-le-Wigford.* Colchester.

(—) (19   b), *St Margaret's Church Hornby.* (No place of publication.)

(—) (19   c), *A Brief History of the Church and Parish of St Nicholas Ipswich.* Ramsgate.

HAND-LIST

GUIDE TO THE ENTRIES

This guide explains the system of presentation of the entries in the Hand-list. For detailed discussion of the principles of distribution and dating of objects, and of the formulae employed in the texts, see the *Introduction*.

Each inscribed object is entered in alphabetical order of its place of finding in modern times and is given a running number. These numbers also appear in the entries, in the plates, and in Indexes I, II, IV and VII; they are omitted from the *Introduction* and Indexes V and VI so as not to cause confusion there. This is followed by a more detailed account of its place of finding and present locality including, where known, the town, the county (except in the case of eponymous county-towns) and the country (where this is other than England). The object's present locality is stated in general if the object is merely housed there, but is particularised if it forms part of the fabric of a building. Thus, for example, a general description is, 'Newent parish church', whereas a particular one is, 'set into the interior north wall of the chancel of Birtley parish church'. For this purpose, stones fixed only to the floor of a building are not taken as part of the fabric, and where an object is stated to be set in a wall, this indicates an exterior wall unless the opposite is stated. The dedications of the parish churches are given only where there is more than one parish church in the town. Stones which are not easily located by reference to a building are given a National Grid reference number. If known, the date of loss of a lost object is stated.

Each entry then continues with a paragraph containing the factual information known about the object. This is presented in abbreviated form in the following order; if any fact is uncertain, this is stated.

i. Find-place and date, where known, with brief details of the find. Unless the contrary is stated, objects are not assumed to have been found *in situ* nor in their present *situs*,[1] nor during controlled excavation.

ii. Extremity measurements in the order height × width, × thickness where known, unless different measurements are stated. The measurements are in centimetres and are correct to one place of decimals, except in the case of very large stones where they are correct only to the nearest centimetre.

iii. Description of the object, including its material and function and the type of stone, where known. Unless the contrary is stated, objects are assumed to be: complete; uncarved and undecorated; to contain neither original nor modern

[1] See further, *Introduction 2. Localisation and Distribution of Inscriptions*.

paint; stones to be rectangular or of rectangular section, but stone sun-dials to be semi-circular.

iv. Description of the text, including its position on the object. A text is described as on 'one face' if only the text distinguishes the faces, and on 'visible face' if the object is set into a wall, if it is lost and illustrations of only the inscribed face remain, or if its situation is otherwise unclear. Unless the contrary is stated, texts are assumed to be: primary; complete; incised, except in the case of gold, silver and niello objects with contrasting texts where the lettering is described; set within framing lines but not within panels. 'Framing lines' are taken to be the lines dividing the lines of texts, 'panels' the lines enclosing a text. However in the case of one-line texts this distinction is sometimes difficult to maintain. The set of the lettering is described only when it is set differently from lines of print. Unless the contrary is stated, texts with the letters facing inwards read clockwise, and outwards anticlockwise. The legibility of the text is described in one of five ways:

illegible: so deteriorated that no meaningful text can be made out.

highly deteriorated: the text consists largely of editorial reconstruction.

rather deteriorated: the text is somewhat damaged, but it can be made out.

slightly deteriorated: the text is a little damaged but its reading is virtually certain.

legible: the reading of the text is certain.

v. Language and formula of the text. The formulae employed are discussed in detail in *Introduction 4. Formulae of Texts.*

vi. Script of the text. The principles are explained in detail elsewhere.[1]

vii. Approximate date of the object. The principles of dating are discussed in detail in *Introduction 3.* Where necessary, a discussion of the date is given in the commentary following the text. The factual date is given in one of five forms, as illustrated here by the eighth century:

A.D. 750–7: a certain date, based on direct evidence.

Eighth century: a certain but unspecifiable date, based on direct evidence.

Probably eighth century: a date suggested by direct evidence, where this is insufficient to make it certain.

Possibly eighth century: a date suggested by indirect evidence, or by one piece of inconclusive direct evidence.

Date uncertain: where insufficient evidence for dating is available.

[1] Okasha (1968), 321–38.

Each entry then continues with a comprehensive bibliography of the object, abbreviated and in chronological order.[1] Next follows the text, transliterated according to the following system:

Non-runic letters are shown in capitals, runic letters in lower case. The letters Ð, Þ, V, Ƿ are retained as in the text. Ligatures, excluding the Old English monophthongs *æ*, *œ*, appear as 'A/B'. Abbreviation and punctuation marks of any sort are shown as '-' and ':' respectively, except where ':' is an abbreviation mark, in which case it remains. Deliberate spaces between letters in the text are indicated by spaces. Ends of lines of texts and ends of complete texts are shown by '|'. Edges of the object and large portions of decoration on it are both taken to end a line of text. Where one text continues on more than one face of an object, the text is printed in rows corresponding to the faces; for this purpose, a circular text is considered to have one face. This should not, of course, be confused with long texts on one face which have to be printed on more than one line. These are printed with all lines after the first indented, while a new face of text is printed without indentation. The following signs are also used:

'*A*': a letter damaged but legible.

'[*A*]': a damaged letter where the restoration is fairly certain.

'[A]': a legible and undamaged letter of unusual form, probably A.

'[. . .]': three letters lost, the number varying according to the number of dots.

'[...]': an indefinite number of letters lost in the text.

'—': a complete loss of text at beginning or end.

The text is then transliterated again with word-division and the insertion of obvious contextual letters, but with no editorial punctuation, and with bracketed letters remaining so. This is followed by a translation, in which all words inserted to make a fluent rendering, with the exception of 'a' and 'the', are bracketed. In the translations, Latin names are normalised, but vernacular names are spelt as in the text. Texts consisting of particularly common personal names, e.g. of the four evangelists, are not normally translated.

Each entry ends with an interpretative commentary, restricted to that which is essential for an understanding of the text. All vernacular names are either commented on, or the persons named are identified. Vernacular names are quoted in the normalised forms used in Index v, with vowel-length marks, since these are essential for the etymology of the elements, except in the cases where the persons are

1 For the principles of selection and arrangement of bibliographical references see the introduction to the *General Bibliography*.

identified, when normalised forms are used. All other length marks in any language are omitted. Where the gender is not stated, vernacular names are to be taken as masculine. Where inscriptions have in addition a runic text, this is transliterated in the commentary only, following the readings of Dr R. I. Page. Vulgate references are quoted by chapter (II) and verse (2), and are taken from M. Hetzenauer, *Biblia Sacra Vulgatæ Editionis...* Rome, Ratisbon 1914.

The following abbreviations are used in the Hand-list. The list excludes commonly accepted abbreviations; it also excludes those abbreviations forming part of the system of transliteration, bibliographical abbreviations, and abbreviations occurring in the texts of the inscriptions. These are explained, respectively, above, in the introduction to the *General Bibliography*, and in Index VI.

Canterbury I	Canterbury, inscription I
Canterbury i	Canterbury inscription, text i
Canterbury I i	Canterbury inscription I, text i
AS	Anglo-Saxon
Cont Gmc	Continental Germanic
LV	*Liber Vitae*; in Sweet (1885)
ME	Middle English
OE	Old English
OIr	Old Irish
ON	Old Norse
OW	Old Welsh
OWN	Old West Norse
RB	Romano-British
TRE	*Tempore Regis Edwardi*
DB	Domesday Book
ring cat. no.	ring catalogue number
BM	British Museum
BMC no.	British Museum Catalogue number; see Grueber and Keary (1893)
V&A	Victoria and Albert Museum
ER	East Riding (of Yorkshire)
NR	North Riding
WR	West Riding

1 Aldbrough

Set in the south side of the interior south aisle of Aldbrough parish church, ER Yorkshire.

First mentioned 1782, in church fabric, possibly in present *situs*. Diam 43·2 cm., thickness 5·1 cm. Carved stone circular sun-dial showing traces of paint when found, which are no longer visible; slightly deteriorated text set right round perimeter on visible face, with letters facing inwards. OE dedication formula. AS capitals. Late tenth to eleventh century.

Brooke (1782), 39–53 & figs.; Pegge (1785), 86–9; Pegge (1787), 21–2 & fig.; Gough (1806), III, 319 & fig.; Poulson (1841), 5–7, 14–15 & fig.; Parker, J. H. (1846), 25 & fig.; Rickman (1862), 101 & fig.; Stephens (1866–7), xxii–xxiii & fig.; Hewitt (1874), 217; Rowe (1874), 210; Haigh (1879), 151–4 & fig.; Taylor, R. V. (1881), 148; Stephens (1894), 24; Gatty (1900), 56–8 & fig.; Collingwood, W. G. (1911), 256–8 & fig.; Collingwood, W. G. (1912), 122, 131; Collingwood, W. G. (1915 *a*), 288, 290; Twycross-Raines (1920), 28–30; Green, A. R. (1928), 511–12; Ekwall (1930), 20; Morris (1932), 51–2; Clapham (1948 *a*), 7; Hofmann (1955), 212–13; Zinner (1964), 31; Taylor, H. M. and Taylor, J. (1965), 20–1 & fig.; Binns (1966), 21 & fig.; Taylor, J. and Taylor, H. M. (1966), 18–19 & fig.; Bradley, H. (1968), 21; Okasha (1969), 26.

✠VLF[. .]TARŒRANCYRICEFORH[A]NVM꒰FORGVN[.A.A]
SAV*LA*|

The text probably reads: ✠ VLF [HE]T ARŒRAN CYRICE FOR H[A]NVM ꒰ FOR GVN [ƿARA] SAVLA, '✠ Vlf ordered the church to be erected for himself and for Gvn[ƿaru]'s soul', where H[A]NVM is probably the ON pronoun used as a reflexive. Alternatively the second word could be [LE]T, 'caused'. The personal names are of ON origin and are recorded; this Vlf may be Ulf the landowner of Aldbrough *TRE*.[1] In view of the small number of *tid*-marks and the shape of the dial, it is possible that it was not intended for practical use.

2 Alnmouth

Alnmouth, Northumberland. Now in the Museum of Antiquities, Newcastle upon Tyne, no. 1958.8.N.

Found July 1789, near ruins of old church. *c.* 86·4 × *c.* 40·6 × *c.* 16·5 cm. Incomplete carved stone shaft in two pieces, with probably complete texts set on three faces in panels; text i legible, ii rather deteriorated, iii illegible. OE texts, i maker formula, ii possibly memorial formula. AS capitals and runes. Probably tenth century.

Brand (1792), 472 & figs.; Richardson (1842), 324 & fig.; Dickson (1852), chapter 3; Haigh (1856–7), 509; Haigh (1857), 173–4, 185–6 & figs.; Tate (1866), 39–40 & figs.; Stephens (1866–

---

[1] DB Yorkshire fo. 324.

7), 461–2 & figs.; Stuart (1867), 65–6 & pl. cxvii; Evans (1873), 333; Haigh (1876), 32; Bruce (1880), 69–71 & figs.; Smith, W. and Cheetham (1880), 1979; Stephens (1884*a*), 441; Stephens (1884*b*), 156, 256 & figs.; Allen and Browne (1885), 343; Sweet (1885), 127; Allen (1889), 211, 221, 222; Bugge (1891–1903), 150; Hodges (1893), 82–3; Payne (1893), 113; Bateson (1895), 489–90 & figs.; Viëtor (1895), 18 n.; Browne (1897), 288; Stevens (1904), 50; Howorth (1917), II, 222; Collingwood, W. G. (1927), 62, 101, index & figs.; Dickins and Ross (1940), 169–78 & fig.; Wise, M. J. and Ross (1953–4), 25; Page, R. I. (1969), 34.

i: MYREDa/H:MEH:ƿO—

ii: *SAV*[...] | [.]AD*V* | [*L*]FESD—

Text i reads: MYREDAH:MEH:ƿO—, probably 'Myredah made me', where the name is Celtic, OIr MUIREDACH. Text ii reads: SAV[... E]ADV[L]FES D —, probably 'The soul of [E]adv[l]f —', where the name is a form of the recorded ĒADWULF. It is uncertain whether these texts are abbreviated or incomplete.

3   Ardwall

Ardwall, Kirkcudbrightshire, Scotland. Now in Dumfries Burgh Museum, no. 1968–93.

Found May 1964[1], during controlled excavation on Ardwall Island, re-used in eighteenth-century building. 137·2 × *c.* 40·6 × *c.* 19·1 cm. Probably complete stone shaft with legible texts set without framing lines on face, text ii probably incomplete. OE personal name or names. Insular majuscule. Probably eighth to ninth century.

Thomas (1964), 35; Wilson, D. M. and Hurst (1965), 177; Thomas (1966), 99, 102–3 & fig.; Thomas (1967), 153–5 & figs.

i: CU[*D*]GAR |

ii: [.]U[.]HGA—

Text i reads: CU[*D*]GAR, or possibly CU[Đ]GAR, a recorded personal name. Text ii may be a variant of this: [H]U[T]HGA —, perhaps with final R, or consist of practice letters. Text i is likely to be primary but ii may not be so. One other stone at Ardwall contains the letters MM, but it is probably seventh century and is unlikely to date from the Anglian period.[2]

4   Athelney

Athelney, Somerset. Now in the Ashmolean Museum, Oxford[3]

Found 1693, in Newton Park near Athelney; possibly in field now called 'Forty Acres'. *c.* 6·4 × *c.* 3·2 × 1·3 cm. Decorated jewel of gold, crystal and enamel, with

---

[1] A. C. Thomas, in a personal communication.
[2] Thomas (1967), 159 & figs. This stone is preserved in Dumfries Burgh Museum, no. 1966–679–8.
[3] The jewel was acquired too early to have an acquisition number.

legible text of gold letters set in panel round thickness, letters facing back. OE maker formula. AS capitals. Probably late ninth to early tenth century.

Musgrave (1698), 441 & fig. opp. p. 429; Hickes (1700–1), 464–9; Hickes (1705), I, 142–4 & figs.; Wotton (1708), 17–21 & figs.; Musgrave (1715), 5–8; Musgrave (1716), 16 & figs.; Wise, F. (1722), 170–2 & fig.; Shelton (1737), 19–21 & figs.; Leland (1745), VII, xxiii–xxiv; Chandler (1763), 143 & figs.; Milles (1773), 79; Pegge (1773), 72–4; Hutchinson (1778), 136 n.; Pegge (1780), 75; (—) (1780), 128; Collinson (1791), 87; Gough (1806), I, 97 & figs.; Gorham (1820), 92–8 & figs.; Gorham (1826), 497–9 & figs.; Silver (1831), vii–viii & figs.; Brayley (1834), 216–17 & figs.; Duncan, P. B. (1836), no. 371, pp. 135–9; Way (1846a), 164–6 & figs.; Akerman (1847), 143–4 & figs.; Giles (1848), appendix 3, pp. 20–3 & figs.; de Laborde (1852), 99 n.; Pauli (1852), fig. p. 414; Giles (1858), 327–35 & figs. (frontispiece); Rix (1858a), 78; Rix (1858b), 357–8; Shaw, H. (1858), pl. 1 (text & 5 figs.); Smith, H. L. (1858), 312–13; (—) (1858a), 46–7; (—) (1858b), 233; Macray (1862), 493; Stephens (1867–8), 586; Labarte (1875), 10; Hübner (1876), add. no. 223, p. 90; Clifford (1877), 21–6; André (1879–80), 80; Jewitt (1879–80), 65–6 & figs.; Allen (1889), 246–7; Robson (1899), 200–2 & figs.; (—) (1899a), 59–61; Earle (1901), passim & figs.; Smith, R. A. (1901), 233; (—) (1901b), 212–16 & fig.; (—) (1901c), 65–7; Molinier (1902), 93–4 & figs.; Dalton (1903–5), 71–7; Michel (1905), 844–5; Smith, R. A. (1906a), 376–80 & figs.; Smith, H. C. (1908), 68–9 & figs.; Jackson, C. J. (1911), 55–6 & figs.; Brown, G. B. (1916), 177–8 & fig.; Browne (1916), 72; Greswell (1922), 80; Brøndsted (1924), 142–3 & fig.; Tyrrell-Green (1928), 154; Hauttman (1929), 57, 702–3 & fig.; Chamot (1930), 2–3, 21–2 & fig.; Saunders (1932), 25–6 & figs.; Hayward (1935), 81; Hackenbroch (1938), 24–5 & fig.; Kendrick (1938), 216–17 & figs.; Saxl and Wittkower (1948), 19 & figs.; Jessup (1950), 87–9 & fig.; Hodgkin, R. H. (1952), II, ix & fig.; Rice (1952), 238–40 & fig.; Stone (1955b), 25–6; Rice (1956), 214–17 & figs.; Lundström (1960), 190–8 & fig.; Wilson, D. M. (1960), 145–6, 220–1 & figs.; Clarke, J. R. (1961), passim & figs.; Wilson, D. M. and Blunt (1961), 107; Wilson, D. M. (1964), 6; Thomas (1965), 247 & fig.; Bakka (1966), 277–82 & figs.; (—) (1968), 21, 381 & fig.; Swanton (1970) 66 n.

✠AELFREDM/ECH/EHTGEVVYRCAN|

The text reads ✠ AELFRED MEC HEHT GEVVYRCAN, '✠ Aelfred ordered me to be made'. Identification with King Alfred the Great has been asserted but not proved.

5 Attleborough

Attleborough, Norfolk. Now in Norwich Castle Museum, no. 61.76.94.

Found pre 1848, during railway construction. Diam. c. 2 cm. Silver ring, with text set without framing lines right round outside. Latin text, possibly descriptive formula, type c. AS capitals and insular minuscule. Possibly eleventh century.

Fitch (1848), 64–5 & figs.; Jones (1877), 413–14 & figs.; Leeney, F. (1909), no. 1077, p. 111.

ETHRALDRICONLVND |

The text probably reads: ETHRALDRIC ON LVND, although it is not certain which is the initial letter. ON LUND[E], 'in London' occurs on coins from the last years of Ethelred II, but is not universal until the last years of Cnut.[1] The first part may be a personal name: AEÐ-, EÐ- and -RĪC are common name elements, though the rest remains unexplained. The text may be a blundered coin legend inscribed for decoration.

6 Auzon

Auzon, Haute-Loire, France. Now in the British Museum, London, no. 1867.1-20.1; the right hand side is in the Museo Nazionale del Bargello, Florence, Carrand Collection no. 25.

First mentioned early nineteenth century, in private possession. 12·9 × 22·9 × 19·1 cm. Incomplete decorated whale-bone casket, originally held together with silver-covered wooden pegs. Runic texts on five faces; legible runic and non-runic text on back, set in relief lettering in panels above carving. Latin descriptive formula, type b. Insular majuscule and runes. Eighth century.

Haigh (1861), 42–4 & figs.; Stephens (1866–7), xxxi–xxxii, 470–6 A & figs.; Maskell (1872), xlix–li & figs.; Maskell (1875), 52–5 & figs.; Stephens (1884a), 200–4; Stephens (1884b), 142–7 & figs.; Sweet (1885), 126–7; Stephens (1894), 7; Wadstein (1900), *passim* & figs.; Napier (1901), 362–81 & figs.; Viëtor (1901), *passim* & figs.; Dalton (1909), no. 30, pp. 27–32 & figs.; Gold-schmidt (1918), nos. 186–7, pp. 56–8 & figs.; Smith, R. A. (1923), 96–8 & figs.; Longhurst (1926), 1–2, 65–7 & figs.; Leclercq (1930), cols. 2397–401 & figs.; Rivoira (1933), 154 & figs.; Kendrick (1938), 121, 122–6 & figs.; Blouet (1954), 16 & fig.; Elliott (1959), 96–109 & figs.; Schneider (1959), 4–20 & fig.; Wilson, D. M. (1960), 92, 121–2, 154, 220 & fig.

HICFUGIANTHIERUSALIM | afitatores |

The text reads: HIC FUGIANT HIERUSALIM AFITATORES, presumably intended as, HIC FUGIUNT HIERUSALIM HABITATORES, 'Here the inhabitants flee from Jerusalem', referring to part of the depicted scene.

The other texts are in OE and runes.[2] The back has also: HER FEGTAÞ TITUS END GIUÞEASU, 'Here fight Titus and the Jews'; DOM, 'judgement'; GISL, 'hostage'. The front reads: HRONÆS BAN FISC : FLODU : AHOF ON FERGEN-BERIG ᚠARÞ GA:SRIC GRORN ÞÆR HE ON GREUT GISᚠOM, 'Whale's bone; the fish beat up the sea(s) on to the cliff; the whale was distressed when he swam on to the shingle'; MÆGI, 'magi'. The lid reads: ÆGILI, 'Egil'. The left side reads:

---

[1] M. Dolley, in a personal communication.

[2] Various translations are possible, and those given are only suggestions; in particular, those of the right side are very tentative.

ROMⱣALUS AND REUMⱣALUS TⱣŒGEN GIBROÞÆR AFŒDDÆ HIÆ ⱣYLIF IN ROMÆCÆSTRI OÞLÆ UNNEG, 'Romulus and Remus, two brothers; a she-wolf fed them in the city of Rome, far from their native land'. The right side reads: HER HOS SITIÞ ON HARMBERGA AGL[.] DRIGIÞ SⱣA HIRÆ ERTAE GISGRAF SARDEN SORGA AND SEFA TORNA, 'Here Hos sits on the sorrow-mound; she suffers distress as Ertae had imposed it upon her, a wretched den of sorrows and of torments of mind'; RISCI, 'rush'; BITA, perhaps a personal name; ⱣUDU, 'wood'.

7 Bath

Pump Room, Bath, Somerset, no. RB 109.

Found 1898, during controlled excavation, east of Roman Baths, south of Abbey. 10·2 × 8·9 × c. 0·2 cm. Decorated lead circular cross. Text i incomplete, slightly deteriorated, set in panels round perimeter of face, letters facing inwards; ii highly deteriorated, set in panels on diagonal arms of cross on face, letters facing downwards; iii illegible, set without framing lines but in panel on vertical and horizontal arms of cross on face, letters facing down and left; iv illegible, set without framing lines but in panel on horizontal arms of cross on back, letters facing left. Latin texts, i and probably ii descriptive formulae, type c. Texts i, ii AS capitals, iii insular minuscule, iv AS capitals and insular minuscule. Date uncertain.

Davis (?1898), *passim* & figs.; Smith, R. A. (1906a), 380–1 & figs.; Clapham (1948a), 9; Rice (1952), 235.

i: *LVCAS | IOHANNES | —*
ii: *ADO[. ...] | E[.] OI | [. .]OE | [. .]ADA[.] |*

Text i reads: LVCAS IOHANNES —, and probably contained the other evangelists' names also. The other texts are now too illegible to be meaningful, though iii begins with A, and contains: — CUNABUL —, while iv begins: ANNO AB —, and contains several groups of legible letters.

On the evidence of early photographs some, but not all, of Smith's readings can be justified.[1] He read the evangelists' names in text i, then text ii as gnostic names of the Deity: ELOE (or ELOI) ADONAI SABAI ϴEOI. He read text iii as follows:

QUI IN VIRTUTE CRUCIS MUNDUM [PURGAVIT]
TARTARA DISRUPIT CLAUSTRA CELESTIA A[PERUIT]
ET OMNIBUS DEDIT PA[CEM] FIDELIBUS SA[LUTEM]

[1] Smith, R. A. (1906a), 381, with his italicised (= inserted) letters here bracketed.

CHRISTE [OMNIUM] H[OMINUM] CUNABULA CUNCTA [DISPONENS]
PUR[IFICA ME] SQUALORE SORDE VOLUTA[TAM]
SUPPLEX TI[BI DOMINE] DEPOSCO MISERERE [MEI],

translating it: 'He who by the power of the Cross redeemed the world, burst asunder the gates of Hell, opened those of Heaven, gave peace to all and salvation to the faithful. O Christ, who orderest the birth of all, purify me who am polluted by the stain of sin, I suppliantly beseech Thee, O Lord have mercy on me.' He read text iv as: ANNO AB INCARNATIONE DOMINI NOSTRI D[IE] XV KAL. OCTOBRIS [...] EADGYVU [...] CONGREGATIONIS SOROR, probably 'In the (...) year after the Incarnation of Our Lord, Eadgyvu died, a sister of the community, on September 17th'.

8 Beckermet

Churchyard of St Bridget's parish church, Beckermet, Cumberland.

First mentioned 1816, probably in present *situs*. Upper part 137·2 × 48·3 × c. 31·8 cm., diam. of lower part c. 56·5 cm. Incomplete carved stone shaft, cylindrical below and rectangular above; incomplete illegible text set in panel on one rectangular face. Language and formula uncertain. Possibly AS capitals and insular minuscule. Probably tenth to eleventh century.

Lysons, D. and Lysons, S. (1816), cci–ccii & fig.; Jefferson (1842), 308; Haigh (1857), 149–50 & fig.; Whellan (1860), 458–9; Addison (1865), 60–2; Stephens (1865), 191–2 & figs.; Allen & Browne (1885), 342, 343; Allen (1889), 217; Ferguson (1892), 495; Calverly (1899), 26–33 & figs.; (—) (1900a), 87–8; Collingwood, W. G. (1901), 264, 281–2 & fig.; Stevens (1904), 48–9; Collingwood, W. G. (1915b), 130–1 & fig.; Collingwood, W. G. (1923), 262; Parker, C. A. (1926), 118–20 & fig.; Brown, G. B. (1937), 271–2 & fig.; Kendrick (1941), 11 & fig.; Kendrick (1949), 70 & fig.; Fair (1950), 94; Pevsner (1967a), 65–6.

The text is now illegible, though one or two letters on the top four lines can be made out. In 1816 Lysons and Lysons described the text as 'in too decayed a state to afford any satisfactory conjecture as to its import'.[1] Nevertheless, since then five translations from three different languages have been suggested.

9 Billingham

Billingham, Durham. Now in the British Museum, London, no. 1880.3–13.5.

First mentioned 1873–4, found during restoration of Billingham parish church, possibly during considerable restoration of 1864–5. c. 19 × c. 16 × c. 6·4 cm. Incomplete carved magnesian limestone slab with incomplete legible texts, letters

1 Lysons, D. and Lysons, S. (1816), cci.

facing inwards, i set round perimeter on face, ii in remaining quadrant of cross.
i Latin memorial formula, ii possibly Latin descriptive formula, type C. Insular
majuscule. Probably eighth to ninth century.

Haigh (1875), 367; Hübner (1876), no. 202 & add., pp. 72, 90 & fig.; Allen (1887), 118; Allen
(1889), 129; Hall, G. R. (1889), 262; Hodges (1905), 221; Lethaby (1913), 152 & figs.;
(—) (1913–14), 199; Howorth (1914), 47; Howorth (1917), III, 304; Brown, G. B. (1921), 69
& fig.; Smith, R. A. (1923), 123 & fig.

i: OR*AT* | EPROF[...] | [... .*I*]NIB̄ |

ii: *A* — |

Text i reads: ORATE PRO F[...]NIB̄, where the abbreviation is of the form B3 =
-BUS, and the last letters end where the first begin. The extant text can be translated:
'Pray for ...', where F may begin a personal name. Haigh reconstructed the text as:
ORATE PRO F[RATRIBUS NOSTRIS ET PRO CUNCTIS XP̄ANIS HO]MINIB.[1]
However, since the size of the letters varies, it is uncertain how many are lost, and
no reconstruction can be other than conjectural. Text ii reads: A —, possibly
representing *alpha*, with *omega* now lost.

10 Birtley

Set into the interior north wall of the chancel of Birtley parish church, Northumberland.

Found autumn 1884, in church fabric. 26 × 20·3 × *c.* 7·6 cm. Carved free-stone slab
with legible text set in quadrants of cross on visible face. Language and formula uncertain, possibly Latin memorial formula. AS capitals. Possibly eighth to ninth century.

Hall, G. R. (1889), 254–67 & fig.; Hodges (1893), 69–70 & fig.; Hodgson, J. C. (1897), 358–9 &
fig.; Brown, G. B. (1921), 69 & fig.; Pevsner (1957), 95.

Ō | R | P | E |

The text probably reads: ŌRPE, though EŌRP is also possible. The abbreviation
mark suggests that an unrecorded personal name *EORP is unlikely, and that the
text is more likely to be all abbreviated. It may be expanded to read: ORA (or
ORATE) PRO E — 'Pray for E —', where P = PRO, also recorded elsewhere
without an abbreviation sign.

11 Bishop Auckland

Parish church of St Andrew, Bishop Auckland, Durham.

Found 1881, in church fabric. 88·9 × 38·1 × 26·7 cm. Incomplete carved stone
cross-shaft, with rather deteriorated texts set in panels on one face, on front of

---

[1] Haigh (1875), 367.

reconstructed cross; text i set above middle carved figure, ii in centre of left hand figure. Latin texts, probably descriptive formulae, type b. AS capitals. Probably eighth to ninth century.

Browne (1885*b*), 158 & fig.; Hodges (1894), 73–5 & figs.; Hodgson, J. F. (1899), 31–4 & figs.; Hodges (1905), 217–18 & figs.; Collingwood, W. G. (1916–18), 37 & figs.; Collingwood, W. G. (1927), 39–40, index & figs.; Collingwood, W. G. (1932), 41–2 & figs.; Brown, G. B. (1937), 195–7 & figs.; Kendrick (1938), 140–1 & figs.; Kurth (1943), 213–14 & figs.; Pevsner (1953), 202 & fig.; (—) (1958), 15 & fig.; Stoll (1967), 328–9 & fig.

i: *PAS* |

ii: *AND* |

Text ii reads: AND, probably 'Andreas'. Text i reads: PAS, possibly 'Paulus' or 'Paulinus'. The possible reading PASSUS EST, 'he suffered' is unlikely since the figure has no cruciform nimbus. The corresponding portions of the third figure are lost, and the significance of the scene is not now clear. None of the other carved pieces of stone forming the reconstructed cross is inscribed.

12   Bishopstone

Set above the door on the south wall of the south porch of Bishopstone parish church, Sussex.

First mentioned 1835, *in situ* and in present *situs*. *c.* 47 × *c.* 35·6 cm. Caen stone sun-dial with legible text set without framing lines on visible face above dial. OE personal name. AS capitals. Eleventh to twelfth century.

Horsfield (1835), 271; Lower (1840), 496 & fig.; Figg (1849), 279; Figg (1854), 60–1 & fig.; Figg (1856), 322 & fig.; Haigh (1857), 179 & fig.; Way & Noyer (1868), 208–9; Cuming (1873), 281 & fig.; St Croix (1875), 274–5; Hübner (1876), no. 168, p. 61 & fig.; Haigh (1879), 135, 196, 198 & fig.; Allen (1889), 201 & fig.; Searle (1897), 186; Gatty (1900), 66 & fig.; Legge (1903), 177–8 & figs.; Day (?1904), 26 & fig.; Leclercq (1910*b*), col. 1543 & fig.; Leeney, O. H. (1911), 373 & fig.; Whitley (1919), 127; Brown, G. B. (1921), 174; Brown, G. B. (1925), 193–4, 444; Green, A. R. (1928), 508–10 & fig.; Cole (1945–7), 77 & fig.; Clapham (1948*a*), 7; Godfrey, W. H. (1948), 167–8; Jackson, E. D. C. and Fletcher (1956), 5–9 & fig.; Godfrey, W. H. (1957), 3 & fig.; Zinner (1964), 3, 46; Nairn & Pevsner (1965), 418; Taylor, H. M. and Taylor, J. (1965), 72; Taylor, J. and Taylor, H. M. (1966), 19, 49; Stoll (1967), 283 & fig.; Okasha (1969), 26–7 & fig.

✠EAD | RI[C] |

The text reads: ✠ EADRI[C], '✠ Eadri[c]', a recorded name. The dial, though probably late, must pre-date the early Norman door which protrudes on to it; it is unlikely to be contemporary with the eighth century porticus. The text may not be primary.

13 Bodsham

Bodsham, Kent. Now in the British Museum, London, no. 1969.6–6.1.

Found August 1968, below ground in field.[1] Diam. *c.* 2·2 cm., ht. of hoop *c.* 0·8 cm. Decorated gold ring, with legible text set in panels right round outside of hoop, letters gold on niello. OE owner formula. AS capitals. Probably ninth century.

Okasha and Webster (1970), 102–4 & figs.

✠[.] | AR | *M*V | ND | ME | CA | HI | M |

The text reads: ✠ [.]ARMVND MEC AH IM, the first part being: '✠ [.]armvnd owns me', where the name is [G]ARMVND or [S]ARMVND. GĀRMUND is a recorded OE name; alternatively SARMUND could be explained as a possible, though unrecorded and odd, anglicised form of ON SÆMUNDR. The significance of IM is uncertain; it could be decorative, to fill up space, an unrecorded abbreviation (e.g. for IHS), or an error due to a misreading of an exemplum as HIM.

14 Bossington

Bossington, Hampshire. Now in the Ashmolean Museum, Oxford.[2]

Found pre 1845, in peat at Wallop's Ford near Bossington. Diam. *c.* 2·6 cm., ht. of bezel *c.* 2·5 cm. Decorated gold ring with legible text set right round bust on exterior of bezel, letters in relief and facing inwards. Latin descriptive formula, type c. AS capitals and insular minuscule. Possibly ninth to tenth century.

(—) (1836–68), 9; Smith, C. R. (1846), 341 & figs.; Akerman (1847), 144 & fig.; Fairholt (1871), 100–1 & figs.; Jones (1877), 63 & figs.; Smith, W. and Cheetham (1880), 1801–2; André (1883–4), 1; Smith, R. A. (1900), 397; Smith, H. C. (1908), 73; Brown, G. B. (1915), 311 & fig.; Sheppard (1923), 44–6 & figs.; Andrews (1926), 9 & fig.; Anscombe (1926–7), 136–9 & fig.; Oman (1931), 105 & fig.; Nelson (1939), 183 & fig.; Jessup (1950), 135 & fig.; Page, R. I. (1964), 75, 90; Page, R. I. (1968), 18.

INXPŌNOMENC[.]LLAFIC̄ |

The text probably reads: IN XPŌ NOMEN C[U]LLA FIC̄, possibly 'In Christ my name has been changed to C[u]lla', where ʜ = U (cf. coins of Burgred of Mercia), XPŌ = CHRISTO and where FIC̄ may = FICTUM EST. Other possible readings of the name are EHLLA, ECLLA, EULLA, but these are difficult to explain; CULLA is recorded once elsewhere, as a byname in the *Hyde Liber Vitae*.[3] Andrews suggested that the ring was episcopal,[4] but it is more likely to be baptismal. On the numismatic parallels, Dolley strongly preferred a ninth century date.[5]

---

[1] I am grateful to Mr and Mrs Frank Smith, who found the ring, for their help with the details of its finding.

[2] The ring was acquired too early to have an acquisition number.

[3] Birch (1892), 32.   [4] Andrews (1926), 9.   [5] M. Dolley, in a personal communication.

15 Breamore I

Set round the interior arch of the south porticus doorway, Breamore parish church, Hampshire.

First mentioned 1897, *in situ* and in present *situs*. Doorway *c.* 305 × 134·6 cm. Probably incomplete, legible text set without framing lines round north face of south porticus stone doorway, letters containing modern paint and facing inwards. OE descriptive formula, type c. AS capitals. Tenth to eleventh century.

Hill, A. du B. (1897*a*), 233 & fig.; Hill, A. du B. (1897*b*), 408–9; Hill, A. du B. (1898), 85–6 & fig.; Allen (1903), 237; Napier (1903–6), 292–3; Förster (1906), 448–9; Moger (1911), 600 & fig.; Brown, G. B. (1925), 351–3 & fig.; Rivoira (1933), 192 n. & fig.; Green, A. R. (?1942), no pagination; Clapham (1947), 160; Clapham (1948*a*), 7; Green, A. R. and Green, P. M. (1951), 6–7 & fig.; Hunter Blair (1956), pl. x; Deanesly (1961), 350–1; Fisher (1962), 392–3 & fig.; Taylor, H. M. and Taylor, J. (1965), 95–6 & fig.; Radford (1966), 203; Taylor, J. and Taylor, H. M. (1966), 11, 50; Pevsner and Lloyd (1967), 143; Okasha (1969), 29.

H/ERSƿVT/ELAÐSEOGECƿYDRÆDN/ESÐE —

The text reads: HER SƿVTELAÐ SEO GECƿYDRÆDNES ÐE —, probably 'Here is shown the agreement (*or* covenant) which —'. Alternatively ÐE could mean 'to you' and the text could then be complete. Deanesly suggested that the text was a legal document,[1] but it seems more likely to be religious. The letters GEC are on a piece of stone which has been renewed. The text is probably primary; it must post-date the arch, but probably by only a short period.

16 Breamore II

On a stone placed beside the chancel arch, on the west-facing interior wall, Breamore parish church, Hampshire.

First mentioned 1898, in present *situs*. *c.* 15·5 × *c.* 20 cm. Incomplete stone with incomplete slightly deteriorated text, set without framing lines on visible face. Language and formula uncertain. AS capitals. Probably tenth to eleventh century.

Hill, A. du B. (1898), 85; Allen (1903), 237; Moger (1911), 600; Green, A. R. (?1942), no pagination; Clapham (1947), 160; Green, A. R. and Green, P. M. (1951), 7; Fisher (1962), 392; Taylor, H. M. and Taylor, J. (1965), 96; Radford (1966), 203; Taylor, J. and Taylor, H. M. (1966), 11; Pevsner and Lloyd (1967), 143; Okasha (1969), 29.

— DE[S] —

The text reads: — DE[S] —, and is too fragmentary to be meaningful. It is dated by comparison with 15 Breamore I. It may have originally formed part of a similar (or the same) text set round another arch.

[1] Deanesly (1961), 350 n.

17   Brussels I

Church of SS Michael and Gudule, Brussels, Belgium.

Deposited in church January 1650; possibly identical with relic of True Cross recorded in Tiel 1315. *c.* 47·6 × *c.* 29·2 × *c.* 0.6 cm. Wooden cross, protected by modern gold cover, containing space for relic; covered with incomplete decorated silver lamina which contains legible texts; i, ii set without framing lines on remaining face, iii set in panels on edges, letters facing remaining silver face and reading from lower left corner. Text i, Latin descriptive formula, type b, ii OE maker formula, iii OE descriptive formula, type a. AS capitals and insular minuscule. Tenth to eleventh century.

Fleury (1870), 317–19; Logeman (1891), *passim* & figs.; Zupitza (1891), 462; Grein (1894), 489; Cook (1905), xlv–xlvii, 29; Cook (1912), 247–9; Cook (1915), 157–61; Browne (1916), 71–2; Hensen (1925), 92–7; Velge (?1925), 363–6 & figs.; Norman (1936), 9–10; d'Ardenne (1939), 145–64, 271–2 & figs.; Dobbie (1942), cxxiii–cxxv, clxxvi, 115, 204; Dickins and Ross (1954), 13–16, 26–7, *passim*; Page, R. I. (1964), 87; Crossley-Holland and Mitchell (1965), 122; Whitelock (1967), 274; Swanton (1969), 422; Swanton (1970) 41–2, 48–9, 66 n.

i: A G N V | S D Ī |

ii: ✠ D R A H M A L | M E ƿ O R H T E : |

iii: ✠ R O D I S M I N N A M A G E O I C R I C N/E C Y N I N/G B Æ R B Y F I G Y N DE

        B| L O D E B E S T E M/E D |

        Þ A |

        S R O D E H E T Æ Þ L M Æ R |

        ƿ Y R I C A N 7 |

        A Ð E |

        L ƿ O L D H Y S B E R O Þ O[.] |

        C R I S T E T O L O F E F O R Æ L F R I C E S S A V L E H Y R A B E R O Þ O R : |

Text i reads: A G N V S D Ī, 'Lamb of God', where D Ī = D E I. The text describes the decoration and the reference is to the Vulgate John I 29. Text ii reads: ✠ D R A H M A L M E ƿ O R H T E :, '✠ Drahmal made me'. The name is of ON or Cont Gmc origin and is discussed in Index v. The first part of text iii is in verse and reads:

        ✠ R O D I S M I N N A M A   G E O I C R I C N E C Y N I N G

        B Æ R B Y F I G Y N D E   B L O D E B E S T E M E D

'✠ Cross is my name. Once, trembling and drenched with blood, I bore the mighty king'. The relationship of this text, the runic text of Ruthwell and the Vercelli Book *Dream of the Rood* is discussed by Dickins and Ross.[1] The rest of the text reads:

[1] Dickins and Ross (1954), 13–19.

ÞAS RODE HET ÆÐLMÆR ƷYRICAN 7 AÐELƷOLD HYS BEROÞO[R] CRISTE TO LOFE FOR ÆLFRICES SAVLE HYRA BEROÞOR:, 'Æþlmær, and Aðelƿold his brother, ordered this cross to be made to the glory of Christ, (and) for the soul of Ælfric their brother'. The personal names AEÐELMĀER, AEÐELWEALD and AELFRĪC are all recorded. The dating of the cross supports Dolley's theory of the resurgence, around A.D. 1010, of devotion to the *Agnus Dei*.[1]

18   Caistor

Caistor, Lincolnshire. Lost.

First mentioned 1773, found 1770 beneath ground on Castle Hill. Probably *c*. 23 × *c*. 46 cm., though measurements differ.[2] Incomplete, probably uncarved stone slab with text set without framing lines on visible face.[3] Figures of text suggest it was incomplete but legible. Latin text, possibly memorial formula. AS capitals and insular minuscule. Date uncertain.

Turner & Bradley, J. (1784), 161–2 & fig.; Gough (1806), II, 386–7 & fig.; Oliver (1829), 221–2; Oliver (1831), 204; Trollope, E. (1862), 152; Radford (1946), 95–9 & fig.

— [IS. . . . ...]│ CRVCISPOL[. ...]│ QUODE[.]BE/REC[...]│INHONOR[. ...]│ [. . T. . .D. .] —

The text reads: — [IS. . . ...] CRVCIS POL[. ...] QUOD E[.]BEREC[...] IN HONOR[E] —, but is too fragmentary to be meaningful. A noun on which depends CRVCIS and QUOD is presumably lost before CRVCIS and a verb after E[C]BEREC — or E[G]BEREC —, which is a personal name. Radford suggested that the text formed part of a dedication stone of a church or altar, though earlier commentators associated it with the dedication by King Ecgberht of Wessex of his battle spoils to the church in A.D. 827.[4] There is a little epigraphic evidence which might suggest an early date.

19   Canterbury I

Canterbury, Kent. Now in the Ashmolean Museum, Oxford, no. 1951–131.

First mentioned 1903, in possession of W. C. Trimnell, found some years previously in Canterbury. Diam. 7·6 cm. Decorated circular silver coin-brooch, with texts in relief lettering facing inwards; text i legible, set round bust on face, ii highly deteriorated set right round cross on back. Latin texts, i maker formula, ii descriptive formula, type c. AS capitals. Tenth century.

1 M. Dolley, in a personal communication.
2 These are the measurements given by the earliest commentators, Turner and Bradley, J. (1784), 161.
3 The description, etc., of the stone is taken from published accounts and figures.
4 Radford (1946), 98–9; Turner and Bradley, J. (1784), 162; Oliver (1831), 204.

Smith, R. A. (1901–3), 210–12 & figs.; Smith, R. A. (1906 c), 374 n.; Smith, R. A. (1908), 382 & figs.; (—) (1930 b), no. 44, p. 22; Jessup (1950), 112 & fig.; (—) (1951 a), 32 & figs.; (—) (1951 b), lot 122, p. 16; Bruce-Mitford (1956), 200; Page, R. I. (1964), 75, 85; Wilson, D. M. (1964), 7–8, 35.

i: ✠ Ᵽ/VDEMANFECIÐ |

ii: NOM[INED]OM[INI] |

Text i reads: ✠ ⱣVDEMAN FECIÐ, '✠ Ⱡvdeman made (me)'. The name is a form of the recorded WUDUMAN; the inflexion of FECIÐ occurs also elsewhere, e.g. BCS 536 (A.D. 873) ABEAÐ = HABEAT.[1] Text ii reads: NOM[INE D]OM[INI], 'In the name of the Lord'. It has been partially obliterated by the addition of strengthening metal strips over-lying the text. By comparison with coins, Dolley suggested a date in the mid tenth century on the evidence of the style of the drapery. He also noted that IN NOMINE DOMINI occurs on Swedish imitative coins of the late tenth century.[2]

20 Canterbury II

Canterbury Cathedral Treasury, Kent.

Found July 1939, below ground in Cathedral Cloister Garth. Rectangular part c. 1·6 × 4·8 × c. 0·3 cm., triangular part c. 1·3 cm. long. Gold and silver decorated portable sun-dial with rectangular and triangular parts; rectangular silver part contains slightly deteriorated texts, i set in panels on faces, ii without framing lines on edges; letters are filled, possibly with niello. Latin texts, i descriptive formula, type a, ii maker and owner formulae. AS capitals. Probably tenth century.

(—) (1950), 1890 & fig.; Ward (1966), 24–5.

i: IAN DEC | FEB NOV | MAR OCT |
   MAI AVG | IVN IVL | APR SEP |

ii: [SA]LVSFACTORI |
    [PA]XPOSSESSOR[I] |

Text i reads: IAN DEC FEB NOV MAR OCT MAI AVG IVN IVL APR SEP, being the months of the year in abbreviated form, presumably in Latin, and presumably in the order necessary to the working of the dial. The unabbreviated forms are given in Index VI. Text ii reads: [SA]LVS FACTORI [PA]X POSSESSOR[I], 'Salvation to the maker, peace to the owner'.

[1] I am indebted to N. P. Brooks, University of St Andrews, for drawing this example to my attention.
[2] M. Dolley, in a personal communication.

21 Canterbury III

St Augustine's Abbey Museum, Canterbury, Kent.[1]

Found March 1924, below ground in south aisle of Abbey nave, during controlled excavation, with bones and remains of lead box. 15·6 × 12·9 × c. 0·2 cm. Lead cross with text i legible on face and ii slightly deteriorated on back; both texts set vertically and horizontally on arms with horizontal letters facing left. Latin texts, i memorial formula, ii descriptive formula, type b. AS capitals. Late eleventh century or post-Conquest.

Potts (1924), 422–5 & figs.; Clapham (1948 a), 7.

i: ANN/O:ML̄ | L:X:III: |
    :V:IDVS:MĀR:MIGRAVITEXHAC:VIT*A* | WLFMÆG:SOROR:
      WLF[*R*]ICI:ABB: |

ii: AXP̄IEX | [.*OC*:ω] |
    SIGNO:C*V*N*A*B*V*L*A*C*V*/N*C(.)A(.)* |

Text i reads: ANNO : ML̄ L : X : III : : V : IDVS : MĀR : MIGRAVIT EX HAC: VITA WLFMÆG : SOROR : WLF[R]ICI : ABB :, 'On 11 March 1063, Wlfmæg, sister of Abbot Wlf[r]ic, departed from this life', where ML̄ = MILLESIMO, MĀR = MARTII, and ABB = ABBATIS. Text ii reads: A XP̄I EX [HOC : ω] SIGNO CVNABVLA CVNC[T]A [.], possibly 'By this *alpha* and *omega* of Christ I mark all resting places', where XP̄I = CHRISTI, A = ALPHA and ω = OMEGA. CUNABULA, however, usually means 'cradle', and SIGNO might be an oblique case of SIGNUM.

The script suggests that this text is not contemporary with the death of Wulfmaeg, sister of Abbot Wulfric, but was inserted later. Support for this is supplied by the two similar lead plates (also in St Augustine's Abbey Museum) commemorating King Lothair (*ob.* A.D. 685) and King Wihtred (*ob.* 725). The epigraphic evidence makes it clear that these texts are not contemporary. All three probably date from Abbot Scotland's translation of various early burials in the early twelfth century,[2] and may be *in situ* of the translation.

22 Canterbury IV

Set in the south wall of St Martin's parish church, Canterbury, Kent.

First mentioned 1898, in present *situs* and probably *in situ*. 9·5 × 24·1 cm. Incomplete and slightly deteriorated text set without framing lines on exterior face of

---

[1] Neither the cross nor the lead plates referred to below have Museum acquisition numbers.
[2] See Goscelinus (1854), cols. 743–64.

stone, possibly sand-stone, forming part of west exterior jamb of blocked AS doorway. Latin text, possibly dedication formula. AS capitals. Date uncertain.

Routledge (1897), 9; Routledge (1898), 56–9; Peers (1901), 413–18; Fisher (1962), 356 & fig.; Okasha (1969), 29.

— [SCE] | ŌMNIV̄ SC̄ORV̄ |

The text reads: — ŌMNIV̄ SC̄ORV̄, that is, — OMNIVM SANCTORVM, '— of all saints', where letters may be lost at the beginning of the second line. The abbreviation mark over the first letter of ŌMNIV̄ is perhaps an error. Taylor and Taylor described the doorway as a Saxon insertion into an earlier Saxon wall, both probably dating from the seventh century.[1] The text in its present position is unlikely to be primary; if the stone has been re-used in building, however, it may originally have been a primary text.

23   Carlisle I

Carlisle Cathedral Fratry, Cumberland.

Found 1857, below ground in Cathedral precincts. 10·8 × 31·8 × 7 cm. Incomplete carved sandstone cross-head, with incomplete but legible text set in panels but without framing lines on both faces. Probably OE memorial formula. AS capitals. Probably eighth to ninth century.

Purday (1858), 85–6 & figs.; (—) (1859), 15; Calverley (1899), 95–6 & figs.; Collingwood, W. G. (1901), 258, 281 & figs.; Collingwood, W. G. (1915b), 125–6 & figs.; Collingwood, W. G. (1923), 230; Collingwood, W. G. (1927), 58, index & figs.; Dahl (1938), 18, 194.

⊬SIG | [......] | TTEDIS | [...... ...] |
AEF | [...S.] | ITBE | [RH....] |

The second s of the first face is set below the line of script. The text can be partially reconstructed by formula comparison to read: ⊬ SIG[...SE]TTE DIS [...] AEF[TER S.]-ITBE[RH...], '⊬ Sig[...] set this [...] in memory of [S.]itbe[rh...]'. The text may be incomplete at the end of one or both faces. The neuter noun following DIS may have been OE BĒACEN, and the second name could possibly be [SꞂ]ITBE[RHT], a form of the recorded SWIÐBEORHT.

24   Carlisle II

Carlisle, Cumberland. Lost.

Found pre August 1882, in St Cuthbert's Lane. 17·8 × 14·3 × 8·6 cm. Incomplete carved stone cross-head, with incomplete slightly deteriorated text set on face,

---

[1] Taylor, H. M. and Taylor, J. (1965), 143.

without framing lines but in panel.[1] Language and formula uncertain. AS capitals. Possibly ninth century.

Collingwood, W. G. (1916), 279–81 & figs.; Collingwood, W. G. (1923), 230; Collingwood, W. G. (1927), 87, index & figs.

— | B*A* | [*D*..] | —

The text reads: — B*A*[D] —, and may have been part of a personal name. Collingwood's reconstruction (see plate) is of course hypothetical.

25 Chester-le-Street

Parish church of SS Mary and Cuthbert, Chester-le-Street, Durham.

Found June 1883, in church fabric. 88·9 × *c.* 22·9 × *c.* 16·5 cm. Carved tenoned stone slab with legible text set without framing lines on face. OE personal name. AS capitals and runes. Probably tenth to eleventh century.

Browne (1883), 182–4 & fig.; Stephens (1884*a*), 461–3 & figs.; Stephens (1884*b*), 246–7 & figs.; Allen and Browne (1885), 342–3; Stephens (1885), 82–92 & figs.; Boyle (1887–8), 298; Allen (1889) 221; Hodges (1894), 76; Viëtor (1895), 18 n.; Searle (1897), 183; Hodges (1905), 222; Pevsner (1953), 66; Page, R. I. (1959*a*), 386; Fyson (1960), 152 & fig.; Jackson, F. H. and Appleton (?1964), 13; Page, R. I. (1964), 76; Spurr (1964), 9 & fig. on back cover; Page, R. I. (1969), 48.

EAD*m* | V*n*D |

The text, which is probably not primary, reads: EADMVND, a recorded name.

26 Crowland

Crowland, Lincolnshire. Standing beside the road, National Grid reference TF 260 149.

First mentioned 1607 at Crowland, later in garden near Brotherhouse toll bar on Spalding road. 86·4 × *c.* 38 × 22·2 cm. Incomplete stone shaft, possibly tenoned at base;[2] incomplete slightly deteriorated text set in panel on one face. Latin descriptive formula, type a. Capitals and uncials. Date uncertain, probably post-Conquest.

Camden (1607), 399–400; Gibson, E. (1695), col. 462; Stukeley (1724), 32 & fig. opp. p. 12; Pownall (1775), 96–100 & fig.; Pegge (1779), 101–5 & fig.; Pegge (1782), 395–9 & figs.; Gough (1806), II, 332, 343–4 & figs. (figs. p. 344 & opp. p. 401); Hübner (1876), no. 171 & add., pp. 63, 90 & fig.; Birch (1879), 393, 395 & figs.; Birch (1881), xxxii–xxxiv & fig.; Canham (1890), 124 & fig.; Canham (1894), 247–8 & fig.; Howorth (1917), II, fig. opp. p. 298.

— HANC | :PET/RĀ: | GVT/HLA | CVSH̄[.] | SIBI :ME | TAM |

The text probably reads: — HANC : PETRĀ : GVTHLACVS H̄[T] SIBI : METAM, '— Guthlacus has this stone as a boundary for himself', where PETRĀ = PETRAM

---

[1] The description, etc., is taken from published accounts.   [2] Moore in Birch (1881), xxxiii n.

and Ħ[T] = HABET; alternatively, HABUIT could be read, or Ħ[C] = HUIC, HANC. The medial rhyme may be intentional. The text is unlikely to be contemporary with St Guthlac, and may refer to the boundary of the Abbey of Croyland. The script suggests that it is post-Conquest. The fourteenth-century pseudo-Ingulphus may have known of the stone since he refers to Abbot Turketul's setting up of Abbey boundary crosses in the late tenth century.[1] The stone may also have been known *c.* 1450: 'de Cruce apud Brothirhowse'.[2]

27 Cuxton

Cuxton, Kent. Now in the British Museum, London, no. 1833.1–1.1.

BM Register 1833 states found Cuxton 1830; first published reference states found Chatham 1814.[3] Diam. 3·5 cm. Circular decorated silver brooch, with legible text set right round perimeter on face, letters facing inwards. OE owner formula. AS capitals. Tenth century.

Stothard (1846), 327; Westwood (1855), 202 & fig.; Stephens (1867–8), 586 & fig. *ad finem*; Evans (1873), 332; Payne (1893), 112; Searle (1897), 9; (—) (1901*a*), 17; Smith, R. A. (1908), 383; Smith, R. A. (1923), 103 & fig.; Jessup (1930), 238 & fig.; Harder (1932), 37; Page, R. I. (1964), 84, 87; Wilson, D. M. (1964), no. 14, pp. 44, 47, 129–30 & fig.; Page, R. I. (1969), 30.

✠ÆLFGIVV MEA[H] |

The text reads: ✠ÆLFGIVV ME A[H], '✠ Ælfgivv owns me', where there is probably a space in the text after the personal name. AELFGIFU is a recorded feminine name.

28 Deerhurst I

Deerhurst, Gloucestershire. Now in the Ashmolean Museum, Oxford.[4]

Found 1675, below ground in orchard adjoining chapel; possibly identical with stone mentioned by Leland.[5] 68·6 × 96·5 × *c.* 15·2 cm. Stone slab containing modern paint, with legible text set without framing lines on one face. Latin dedication formula. AS capitals. A.D. 1056.

Camden (1607), 253; Gibson, E. (1695), cols. 233–4, 245–6; Leland (1744), VI, 71–2 (original numbering, VI, fo. 81); Chandler (1763), cxxxv & fig.; Pegge (1787), 16–19 & fig.; Gough (1806), I, 380, 390 & fig. opp. p. 344; Wright (1845), 33; Haigh (1846*b*), 10–12; Parker, J. H. (1846), 26–7 & fig.; Westwood (1846), 250–1; Rickman (1862), 88–9 & fig.; Butterworth (1876), 97–9; Butterworth (1878), 5–6, 22–6; Butterworth (1885), 413–18 & fig.; Middleton (1885–7), 15–19 & fig.; Butterworth (1886–7), 105–16 & fig.; Middleton (1887), 69–71 & fig.; Butterworth (1888), 98–107 & fig.; Allen (1889), 202–3; Plummer (1899), 238; Taylor, C. S. (1902), 230–6;

---

[1] Cf. Colgrave, B. (1956), 7–8.   [2] Quoted in Birch (1881), xxxiii.   [3] Stothard (1846), 327.
[4] The stone was acquired too early to have an acquisition number.   [5] See below.

Howorth (1917), II, 388–9; Brown, G. B. (1925), 307–8; Rivoira (1933), 174; Clapham (1948 a), 7; Gilbert (1964), 11–12 & fig.; Taylor, H. M. & Taylor, J. (1965), 209–11; Mee (1966), 116.

⊹ODDA : DVXIVSSI : TH/ANC | REGIAMAVLAM[:]CONSTRVI[:] | ATQVE : DED/IC/ARIINHONO | RES̄[:]TRINITATIS[:] | PROANIMAG/ER | MANISVIÆLFRICIQ/VE[:]DEHOC | LOC/O[:] | ASV̄PTAEALDREDVSVERO | EP̄SQVI[:]EANDĒ[:] | D/ED/ICAVITIIID/I | BVS : APL̄XIIIIAVT/EANNO$REG| NIEADWARDREGISANGLORV̄|

The text reads: ⊹ODDA : DVX IVSSIT : HANC REGIAM AVLAM[:] CONSTRVI[:] ATQVE : DEDICARI IN HONORE S̄[:] TRINITATIS [:] PRO ANIMA GERMANI SVI ÆLFRICI QVE [:] DE HOC LOCO [:] ASV̄PTA EALDREDVS VERO EP̄S QVI [:] EANDĒ [:] DEDICAVIT II IDIBVS : APL̄ XIIII AVTE ANNO $ REGNI EADWARD REGIS ANGLORV̄, '⊹Earl Odda ordered this royal church to be built and dedicated in honour of the Holy Trinity for the soul of his brother Ælfric which (was) taken up from this place. And Ealdred was the Bishop who dedicated the same on 12 April and in the fourteenth year of the reign of Eadward King of the English', where $ is presumably an error, EADWARD is uninflected, and the date is 1056. The following abbreviations are used: S̄ = SANCTI; ASV̄PTA = ASSUMPTA; EP̄S = EPISCOPUS; EANDĒ = EANDEM; APL̄ = APRILIS; AVTE = AUTEM; ANGLORV̄ = ANGLO-RUM. The third I of TRINITATIS is small in size and inserted between the T and the S.

Earl Odda of Devonshire, whose name is of ON origin, a relative of Edward the Confessor (A.D. 1042–66), died in 1056, and his brother Aelfric in 1053. Ealdred became Bishop of Worcester in 1047 and Archbishop of York in 1060. It is not certain whether the REGIA AVLA, presumably 'royal church' not 'royal hall', refers to the church or chapel at Deerhurst.

Leland referred to two inscriptions from Deerhurst: Odda's coffin, found 1259, which no longer exists,[1] and the tomb of Almaric, brother of Oddo and Doddo (allegedly living in the eighth century) which had a text saying that Doddo consecrated the church to the Virgin for Almaric's soul.[2] Leland's source was the sixteenth century Tewkesbury Chronicle whose writer said he had seen Almaric's tomb.[3] This seems to be a garbled description of the stone under discussion, suggesting that it was known before 1675.

[1] Leland (1770), I, 244.
[2] Leland (1744), VI, fo. 81.
[3] BM MS *Cotton Cleopatra* C iii, fo. 220a.

29 Deerhurst II

Set in an interior wall of the Saxon chapel, Deerhurst, Gloucestershire.

Found 1885, set in exterior of sixteenth century chimney stack built on to Saxon chapel, cut to form window. 52·1 × 43·2 cm. Incomplete stone slab with incomplete legible text set without framing lines on visible face. Latin text, probably dedication formula. AS capitals. Possibly early to mid eleventh century.

Butterworth (1885), 413–18 & figs.; Middleton (1885–7), 15–19; Butterworth (1886–7),105–16 & figs.; Middleton (1887), 69–71 & figs.; Butterworth (1888), 93–107 & figs.; Routledge (1897), 9; Clapham (1948a), 7; Gilbert (1964), 11; Taylor, H. M. and Taylor, J. (1965), 209–11; Mee (1966), 116.

— [.]HONO | [... .]Ē:TRI | [...]HOC | [... .]E[:]DE | [...]ATV̄:Ē: |

The text can be read: [. IN] HONO[RE SC]Ē : TRI[NITATIS] HOC [... :] DE[DIC]-ATV̄ : Ē :, probably '✠ In honour of the Holy Trinity this [church, altar] was dedicated', where DE[DIC]ATV̄ : Ē : = DEDICATUM : EST :, [SC]Ē probably = SANCTAE, and where the left hand side of the stone is taken to be original. If this is not so, more letters would be lost and the text would not then be recoverable. It is not certain whether the text refers to the church or chapel at Deerhurst, but from its location perhaps the latter; it is tentatively dated by comparison with 28 Deerhurst I and by the date of the chapel.

30 Dewsbury I

Dewsbury, WR Yorkshire. Now in the British Museum, London, no. 1882.7–7.1.

Found c. 1830, near parish church. 10·2 × 11·4 × 5·1 cm. Carved sandstone, probably incomplete cross-shaft, with incomplete slightly deteriorated text set without framing lines on one face. OE memorial formula. Insular majuscule. Eighth to ninth century.

Ellis (1849–53), 94; Ellis (1852), 437 & figs.; Haigh (1856–7), 519; Haigh (1857), 155–6 & fig.; Stephens (1866–7) xxviii, 464, & fig.; Fowler (1870), 223–5 & fig.; Haigh (1877), 419–20; Smith, W. and Cheetham (1880), 1979, 1987 & fig.; Stephens (1884a), 200; Stephens (1884b), 140 & fig.; Sweet (1885), 129; Frank (1888), 42; Allen (1889), 217–18, 220, 222; Stephens (1894), 10; Chadwick (1901), 82; Collingwood, W. G. (1912), 129; Lethaby (1913), 152–3, 158–9 & figs.; Collingwood, W. G. (1915a), 167–8, 290 & figs.; Smith, R. A. (1923), 124–5 & figs.; Collingwood, W. G. (1927), 59, 109, index & figs.; Collingwood, W. G. (1929), 30 & figs.; Olsen (1930), 286; Dahl (1938), 15, 193; Page, R. I. (1958), 149.

— RHTAEBE | CUNA[E]FT | ERBEOR | NAEGIBI | DDADD | [A]ERSA | ULE |

The text reads: — RHTAE BECUN A[E]FTER BEORNAE GIBIDDAD D[A]ER SAULE, '— a monument in memory of his child (*or* lord); pray for the (= his) soul'. The incomplete first word is probably part of an OE name in the dative singular. BEORNAE may be OE BEARN, 'child' or BEORN, 'lord'.

31 Dewsbury II

Dewsbury parish church, WR Yorkshire.

Found 1766–7, in church fabric. 61 × 25·4 × c. 12·7 cm. Incomplete carved free-stone slab, with figure's eyes filled with white material when found;[1] legible text set in panel above carving on face. Latin descriptive formula, type b. AS capitals. Possibly late ninth century.

Whitaker (1816), 301 & fig.; Haigh (1856–7), 509–11 & fig.; Haigh *et al.* (1859), 224–9; Fowler (1870), 222–3 & fig.; Collingwood, W. G. (1912), 113, 129; Collingwood, W. G. (1915a), 162–3, 289 & figs.; Collingwood, W. G. (1927), 6–8, 33, 73–4, index & figs.; Collingwood, W. G. (1929), 24–30 & fig.; Elgee, F. & Elgee, H. W. (1933), 196; Brown, G. B. (1937), 185–7 & figs.; Pevsner (1967b), 179.

[·]IHSXPVS: |

The text reads: [.] IHS XPVS :, possibly with a preceding cross. This abbreviation of the *nomina sacra* presumably refers to the figure carved beneath. Collingwood suggested that this stone and 32 Dewsbury III formed part of the same cross-shaft.[2]

32 Dewsbury III

Dewsbury parish church, WR Yorkshire.

Found 1766–7, in church fabric. 58·4 × 25·4 × c. 20·3 cm. Incomplete carved free-stone slab, with figures' eyes filled with white material when found;[3] probably incomplete, rather deteriorated texts set in panels above each row of figures on face. Latin descriptive formulae, type b. AS capitals. Possibly late ninth century.

Whitaker (1816), 301 & fig.; Haigh (1856–7), 509–11 & fig.; Haigh *et al.* (1859), 224–9; Fowler (1870), 222–3 & figs.; Smith, W. and Cheetham (1875), 849–50; Collingwood, W. G. (1912), 113, 129; Collingwood, W. G. (1915a), 164–5, 289 & figs.; Collingwood, W. G. (1916–18), 46 & fig.; Collingwood, W. G. (1927), 6–8, 33, 73–4, index & figs.; Collingwood, W. G. (1929), 24–30 & figs.; Elgee, F. and Elgee, H. W. (1933), 196 & fig.; Brown, G. B. (1937), 185–7 & figs.; Pevsner (1967b), 179.

i: [.]VMF[ECIT] —
ii: — [.]TD VOPIS: |

---

[1] Whitaker (1816), 301.   [2] Collingwood, W. G. (1927), 6–7.   [3] Whitaker (1816), 301.

The texts read: [.]ѴM F[ECIT]—and—T DVO PIS :. In 1915 Collingwood read substantially more of these texts, *viz.*, [VI]NVM FECIT EX A. and [V P]ANES ET DVO PIS., taking A. as AQUA and PIS. as PISCES.[1] These can be translated as 'he made wine from water' and 'loaves and two fishes'. Collingwood took these texts as referring to the carvings of the miracles of the feast at Cana and of the loaves and fishes, respectively the Vulgate John II 1–11 and Mark VI 35–44. However the texts are now too deteriorated either to confirm or deny this ingenious suggestion. Collingwood also suggested that this stone and 31 Dewsbury II formed part of the same cross-shaft.[2]

33 Driffield

Driffield, ER Yorkshire. Lost.

Found 1867, in field. Diam. *c.* 2·2 cm. Decorated gold ring with legible text set round bezel and hoop; letters enamel (probably lead and sulphur) on gold set in panels.[3] Latin descriptive formula, type c. AS capitals. Possibly ninth century.

Fowler (1869–70), 157–62 & figs.; Hübner (1876), no. 225 & add., pp. 81–90; Wilson, D. M. (1964), 23 n.

⯌E | C | C | E |
AG | NV[S] | DĪ |

The text reads: ⯌ ECCE AGNV[S] DĪ, '⯌ Behold the Lamb of God', where DĪ = DEI. The reference is to John I 29, in the Vulgate, *Ecce agnus Dei, qui tollit peccatum mundi.*

34 Durham I

Durham Cathedral Library.[4]

Found May 1827, in Cathedral,[5] during controlled excavation;[6] presumably identical with Cuthbert's *theca.*[7] 46·4× 168·9× *c.* 39 cm., thickness *c.* 2 cm.[8] Incomplete carved oak coffin, with incomplete texts set without framing lines; text i rather deteriorated, set on lid; ii highly deteriorated, set on smaller end; iii highly deteri-

---

[1] Collingwood, W. G. (1915a), 164–5.   [2] Collingwood, W. G. (1927), 6–7.
[3] The description, etc., is taken from Fowler (1869–70), 157–62 & figs.
[4] The coffin has no acquisition number.
[5] The coffin was re-interred *c.* 1542 behind the High Altar, probably in the same place that it came from. It was found there in 1827.
[6] This 1827 investigation seems to have been rather unscientific and, on the investigators' own admission, in parts hasty.
[7] Bede (1940), 292, 294.
[8] These original overall outer measurements are given by Kitzinger (1956), 215–16.

5-2

orated, set on larger end; iv highly deteriorated, set on archangel side; v slightly deteriorated, set on apostle side. Latin descriptive formulae, type b. AS capitals and runes. *c.* A.D. 698.

Milner (1812), 17–18; Raine, James the elder (1828), 183–228, *passim* & figs.; Reginald (1835), 84–90; Lingard (1845), 73–81; Stephens (1866–7), xxxi, 449–55 & figs.; Westwood (1868), 154; Hübner (1876), no. 229(a), p. 82; Stephens (1884*b*), 133–5 & figs.; Browne (1886), 32; Consitt (1887), 234–8; Eyre (1887), 141–219 & *passim*; Allen (1889), 233–43; Brown, W. (1899), 74–88, 117–32 & fig., 256–60 & figs.; Haverfield and Greenwell (1899), 133–56 & figs.; (—) (1900*b*), 69 & figs.; Kitchin (1905), 241–53 & figs.; Leclercq (1910*a*), cols. 3287–91 & figs.; Cook (1912), 304 & figs.; Lethaby (1913), 150 & fig.; Peers *et al.* (1914–15), 137; Collingwood, W. G. (1916–18), 36–7; Howorth (1917), III, 94–8 & figs.; Brown, G. B. (1921), 397–411 & figs.; Hughes and Falkner (1925), 69–76 & fig.; Clapham (1930), 43, 56 & figs.; Porter (1931), 96–7 & fig.; Rivoira (1933), 154–6; Saxl (1943), 19 & fig.; Pevsner (1953), 113; Colgrave, H. (1955), 60–1 & fig. opp. p. 14; Battiscombe (1956), *passim* & figs.; Dickins (1956), 305–7 & figs.; Kitzinger (1956), 202–304; Plenderleith (1956), 539–40 & *passim*; Wilson, D. M. (1960), 64, 154, 220 & fig.; Wilson, D. M. and Blunt (1961), 107; Page, R. I. (1962), 901; Bruce-Mitford (1969), 23 & fig.; Page, R. I. (1969), 46, 48.

i: m/ath[...]s | m/*arcus* | *L V C A S* | [...]h*an*[...]s |

ii: i*h*[...]x$\bar{\mathrm{p}}$s | — [*A*] —

iii: — [. . *M I . H . . L*] | — *A B R*[*.*]*E L* |

iv: — [*S* ...]*R A*[. .]*A E L* | [*S*]*C S   V R I A*[...] | *S C S* —

v: — *N V S* | *B A R*[...] | ... .*A* . .*B V S*] | *I O H A N N I S* | *A N D R E A S* | *P E T R V S* |
      M A T H[*E*]*Æ* | *T H O M A S* | [*P A*] —

Two inscribed fragments are unplaced:

— *V* m I *A* —

— [*P P*]*V S* —

The texts are all descriptive, referring to the carved figures. The unplaced fragments probably originally belonged to texts iv or v; the second could be the ending of [PHILIPP]VS, while the first reads: — VMIA —. The other texts read:

i: MATH[...]s MARCUS LVCAS [...]HAN[...]s, the four evangelists.

ii: IH[...] X$\bar{\mathrm{P}}$s [...]A[...], the abbreviations for the *nomina sacra*, and possibly Mary.

iii: [..MI.H..L ...]ABR[.]EL, the archangels Michael and Gabriel.

IV: — [S ...] RA[..]AEL [S]CS VRIA[...] SCS —, probably the archangels Raphael, Uriel and another, where SANCTUS is abbreviated.

v: —NVS BAR[... .A..BVS] IOHANNIS ANDREAS PETRVS MATH[E]Æ THOMAS [PA] —, presumably the names of the twelve apostles.

Kitzinger suggested that text v contained the names of the apostles following the canon of the Roman Mass: Petrus, Paulus, Andreas, Jacobus, Johannes, Thomas, Jacobus, Philippus, Bartholomaeus, Mathaeus, Simon Cananaeus, Taddaeus; Kitzinger also examined the iconography and suggested Mediterranean models.[1] It is uncertain why both runes and capitals are used in the texts; on the evidence of xp̄s, Page demonstrated that the runes are secondary.[2] The coffin is likely to date from A.D. 698 rather than from 687, since the earlier coffin was stone.[3] In 1104, Reginald described the coffin as being carved very finely outside: 'Hæc tota exterius præmirabili cælaturâ desculpitur'.[4]

35 Durham II

Durham Cathedral Library.[5]

Found May 1827, *in situ*, during controlled excavation,[6] inside 34 Durham I (St Cuthbert's coffin), on breast of skeleton; presumably silver altar mentioned in 1104.[7] c. 5·7 × c. 3·8 × c. 0·3 cm.[8] Incomplete carved oak slab, with incomplete decorated silver covering. Text i incomplete but legible, set on one face of wood; ii, iii incomplete but legible, set in relief lettering in silver covering from both sides of wood, iii from covering of inscribed side. Text i, Latin memorial formula, ii, iii uncertain. AS capitals. Wood probably c. A.D. 698, silver covering possibly tenth century.

Raine, James the elder (1828), 199–201 & figs.; Reginald (1835), 89; Lingard (1845), 77, 81; Westwood (1868), 155; (—) (1868), 193; Smith, W. and Cheetham (1875), 69 & figs.; Hübner (1876), no. 229 (b), p. 82; Eyre (1887), 205–6; Allen (1889), 243; Browne (1896), 227; Browne (1897), 105, 276–9; Kitchin (1905), 255–6 & fig.; Leclercq (1907a), col. 3187; Lethaby (1913), 149 & fig.; Browne (1916), 33–4; Howorth (1917), III, 100–1 & fig.; Brown, G. B. (1921), 400–1 & fig.; Braun (1924), 422–4 & fig.; Hughes and Falkner (1925), 85; Brown, G. B. (1930), 10–17 & figs.; Kendrick (1938), 121; Battiscombe (1956), *passim*; Plenderleith (1956), 540–2 & *passim*; Radford (1956), 326–35 & figs.; Oman (1957), 96–7 & fig.; Wilson, D. M. (1960), 63; Wilson, D. M. and Blunt (1961), 107; Bruce-Mitford (1969), 23 & fig.

i: [.]INH/ONOR[. . .]SPETRV |

ii: — IASECSER[A] —

iii: — P[... A ...]OS[...]S —

---

[1] Kitzinger (1956), 269–73; 278 (conclusions summarised).   [2] Page, R. I. (1962), 901.

[3] Bede (1940), 288.   [4] Reginald (1835), 90.   [5] The altar has no acquisition number.

[6] This 1827 investigation seems to have been rather unscientific and, on the investigators' own admission, in parts hasty.

[7] Both accounts of the translation of 1104 mention a silver altar, Reginald stating: 'Præterea habet secum in sepulcro altare argenteum', Reginald (1835), 89.

[8] Plenderleith (1956), 540 says the wood has shrunk from c. 13·6 × c. 12·2 × c. 0·6 cm.

Text i reads: [.]IN HONOR[. . .]S PETRV, either: [.]IN HONOR[E SC]S PETRV, or: [.] IN HONOR[EM] S PETRV, '[.] in honour of St Peter' where PETRV = PETRI, or the undeclined PETRUS, SANCTUS is abbreviated, and possibly undeclined, and the first letter may be a cross. This is presumably the text of a portable altar. Text ii reads: — IA : EC : ERA —, taking the reversed s symbols as word-divisions. Brown expanded the words to: [OMN]IA HAEC ERA[NT], assuming the silver to have been added later to form a reliquary.[1] Text iii is too fragmentary to be meaningful.

Bede made no mention of the altar, but it is likely to have been added at Cuthbert's reburial in A.D. 698, rather than at his burial in 687. The silver covering must post-date the wood; it might do so by only a few years, but it is perhaps more likely to be tenth century.

36 Essex

Lost.

First mentioned May 1846, in possession of A. Way Esq.; probably passed to Franks and possibly lost by 1897 when Franks' Collection passed to BM. Dimensions uncertain. Decorated silver ring with legible text set without framing lines on exterior of hoop.[2] OE text, possibly personal name. Insular majuscule. Date uncertain.

Way (1846b), 201; Braybrooke (n.d.), no. 170, p. 47; Braybrooke (1860), no. 158, p. 46; Braybrooke (1863), 64; Jones (1877), 57.

DOLGBOT |

The text reads: DOLGBOT. It is perhaps an unrecorded name *DOLGBŌT, since taking it as the OE noun 'compensation for a wound' seems less meaningful.

37 Exeter

Exeter, Devon. Now in the British Museum, London, no. 1875.6–17.15.

Found 1833, beneath house in South Street. c. 1 × c. 8 × c. 0·6 cm. Decorated bronze sword-guard with probably complete, slightly deteriorated text set in panels on convex face; two lines of text upside down with respect to each other, second line to left and first line to right of sword hole. Latin, probably maker formula. AS capitals. Probably ninth to eleventh century.

Shortt (1836), 156; Shortt (?1841), 143–5 & figs.; Way (1845), xlii–xliii; Watkin (1874), 352; (—) (1899b), 189–92 & figs.; Smith, R. A. (1906c), 373–4 & figs.; Smith, R. A. (1923), 94–5

1 Brown, G. B. (1930), 12.
2 The description, etc., is taken from published accounts and the published figure pasted in the British Museum copy of Braybrooke (1860), 46.

& figs.; Wilson, D. M. (1960), 109 & figs.; Davidson (1962), 80–1, 82, 112 & figs.; Page, R. I. (1964), 79, 84–5; Wilson, D. M. (1964), no. 17, pp. 64, 130–1 & figs.; Evison (1965), 289; Evison (1967), 171–2 & figs.

EOFR[I] |

MEF[E] |

The text reads: EOFR[I] ME F[E], presumably a form of EOFRI ME FECIT, 'Eofri made me'. The name is probably a shortened form of *EOFOR(R)IC or *EOFRIÐ. Though neither name is recorded, both contain well-attested elements. It is not certain whether the object is an upper or lower sword-guard.

38 Eye

Eye, Suffolk. Now in the British Museum, London, no. 1822.12–14.1.

Found pre 1822, below ground in garden. Base diam. *c.* 3·2 cm., ht. *c.* 7 cm. Decorated conical bronze seal-die; legible text set right round base with letters laterally displaced, facing inwards and reading anti-clockwise. Latin descriptive formula, type a. AS capitals. Probably early to mid ninth century.

Gurney (1824), 479–83 & figs.; Madden (1856), 369–70; Birch (1887), nos. 1488–9, p. 213; (—) (1901 *a*), 18; Smith, R. A. (1911), 352; Stevenson (1912), 6 n.; Smith, R. A. (1923), 110 & fig.; Leclercq (1930), cols. 2403–4 & figs.; Tonnochy (1952), no. 1, pp. xviii, 1 & figs.; Wilson, D. M. and Blunt (1961), 107; Page, R. I. (1964), 80–1; Wilson, D. M. (1964), no. 18, pp. 31, 34, 60, 131–2 & figs.

⊕SĪGEÐILVVALDIEP̄ |

The text reads: ⊕ SĪG EÐILVVALDI EP̄, '⊕ The seal of Bishop Eðilvvald', where SĪG = SIGILLUM and EP̄ (with the abbreviation mark following the P) = EPI-SCOPI. This may refer to Ethelwald, Bishop of Dunwich A.D. 845–70, although Page stressed the early ninth century date suggested by the form EÐIL-.[1] Dolley drew attention to the virtual identity of this to the reverse type of certain coins of Ethelberht struck at Canterbury *c.* A.D. 865.[2]

39 Falstone

Falstone, Northumberland. Now in the Museum of Antiquities, Newcastle upon Tyne, no. 1956. 224.A.

Found *c.* 1814, below ground in field near Falstone. 15·2 × 33 × 6·4 cm. Incomplete carved stone, possibly containing traces of original paint; rather deteriorated text set in panel on left side of face, with virtually identical runic text on right side; last

[1] Page, R. I. (1964), 81.
[2] M. Dolley, in a personal communication.

eight letters of text set below runic text. OE memorial formula. Insular majuscule. Eighth to ninth century.

Wood (1822), 103–4 & figs.; (—) (1822), 'Donations', p. 6; Charlton (1855–7), 70–1; Haigh (1856–7), 519–20; Haigh (1857), 155–6 & fig.; Haigh (1861), 41–2 & fig.; Stephens (1866–7), xxviii, 456 & fig.; Haigh (1869–70), 217; Ellison (1876), 272–3; Haigh (1877), 419–20; Smith, W. and Cheetham (1880), 1979; Stephens (1884*b*), 136 & fig.; Sweet (1885), 127; Sweet (1887), 88; Allen (1889), 211–12, 220, 221, 222; Hall, G. R. (1889), 267–9 & fig.; Hodges (1893), 71; Stephens (1894), 24; Viëtor (1895), 17–18 & fig.; Searle (1897), 302; Grienberger (1900), 297; Chadwick (1901), 83–4; Lethaby (1913), 153; Collingwood, W. G. (1927), 165, index; Flom (1930), 287; Olsen (1930), 286; Ross (1933), 152; Dahl (1938), 17, 193–4; Dodds (1940), 256–7 & fig.; Page, R. I. (1958), 149; Elliott (1959), 71, 86 & figs.; Page, R. I. (1959*a*), 405; Page, R. I. (1961), 76–8; Page, R. I. (1962), 900, 901–2.

[✠E...T....]‖ A[EAEFT...] | HROETHBERH[T.]| BECUNAEFTAER | EOMAEGEBIDAEDDERSAU [..] |

The text can be read: [✠ E...T...]A[E AEFTAER] HROETHBERH[TE] BECUN AEFTAER EOMAE GEBIDAED DER SAU[LE], '—in memory of Hroethberh[t], a monument in memory of (his) uncle; pray for the (= his) soul'. The personal name HRÈÐBEORHT is recorded. The first words, also deteriorated on the runic text, presumably contained a verb and the commissioner's name. The runic text reads: ✠ [...] ÆFTÆR ROE[...]TÆ [BEC]UN ÆFTÆR E[...] GEB[...]ÆD ÞE[...] SAULE. The reason for the biliteral text may have been artistic, to exhibit knowledge, or because runes had become to some extent traditional on grave-stones.

40 Gainford

Gainford, Durham. Now in Durham Cathedral Library, no. 46.

First mentioned 1896, in Library. 26·7 × 68·6 × *c.* 10·2 cm. Incomplete carved stone, with incomplete rather deteriorated text set without framing lines on one face. OE text, probably memorial formula. AS capitals. Probably ninth century.

Haverfield and Greenwell (1899), no. XLVI, pp. 108–9 & figs.; Hodges (1905), 230; Cramp (1965*a*), no. 46, p. 7.

— A[.]RIHCSETAE —

The text reads: — A[L]RIHC SETAE —, '— a[l]rihc set —'. The name is explicable with the second element probably a form of -RĪC, and the first a form of EALH-, AELF-, AEÐEL-, or possibly, with a letter lost, of e.g. CAL-, HAL-.

41   Great Edstone

Set in the south wall above the doorway, Great Edstone parish church, NR Yorkshire.

First mentioned 1817, in present *situs. c.* 10·2 × *c.* 53·3 cm. Carved stone sun-dial, with text i legible but probably incomplete set on left of dial on visible face; ii rather deteriorated set in panel along horizontal diameter of dial. Text i OE maker formula; ii Latin descriptive formula, type a. AS capitals. Tenth to eleventh century.

Young (1817), 747–8 & fig.; Way and Noyer (1868), 210; Rowe (1874), 209 & fig.; Hübner (1876), no. 181, p. 66 & fig.; Tudor (1876), 9 & fig.; Haigh (1879), 146–9 & fig.; Taylor, R. V. (1881), 147; Stephens (1884a), 386; Frank (1888), 150–1; Allen (1889), 201–2; Stephens (1894), 14; Gatty (1900), 55–6 & fig.; Collingwood, W. G. (1907), 329 & fig.; Leclercq (1910b), cols. 1543–4 & fig.; Collingwood, W. G. (1912), 122, 124; Gaye & Galpin (1912), 127–32 & fig.; Morewood (1914), 477; Collingwood, W. G. (1915a), 288, 290; Home (1915), 80–1 & fig.; Green, A. R. (1926), 15–16; Green, A. R. (1928), 510 & fig.; Morris (1931), 151; Page, R. I. (1964), 83; Zinner (1964), 4, 74; Taylor, J. and Taylor, H. M. (1966), 21–2; Okasha (1969), 27 & fig.; Page, R. I. (1969), 31.

i: ✠LOÐAN | MEⱣRO | HTEA —
ii: ORLOGIV [....]TORIS |

Text i reads: ✠ LOÐAN ME ⱣROHTE A —, '✠ Loðan made me —'. The recorded name is of ON origin. The text is probably unfinished and might have continued A[ND —]; cf. 64 Kirkdale iii. Text ii reads: ORLOGIV[...]TORIS, probably ORLOGIV[M VIA]TORIS, 'the traveller's clock'. Similar texts occur on contemporary MS drawings of sun-dials, for example, *Basel F. III*, 15a, fo. 23 v (in the Universitätsbibliothek, Basel) and *Laon 422*, fo. 53 (in the Bibliothèque de Laon).

42   Hackness

Hackness parish church, NR Yorkshire.

First mentioned 1848 in church, discovered 'some years past' in outbuilding at Hackness Hall.[1] *c.* 147 × *c.* 43 × *c.* 43 cm. Incomplete carved limestone shaft in two pieces; text i illegible, set probably in panel on one face of lower stone; ii, iii virtually illegible, set in panels on faces of upper stone; iv illegible, set on one face of upper stone. Latin texts, perhaps memorial formulae. AS capitals. Probably eighth to ninth century.

Harcourt (1848), 108–10; Poole and Hugall (1848), 44–6 & fig.; Haigh (1855–7), 176–8; Haigh (1856–7), 520; Haigh (?1858), 29–40; Scarth (1860), 115–21 & figs.; Stephens (1866–7), xxviii, 467–8 & fig.; Haigh (1875), 372–91 & figs.; Hübner (1876), nos. 182–4, pp. 66–7 & figs.; Smith, W. and Cheetham (1880), 1979; Stephens (1884a), 215; Stephens (1884b), 155; Allen

---

[1] Poole and Hugall (1848), 44.

and Browne (1885), 342, 343; Browne (1885a), 79–80; Frank (1888), 214–18 & fig.; Allen (1889), 214–15, 221, 222; Browne (1897), 280–2; Chadwick (1901), 82; Stevens (1904), 50–1; Collingwood, W. G. (1907), 329–30 & figs.; Collingwood, W. G. (1911), 278–80 & figs.; Collingwood, W. G. (1912), 124 & figs.; Collingwood, W. G. (1915a), 289; Collingwood, W. G. (1916–18), 38 & figs.; Howorth (1917), III, 201–4 & figs.; Russell and Clapham (1923), 531; Collingwood, W. G. (1927), 59–61, 116, index & figs.; Brown, G. B. (1930), 52–75 & figs.; Clapham (1930), 127; Morris (1931), 174–5; Collingwood, W. G. (1932), 51 & figs.; Elgee, F. and Elgee, H. W. (1933), 191–3; Clapham (1948b), 82; Elliott (1959), 83–6 & fig.; Grosjean (1961), 340–3; King (1964), no pagination.

Texts i, ii, iii are now virtually illegible, though some words can be made out in ii: SEMPER TENENT...MATER AMANTISSIMA, and iii appears to begin: OEDIEBV... BEATA—. Text iv contains ORA—, following two lines of badly preserved runes (possibly '⊹[...]mc[..]œgn[...]œ[...]') and three and a half lines of very indistinct *hahal*-runes. The stone also contains an ogham text. The non-runic texts have probably deteriorated recently, since Brown's photographs to some extent support his readings.[1] With his corrections and abbreviation expansions added, these are:

i: — TREL ... OSA ABBATISSA OEDILBURGA ORATE PRO —, '— abbess Oedilburga, pray for —'

ii: — [OEDI]L[BUR]GA SEMPER TENENT MEMORES COMMUNITATES TUAE TE MATER AMANTISSIMA, '— Oedilburga, thy communities hold thee ever in memory, most loving mother'.

iii: OEDILBURGA BEATA AD SEMPER—', 'Blessed Oedilburga, for ever —'.

43 Haddenham

Haddenham, Cambridgeshire. Now in Ely Cathedral.

First mentioned 1724, possibly *c.* 1706, used as horse-block near church. Base *c.* 45× *c.* 76× *c.* 76 cm., shaft *c.* 107× *c.* 30·5× *c.* 30·5 cm. Incomplete probably uncarved stone cross-shaft in base with legible text set in panel on one face of shaft. Latin memorial formula. AS capitals. Date uncertain.

Stukeley (1724), 10 & fig.; Bentham (1771), 50–1 & fig.; Gough (1806), II, 234 & fig. opp. p. 401; Millers (1808), 57–8; Stuart (1867), xlvi; Smith, W. and Cheetham (1875), 846 & fig.; Hübner (1876), no. 169, p. 61 & fig.; Birch (1879), 388–96 & figs.; Smith, W. and Cheetham (1880), 1987 & fig.; Browne (1896), 213–14; Stevens (1904), 54; Conybeare (1906), 53–4; Browne (1916), 35–6; Howorth (1917), III, 218–19, 388 & fig. opp. p. 203; Bond (1919), 23 & fig.; Brown, G. B. (1921), 154 & fig.; Lethbridge (1938), 321; Hampson and Atkinson (1953), 76; Wells (1953), 140; Pevsner (1954), 287; Bede (1969), 338.

1 Brown, G. B. (1930), 52–75.

:LVCEM:TVAM:OVINO | DA:DEVS:ET:REQVIĒ | AMEN: |

The text reads: : LVCEM : TVAM : OVINO DA : DEVS : ET : REQVIĒ AMEN :,
'O Lord, grant your light and peace to Ovin, Amen' where REQVIĒ = REQVIEM.
The text is a pentameter verse. OVIN is a recorded name, either an anglicisation of
OW OUE(I)N, or a form of ŌWINE. There is little evidence to connect this with
Ovin, steward to Queen Ethelthryth,[1] as has been suggested, and the script suggests
that the text is later than the seventh century. There is no evidence to support
Birch's suggestion that Stukeley recut the text in 1706.[2]

HARTLEPOOL STONES, BIBLIOGRAPHY

(—) (1833), 218–20	(O)
Gage (1836), 479–82 & figs.	(O, IV)
(—) (1838), 536 & fig.	(VI)
(—) (1844), 187–8 & figs.	(O, IV, VI, VII, VIII; figs. of VII, VIII)
Haigh (1846a), 185–96 & figs.	(General)
Boutell (1849), 2	(General)
Sharp (1851), *Supplemental History*, 25–33 & fig.	(O, III, IV, V, VI; fig. of VI)
(—) (1855), 'Donations', p. 5.	(IV)
Haigh (?1858), 16–27 & figs.	(General)
Greenwell and Westwood (1869), 282	(O, I)
Haigh (1869–70), 214–15	(VIII)
Haigh (1875), 365, 370 & figs.	(General; figs. III–VIII)
Hübner (1876), nos. 188–96, pp. 69–70 & figs.	(General)
Smith, W. and Cheetham (1880), 1979	(O, III, IV, V)
Browne (?1886), 12	(General)
Allen (1887), 117–18	(General)
Frank (1888), 43	(General)
Pettigrew (1888), 26–32 & figs.	(General)
Allen (1889), 215–16 & fig.	(General; fig. of IV)
Hall, G. R. (1889), 259–61	(General)
Hodges (1894), 2–8 & figs.	(III–VIII; figs. of IV, VI)
Hodgson, J. F. (1895), 205–7 & figs.	(General; figs. of IV, VI)
Viëtor (1895), 18 & fig.	(IV)
Searle (1897), 58, 88, 458, 475	(III, IV, VI)
Haverfield and Greenwell (1899), no. XXVIII, pp. 93–4 & fig.	(VI)
Chadwick (1901), 83	(General)
Collingwood, W. G. (1903–4), 223 & fig.	(General; fig. of IV)
Hodges (1905), 212–13 & figs.	(General; figs. of III, VII, VIII)

[1] Bede IV 3, (1896), 207–8.   [2] Birch (1879), 392–3.

Lethaby (1913), 152 & fig.	(General; fig. of O)
Peers *et al.* (1914–15), 132–7	(General)
Howorth (1917), I, 92–3; III, 189–92 & figs.	(General; figs. of O, VI, VII, VIII)
Brown, G. B. (1919), 195–228 & figs.	(General)
Brown, G. B. (1921), 58–101 & figs.	(General)
Smith, R. A. (1923), 121–2 & figs.	(General; figs. of III, V, VII, VIII)
Hughes and Falkner (1925), 105	(VI)
Peers (1925), 258–9 & fig.	(General; fig. of IV)
Collingwood, W. G. (1927), 10–12, index & figs.	(General; figs. of V, VI, VIII)
Clapham (1930), 74–5	(General)
Friesen (1933), 51–2	(III, IV, VI)
Rivoira (1933), 153	(General)
Pfeilstücker (1936), 127	(General)
Dahl (1938), 9–10, 188	(General)
Kendrick (1938), 110	(General)
Henry (1940), 75–6	(General)
Åberg (1943), 104 & fig.	(General; fig. of O)
Bæksted (1943), 44	(General)
Hodgkin, R. H. (1952), I, 296 & figs.	(V, VII)
Cramp (1956a), no. 28, p. 6	(VI)
Scott (1956), 196–212 & fig.	(General; fig. of O)

44 Hartlepool O

Hartlepool, Durham. Lost.

Found July 1833, *in situ* in field 'Cross Close' adjoining Hartlepool Moor. Diam. *c.* 35·6 cm. Incomplete carved circular stone in five pieces, with incomplete rather deteriorated text set in panel round perimeter on face, letters facing inwards.[1] Latin text, possibly memorial formula. AS capitals. Eighth century.

For Bibliography, see *Hartlepool Stones, Bibliography*.

— [. .]V*IE*SC[*I*]T[... .]CO —

The text reads: — [Q]VIESC[I]T [...] CO —. It may have been of the form, HIC IN SEPULCRO REQUIESCIT CORPORE, but it is too fragmentary to be certain. All the Hartlepool stones, 44–50, may pre-date the sacking of Hartlepool by the Danes, A.D. 800, but need not necessarily do so.

1 The description, etc., is taken from rubbings preserved in the Library of the Society of Antiquaries.

45 Hartlepool III[1]

Hartlepool, Durham. Now in the British Museum, London, no. 1880.3–13.4.

Found July 1833, *in situ* in field 'Cross Close' adjoining Hartlepool Moor. 19·1 × 14 × 3·8 cm. Carved magnesian limestone slab, with rather deteriorated text set without framing lines in two lower quadrants of cross on face. OE personal name. Probably AS capitals. Eighth century.

For Bibliography, see *Hartlepool Stones, Bibliography*.

ED[*IL*] | [*UINI*] |

The text reads: ED[ILUINI], a form of the recorded name AEÐELWINE.

46 Hartlepool IV

Hartlepool, Durham. Now in the Museum of Antiquities, Newcastle upon Tyne, no. 1845.8.

Found July 1833, *in situ* in field 'Cross Close' adjoining Hartlepool Moor. 21·6 × 17·1 × 2·5 cm. Carved stone slab, probably magnesian limestone; slightly deteriorated text set without framing lines in four quadrants of cross on face. Latin memorial formula. AS capitals. Eighth century.

For Bibliography, see *Hartlepool Stones, Bibliography*.

OR/A | PRO | UER | MU/ND | T/ORHT | SUID |

The text reads: ORA PRO UERMUND TORHTSUID, 'Pray for Uermund (and) Torhtsuid', where the names are uninflected. The text reads left to right but quadrant by quadrant, not line by line, that is in the order:

1 2
3 5
4 6

WÆRMUND is a recorded name and the feminine *TORHTSWĪÐ, though un-recorded, is quite explicable.

47 Hartlepool V

Hartlepool, Durham. Now in the British Museum, London, no. 1880.3–13.3.

Found July 1833, *in situ* in field 'Cross Close' adjoining Hartlepool Moor. 21·6 × 17·8 × 3·2 cm. Carved magnesian limestone slab, with highly deteriorated texts set

---

[1] The stones are numbered according to Haigh (1846a), 185–96. More stones may have been found which are now lost. Hartlepool I and II have runic texts which read, respectively, Aω HILDIÞRYÞ and HILDDIGYÞ, both feminine names. Hartlepool I is preserved in St Hilda's Church, Hartlepool, and Hartlepool II in the Museum of Antiquities, Newcastle upon Tyne, no. 1845.7.

without framing lines on face; i set in upper quadrants of cross, ii in lower quadrants. Latin memorial formulae. Probably AS capitals. Eighth century.

For Bibliography, see *Hartlepool Stones, Bibliography*.

i: ORA | —
ii: ORA | TEPRO | [GE]R[.] | [...] | [.]ED[.E] | [.]U[ID] |

Text i reads: ORA —, 'Pray for —'. Text ii reads: ORATE PRO [GE]R[...] ED[LES]U[ID], 'Pray for [Ge]r[...] (and) Ed[les]u[id]', where the names are uninflected. Text ii reads in the order:

$$
\begin{matrix}
1 & 2 \\
3 & 5 \\
4 & 6
\end{matrix}
$$

Cf. 46 Hartlepool IV where, however, the order is rationalised by the cross-arms. ED[LES]U[ID] may be explained as a variant of the recorded feminine name AEÐELSWĪÐ; if the reading is [GE]R-, this is also a recorded name element.

48   Hartlepool VI

Hartlepool, Durham. Now in Durham Cathedral Library, no. 28.

Found October 1838, below ground in South Terrace, probably *in situ*. 29·2× 25·4× *c.* 7·6 cm. Carved stone slab, probably magnesian limestone, with legible texts set without framing lines on face; i set in upper quadrants of cross, ii in lower quadrants. Text i, Latin descriptive formula, type c, ii OE personal name. Text i probably AS capitals, ii insular majuscule. Eighth century.

For Bibliography, see *Hartlepool Stones, Bibliography*.

i: A | ω |
ii: BERCHT | GYD |

Text i reads: Aω, the abbreviations of *alpha* and *omega*, with the odd form = OMEGA. The reference is to the Vulgate Revelations XXII 13. Text ii reads: BERCHTGYD, a form of the recorded feminine name BEORHTGȲÐ.

49   Hartlepool VII

Hartlepool, Durham. Now in the British Museum, London, no. 1880.3–13.2.

Found September 1843, probably *in situ* near South Terrace. 22·9× 19·7× *c.* 5·1 cm. Carved magnesian limestone slab; highly deteriorated text set without framing lines in lower quadrants of cross on face. Probably OE personal name. AS capitals. Eighth century.

For Bibliography, see *Hartlepool Stones, Bibliography*.

[H]A N/E | [. .]E V[B] |

The text reads: [H]A N E[. .]E V[B], presumably a personal name, of uncertain form.

50   Hartlepool VIII

Hartlepool, Durham. Now in the British Museum, London, no. 1859.7–7.1.

Found October 1843, below ground near South Terrace, possibly *in situ*. 27·3× 22·9× 10·8 cm. Carved magnesian limestone slab; incomplete but legible text set without framing lines in lower quadrants of cross on face. Probably OE personal name. Insular majuscule. Eighth century.

For Bibliography, see *Hartlepool Stones, Bibliography*.

— [.] | U G U I D |

The text reads: — U G U I D, presumably a personal name with the second element the recorded feminine element -G Ȳ Ð. Text may also have been lost from the upper quadrants.

51   Hauxwell

Churchyard of Hauxwell parish church, NR Yorkshire.

First mentioned 1823, in churchyard, presumably in present *situs*. c. 118× 26·7× 15·2 cm. Incomplete carved stone cross-shaft with illegible text set in panel on face. Language, formula and script uncertain. Probably tenth to eleventh century.

Whitaker (1823), 323–4; (—) (1846), 259 & figs.; Haigh (1857), 184–5 & figs.; Hübner (1876), no. 186, p. 69; Browne (1884–8), 14–16 & fig.; Allen and Browne (1885), 342, 343; Allen (1889), 129, 218, 221; Browne (1896), 215–22 & fig.; Stevens (1904), 50; Collingwood, W. G. (1912), 124; Russell (1914*b*), 249; Browne (1915), 199–200; Collingwood, W. G. (1915*a*), 289; Browne (1916), 35; Green, V. H. H. (19   ), 2, 3–4 & fig.

Haigh read the following text from a squeeze, though commentators before and after him considered it to be illegible: HAEC EST CRVX S̄C̄ GACOBI,[1] presumably 'Here is the cross of St James'. Although the panel looks as if it were intended to contain a text, there now remain no traces at all of lettering.

[1] Haigh (1857), 185.

52 Hexham I

Hexham Abbey, Northumberland.

Found January 1911, below ground in Beaumont Street. 22·9 × 31·8 × c. 7·6 cm. Carved semi-circular stone slab, with legible text set without framing lines on arms of cross on face, letters facing inwards. OE personal name. AS capitals. Probably eighth to ninth century.

Gibson, J. P. (1911–12), 1–2 & fig.; Hodges & Gibson, J. (1919), 68; Hodges (1921), 34–5 & fig.; Collingwood, W. G. (1927), 12, index & fig.; Dahl (1938), 10, 188; Taylor, H. M. and Taylor, J. (1961), 123; Taylor, H. M. and Taylor, J. (1965), 305.

TV | ND | VI | NI |

The text reads: TVNDVINI. TUND- is not recorded as a name element, but the name may be a form of the recorded TONDWINE.

53 Hexham II

Hexham Abbey, Northumberland.

First mentioned 1860, found in choir foundations. Cross-section 26·7 × 35·6 cm. Incomplete stone tegulated roof, with incomplete slightly deteriorated text set in panels along ridge-pole on both faces. Language and formula uncertain. AS capitals. Date uncertain, perhaps post-Conquest.

Longstaffe (1861), 153; Hodges (1921), 75; Collingwood, W. G. (1925), 90.

✠EMI[...] |
SENT —

The text reads: ✠ EMI[...]SENT —, and is too fragmentary to be meaningful.

54 Hexham III

Hexham Abbey, Northumberland.

Found in four pieces: i 1858, behind high altar of Abbey; ii c. 1870, under foundation of house near west end of St Mary's church; iii pre 1896, in fabric of cottage at Dilston; iv after 1896, of unknown provenance. c. 335 × 34·3 × c. 25·4 cm. Incomplete carved stone cross-shaft with incomplete illegible text set on one face, probably without framing lines but in panel. Language, formula and script uncertain. Possibly eighth century.

Longstaffe (1861), 152–3; Wilson, F. R. (1862–8), 22; Raine, James the younger (1864), xxxiv & figs.; Stuart (1867), xlvi, 47–50 & pls. xciii, xciv; Symeon (1867), 14; Hübner (1876), no. 204, p. 73; Browne (1885a), 81–2 & figs.; Hodges (1893), 11; Hinds (1896), 181–2 & figs.; Browne

(1897), 257–61 & fig.; Haverfield and Greenwell (1899), no. III, pp. 53–9 & figs.; (—) (1900*b*), 67–8; Conway (1912), 193; Prior and Gardner (1912), 111, 118; Howorth (1914), 56; Collingwood, W. G. (1916–18), 36 & figs.; Howorth (1917), III, 144–7 & figs.; Hodges & Gibson, J. (1919), 73 & fig.; Hodges (1921), 66–8 & fig. on p. 111; Hodges (1921–2), 293–4; Collingwood, W. G. (1925), 76–8; Collingwood, W. G. (1927), 29–32, index & figs.; Clapham (1930), 55, 57, 64–5 & fig.; (—) (1930*a*), no. 2, p. 1; Porter (1931), 99 & fig.; Collingwood, W. G. (1932), 37–9 & figs.; Rivoira (1933), 150 & fig.; Fisher (1959), 67 & fig.; Taylor, H. M. and Taylor, J. (1961), 121–2; Cramp (1965*a*), no. 3, p. 3; Taylor, H. M. and Taylor, J. (1965), 305.

The text has never been completely legible and is now illegible. Hinds read: A C C A [...] V N I G E N I T O F I L I O D E I,[1] and similar texts were recorded by Browne, Collingwood and Greenfield. Traditionally the cross has been regarded as one of the two which Symeon of Durham described as standing at either end of the grave of Acca, *ob. c.* A.D. 740.[2] However not every early scholar read ACCA on the stone, and there is now no direct evidence to support this theory.

55   Hornby I

Hornby parish church, Lancashire.

First mentioned 1903, built into barn wall on site of priory. 17·8 × *c.* 20·3 × *c.* 10·2 cm. Incomplete carved sandstone cross, with incomplete slightly deteriorated text set in panel on one face. Language and formula uncertain. Probably AS capitals. Date uncertain.

Taylor, H. (1903), 103 & figs.; Collingwood, W. G. (1904), 39–41 & fig.; Taylor, H. (1906), 395 & figs.

[. .]*O E D*[H] |

The text reads: — O E D[H], but is too fragmentary to be meaningful. Collingwood suggested that it was an abbreviated form of I N N O M I N E D O M I N I,[3] but this does not seem very likely.

56   Hornby II

Hornby parish church, Lancashire.

First mentioned 1903, found some years previously built into interior wall of barn at priory farm. 71·1 × 20·3 × 14·6 cm. Incomplete carved stone slab with incomplete illegible text set, probably within panel, on back below carving. Language, formula and script uncertain. Probably ninth century.

[1] Hinds (1896), 182.   [2] Symeon (1867), 14.
[3] Quoted in Taylor, H. (1903), 103.

Taylor, H. (1903), 99–103 & figs.; Collingwood, W. G. (1904), 36–9 & figs.; Garstang (1906), 267 & figs.; Taylor, H. (1906), 391–5 & figs.; Farrer *et al.* (1914), 200; Collingwood, W. G. (1916–18), 46 & figs.; Collingwood, W. G. (1927), 57–8, index & figs.; (—) (19   b), no pagination.

The text is now illegible, though the centre of the line might have contained ✠E. However Collingwood read: '[?D]N . dIRI[GE ?]', which he described as 'possibly, but not by any means certainly, the opening of the Dirge or Antiphon in the Office for the Dead'.[1]

57 Inglesham

Set into the interior south wall of the south aisle of the nave of Inglesham parish church, Wiltshire.

First mentioned 1899, set in church fabric; traditionally from church in Lechlade. *c.* 111·8 × *c.* 61 cm. Incomplete carved stone slab, with incomplete rather deteriorated text set above carving on visible face, probably within panel; traces of paint of uncertain date remain on carving. Probably Latin descriptive formula, type b. AS capitals. Probably eleventh to twelfth century.

Hall, S. C. and Hall, A. M. (1859), 40–1 & fig.; Keyser (1921), 35–6 & fig.; Maclagan (1923), 484; Keyser (1927), xxx, liii–liv, 26 & fig.; Knowles (1931), 197 & fig.; (—) (1931), 59; Rice (1947), 9–10; Kendrick (1949), 43–4 & fig.; Rice (1952), 85, 106 & fig.; Saxl and Swarzenski (1954), 70; Pevsner (1963), 247; Taylor, H. M. and Taylor, J. (1965), 332–3.

[✠]*MARIA*[.] —

The text reads: [✠] MARIA —, and is probably complete at the beginning. It presumably refers to the figure of the Virgin carved beneath. The later sun-dial carved on the stone suggests that it was once set in an exterior wall, probably the south.

58 Ipswich I

Set in an artificial interior wall in the north aisle of St Nicholas' parish church, Ipswich, Suffolk.

First mentioned 1764, in outer fabric of church. *c.* 53·3 × *c.* 86·4 × 15·2 cm. Carved Caen stone slab in two pieces, with texts set without framing lines on face; i slightly deteriorated, set between figures, ii rather deteriorated, set on left side, iii highly deteriorated, set along top. Texts i, ii OE descriptive formulae, type b. AS capitals. Eleventh century.

Kirby (1764), 46; Pegge (1787), 106 & fig. opp. p. 81; Clarke, G. R. (1830), 234; Waller (1846), 146–7 & fig.; Drummond (1848), 21–8 & figs.; Westwood (1849), 76; Wodderspoon (1850),

[1] Collingwood, W. G. (1927), 57.

332–3; Allen (1883–4), 429 & fig.; (—) (1886), 478–80 & fig.; Allen (1887), 273–4 & fig.; Keyser (1905), 142; Prior and Gardner (1912), 129–30 & fig.; Keyser (1927), xxx, 27 & fig.; Cautley (1937), 280; (—) (?1938), 63; Clapham (1948a), 7; Kendrick (1949), 123 & fig.; Dufty (1952), 136–7 & fig.; Rice (1952), 130; Pevsner (1961b), 271; Stoll (1967), 345 & fig.; Galbraith (1968), 173–6 & fig.; (—) (19 c), 3 & fig.

i: [:]HER: SC̃E | [M]IHA[E]L: FEHTʄIÐ | ÐANE:DRACA: |
ii: [SC]E | [.]IHA | EL: |
iii: : [.]SO[.....]: [A..] —

Text i, which describes the whole scene, reads: [:] HER : SC̃E [M]IHA[E]L : FEHT ʄIÐ ÐANE : DRACA : (or DRACĀ :), 'Here St Michael fights (or fought) against the dragon', where SC̃E = SANCTUS and DRACA or DRACĀ = DRACAN. Phonologically the verb can be explained as present or preterite and comparable inscriptions and manuscript captions evidence both usages. Text ii reads: [SC]E [M]IHAEL :, 'St Michael', where [SC]E = SANCTUS, the text referring to the left hand figure. Text iii might then be expected to describe the dragon, but it is now virtually illegible. The Vulgate account of this episode is Revelations XII 7–9; it is uncertain how far this was considered to be symbolic, how far historical fact.

59   Ipswich II

Set in an artificial interior wall in the north aisle of St Nicholas' parish church, Ipswich, Suffolk.

First mentioned 1764, in outer fabric of church. c. 50·8 × c. 87·6 cm. Carved semi-circular Barnack stone, possibly tympanum, with highly deteriorated text set without framing lines round semi-circular perimeter of face, letters facing inwards. Latin text, probably dedication formula. AS capitals. Probably eleventh century.

Kirby (1764), 46; Pegge (1787), 106 & fig. opp. p. 81; Clarke, G. R. (1830), 234–5; Waller (1846), 146–7 & fig.; Drummond (1848), 21–8 & figs.; Westwood (1849), 76; Wodderspoon (1850), 332–3; (—) (1886), 478–80 & fig.; Allen (1887), 385 & fig.; Prior and Gardner (1912), 129–30; (—) (1924), 247; Keyser (1927), xxviii, xli, 27 & fig.; Clapham (1934a), 136; Clapham (1936), 151; (—) (?1938), 63; Kendrick (1949), 123 & fig.; Dufty (1952), 136–7; Rice (1952), 155; Pevsner (1961b), 270–1; Galbraith (1968), 176–8 & figs.; (—) (19 c), 5 & fig.

✠ INDEDI:CAT[IO.E]: E[CL]E[SIE]:OM[N..........]R[V]M—

The text reads: ✠ IN DEDI: CAT[IONE] : E[CL]E[SIE] : OM[N...]R[V]M—. There may be c. 2 letters lost at the end of the text; the division mark in the middle of DEDI: CAT[IONE] is presumably an error. The text is perhaps to be translated, '✠ At the dedication of the church of all [?saints]', where E[CL]E[SIE] = ECCLESIAE. Early drawings suggest that the text has been worn since c. 1885, but it noticeably deteriorated between 1967 and 1969.

83

6-2

60 Ipswich III

Set in an artificial interior wall in the north aisle of St Nicholas' parish church, Ipswich, Suffolk.

Found summer 1848, in inner fabric of church. *c.* 25·4 × 55·9 cm. Incomplete carved Barnack stone slab in three pieces with original paint; two contain incomplete texts set in panels in crosses on face, set sideways to figures, letters facing left. Text i slightly deteriorated, ii legible. Latin descriptive formulae, type b. AS capitals. Possibly eleventh century.

Drummond (1848), 21–8 & figs.; Westwood (1849), 76; Wodderspoon (1850), 333–4; (—) (1886), 478–80 & fig.; Allen (1887), 315 & fig.; (—) (1924), 247; Keyser (1927), xxx, 27; Cautley (1937), 280; (—) (?1938), 63; Dufty (1952), 137 & fig.; Okasha (1967), 249; Galbraith (1968), 178–84 & fig.; (—) (19 *c*), 5 & fig.

i: — *TO[L]VS[:]* |
ii: — OSTOLVS |

The texts read: — TO[L]VS[:] and — OSTOLVS, presumably the endings of APO-STOLUS, preceded by personal names of differing lengths. The texts are complete as they stand, and the rest must have been on stone now lost. There is too little remaining of the third cross to tell whether it was inscribed or not.

Drummond stated that other carved fragments were found at the same time, including one inscribed L.V.S., and that these would be preserved by inserting them into the church fabric.[1] These stones are not now visible, but drawings of various inscribed fragments from the church are preserved in Ipswich Museum.[2] These texts appear to read:

— TOLV —

✠ IA —
— DEI : DEXTE[...]ED[...] NAOSAREN —
— RIA [...]ACOR —
IVD[...] MAR [...] M[.] —

The first two are probably part of the name of one, or two, more apostles, but the meanings of the rest are obscure.[3]

[1] Drummond (1848), 25.
[2] See plates 60 *b* and 60 *c*. I am grateful to Miss K. J. Galbraith, Birkbeck College, London, for bringing these to my attention.
[3] A fuller discussion will appear in my article in *Proceedings of the Suffolk Institute of Archæology for 1970.*

61 Jarrow I

Set in the west-facing interior wall, above the chancel arch, of Jarrow parish church, Durham.

First mentioned 1607, in north wall of church, i.e. of old church.[1] 52·1 × 64·8 cm. Stone slab in two pieces, with slightly deteriorated text set on visible face without framing lines but within panels. Latin dedication formula. AS capitals. *c.* A.D. 685.

Camden (1607), 606 & fig.; Gibson, E. (1695), cols. 779–80; Bede (1722), 296 n.; Leland (1770), IV, 42 (original numbering, III, 39); Grose (1784), 102; Hutchinson (1787), 475–6; Pegge (1787), 14–15 & fig.; Brand (1789), 50 n.–51 n. & fig.; Gough (1806), III, 353, 371; Dugdale (1817), 503; Surtees (1820), 67–8; Boyle (?1822), 587–8; Parker, J. H. (1846), 8 & fig.; Raine, James the younger (1854), xxvi; Stuart (1867), 44–5; Hewitt (1874), 217; Smith, W. and Cheetham (1875), 850; Hübner (1876), no. 198, p. 71 & figs.; Browne (1884–8), 8 & fig.; Boyle (1885), 199–201, 209 & fig.; Allen (1887), 93–4 & fig.; Allen (1889), 202; Hodges (1893), 148–9 & fig.; Bede (1896), II, 361; Browne (1896), 208–9 & fig.; Savage (1900), 33–6 & fig.; Stevens (1904), 38; Hodgson, J. F. (1906–11), 131–2 & fig.; Quentin (1908), 128; Rose (1909), 22–3 & figs.; Hodgkin, J. E. (1913), 174; Browne (1916), 34–5 & fig.; Howorth (1917), II, 287 & fig.; Brown, G. B. (1925), 133–5; Diehl (1925), no. 1820A, p. 358; Clapham (1930), 39; Rivoira (1933), 145; Booth (?1936), 29–33 & fig.; Levison (1946), 262, 273 n.; Saxl and Wittkower (1948), 11 & fig.; Gilbert (1951–6), 316, 319, 320; Pevsner (1953), 175 & fig.; Radford (1954a), 204; Hunter Blair (1956), 156, 319 & fig.; Colgrave, B. and Romans (1962), 18 & fig.; Fisher (1962), 76–7 & figs. 12, 16; Taylor, H. M. and Taylor, J. (1965), 338, 347.

✠DEDICATIOBASILICAE | SCIPAVLIVIIIIK̄LMAI | ANNOXVECFRIDIRĒG | CEOLFRIDIABB̄EIVSD̄EM̄Q | Q:ECCLESD̄OAVCTORE | CONDITORISANNOIIII |

The text reads: ✠ DEDICATIO BASILICAE SCI PAVLI VIIII K̄L MAI ANNO XV ECFRIDI RĒG CEOLFRIDI ABB̄ EIVSD̄EM̄ Q Q: ECCLES D̄O AVCTORE CONDITORIS ANNO IIII, '✠ The dedication of the church of St Paul (was) on 23 April in the 15th year of King Ecfrid and the 4th year of Ceolfrid the Abbot and, under God's guidance, founder of this same church'. The abbreviations are: SCI = SANCTI; K̄L = KALENDAS; MAI = MAII; RĒG = REGIS; ABB̄ = ABBATIS; Q: = QUE; ECCLES = ECCLESIAE; D̄O = DEO. The first Q and the abbreviation marks in EIVSD̄EM̄ are presumably errors or accidental marks unless QQ: = QUE; the abbreviation sign in D̄O is set between the letters. Bede recorded that King Ecgfrith was killed on 20 May 685, in the fifteenth year of his reign.[2] There is no textual evidence to suggest that the inscription is not contemporary with the event described. The church retains the dedication to St Paul.

[1] Leland (1770), IV, 42, ed. Hearne, noted the existence of the stone, and the tradition that it was known by a twelfth century monk of Whitby. This may be Hearne's observation, but if it is Leland's it dates the first mention of the stone to pre 1552, and possibly to the twelfth century.   [2] Bede IV 26, (1896), 266–7.

It seems likely that the text was cut on two pieces of stone, each containing three lines of text, and that these may have been originally separated, cf. 64 Kirkdale. The normal position for a dedication stone would be above the altar or the entrance. Gilbert concluded that the Old, i.e. Ceolfrith's, church (destroyed 1783) contained an Anglian core, and that Aldwine had built this stone into its northern wall.[1]

62 Jarrow II

Jarrow, Durham. Now in the Museum of Antiquities, Newcastle upon Tyne, no. 1956.222.A.

Found December 1782, at parish church. 19·7 × 21·6 × 8·9 cm. Incomplete stone slab, with incomplete but legible text set without framing lines but in panel on one face. Latin text, possibly memorial formula. AS capitals. Possibly eighth century.

Brand (1789), 64 n.; Surtees (1820), 68; Stuart (1867), 65 & pl. cxvi; Hübner (1876), no. 200, p. 72 & fig.; Browne (1884–8), 9–11 & figs.; Boyle (1885), 201–2 & fig.; Browne (1886), 28–30 & fig.; Allen (1889), 214, 222.

— BERCHTI: | [...]EDVERI: | [... C]:CRVCEM: |

The text reads: — BERCHTI : [...] EDVERI : [... c] : CRVCEM :, and may contain personal names in the genitive dependent on CRVCEM; -BERCHTI and -VERI could be respectively forms of -BEORHT and the possibly recorded -WĀER, while [-]ED- could be one of the elements ĒD-, ĒAD-, ĀED- or have a letter lost, e.g. RĀED-. There is no evidence to support Browne's long reconstruction.[2] The stone may pre-date the sacking of Jarrow by the Danes, A.D. 794, but need not necessarily do so.

63 Jarrow III

Jarrow parish church, Durham.

First mentioned 1782, built with text inwards in inner fabric of church; redis-covered 1866 during repairs. 81·3 × c. 50·8 × c. 25 cm. Incomplete carved stone slab with carved cross continued on side of re-used RB stone (Museum of Anti-quities, Newcastle upon Tyne, no. 1851.11). Probably complete, rather deteri-orated text set without framing lines in lower quadrants of cross on visible face. Latin descriptive formula, type b. AS capitals. Possibly eighth century.

Brand (1789), 64 n. & fig.; Surtees (1820), 68 n.; Boyle (?1822), 588; Hübner (1876), no. 199, p. 72 & fig.; Browne (1884–8), 7–9 & fig.; Boyle (1885), 210 & fig.; Browne (1886), 27–8, 32; Allen (1889), 214; Browne (1896), 206–7, 229–32 & fig.; Savage (1900), 35–6 & fig.; Hodges (1905), 234; Hodgson, J. F. (1906–11), 131–2 & figs.; Rose (1909), 24; Hodgkin, J. E. (1913),

---

[1] Gilbert (1951–6), 319.   [2] Cf. Browne (1884–8), 11.

173–4; Booth (?1936), 47–9 & figs.; Levison (1943), 121–6 & fig.; Colgrave, B. and Romans (1962), 22–3 & fig.; Cramp (1965b), 4–5; Swanton (1970), 47.

INHO | CS[..] | GVLA | R[....] | NOVI | TAR[E.] | DITVR | MVN[DO] |

The text is likely to be complete and can be read: IN HOC S[IN]GVLAR[I SIG]NO VITA R[ED]DITVR MVN[DO], 'In this unique sign life is given back to the world', where the 'sign' is presumably the carved cross. The origin of the formula was discussed by Levison, who suggested that the first four words may come from Rufinus's edition of Eusebius.[1] The text is not primary. The stone may pre-date the sacking of Jarrow by the Danes, A.D. 794, but need not necessarily do so.

64   Kirkdale

Set in the south wall above the doorway of the parish church, Kirkdale, NR Yorkshire.

First mentioned 1771, in present *situs*, probably *in situ*. 50·8 × 236·2 cm. Carved stone sun-dial, with text i set in panels to left and right of dial on visible face, ii in panel along horizontal diameter and part of arc of dial, letters facing outwards, iii in panel below dial. Texts contain modern paint; i legible, ii and iii slightly deteriorated. OE texts; i dedication formula, ii descriptive formula, type a, iii maker formula. AS capitals. A.D. 1055–65.

Brooke (1779), 188–205 & fig.; Pegge (1787), 20–1 & fig.; Gough (1806), III, 330 & fig.; Young (1817), 741–7 & fig.; Parker, J. H. (1846), 28–9 & fig.; Rickman (1862), 65 & fig.; Way and Noyer (1868), 209; Haigh (1870), 51–3; Cuming (1873), 281;[2] Evans (1873), 333; Hewitt (1874), 217; Rowe (1874), 208–9 & fig.; Hübner (1876), no. 180, p. 65 & fig.; Tudor (1876), 10 & figs.; Haigh (1879), 149–51, 158 & fig.; Taylor, R. V. (1881), 147–8; Frank (1888), 137–42 & fig.; Allen (1889), 201–2; Hodges (1894), 198–9 & fig.; Stephens (1894), 14; Browne (1896), 194–6 & fig.; Micklethwaite (1896), 320–1; Gatty (1900), 54–5 & fig.; Savage (1900), 35; Stephens (1901), 103 & fig.; (—) (1903), 239–40 & fig.; Förster (1906), 446–8; Collingwood, W. G. (1907), 344 & fig.; Powell, F. W. (1909), 12–18 & figs.; Leclercq (1910b), cols. 1543–4; Collingwood, W. G. (1912), 122, 125; Gaye and Galpin (1912), 127–32 & fig.; Russell (1914a), 521 & fig.; Collingwood, W. G. (1915a), 288, 290; Home (1915), 79–82 & fig.; Pilkington (1915), 32 & fig.; Browne (1916), 37–8 & fig.; Howorth (1917), III, 308; Whitley (1919), 127; Brown, G. B. (1925), 308; Brown, G. B. (1926), 355–7 & fig.; Green, A. R. (1926), 13–15 & fig.; Green, A. R. (1928), 491, 506–7 & figs.; Tolkien (1929), 120; Clapham (1930), 112–13; Ekwall (1930), 20; Morris (1931), 223–6; Elgee, F. and Elgee, H. W. (1933), 225–6 & fig.; Rivoira (1933), 175; Shaw, M. B. (1939), 321–2; Clapham (1948a), 7; Rice (1952), 151–2; (—) (1952a), 537 & fig.; Hofmann (1955), 211–12; Hunter Blair (1956), 192 & fig.; Penn *et al.* (1961), & fig. (no pagination); Page, R. I. (1964), 83; Zinner (1964), 4, 110; Taylor, H. M. and Taylor, J. (1965), 359–61; Taylor, J. and Taylor, H. M. (1966), 22, 50; Ward (1966), 13; Okasha (1969), 28 & fig.

[1] Levison (1943), 122–6.   [2] The figure stated to be of Kirkdale is not so.

i: ✠ORM:GAMAL: | SVNA: BOHTE:SC̄S | GREGORIVS: MIN |
STER: ÐONNEHI | T: ꝠESÆL:TOBRO |
CAN: ꝋTOFALAN:ꝋH/E | HITLET[:]MACAN[:]NEꝠAN: FROM |
GRVNDEXꝢE:ꝋ/SCS/GREGORI | VS:IN:EADꝠARD:DAGVM:
CN̄G | ꝋNTOSTI[:]DAGVM:EORL✠ |

ii: ✠ꝐIS[:]IS[:]DÆGES:SOLMERCA✠ | ÆTILCVM[:]TIDE✠ |

iii: ✠ꝋHAꝠARÐ[:]MEꝠROHTE:ꝋBRAND | PR̄S |

Text i reads: ✠ ORM : GAMAL : SVNA : BOHTE : SC̄S GREGORIVS : MINSTER:
ÐONNE HIT : ꝠES ÆL : TOBROCAN : ꝋ TOFALAN : ꝋ HE HIT LET [:] MACAN
[:] NEꝠAN : FROM GRVNDE XꝢE : ꝋ SCS GREGORIVS : IN : EADꝠARD : DAGVM :
CN̄G ꝋ N TOSTI [:] DAGVM : EORL ✠, '✠Orm Gamal's son bought St Gregory's
church when it was completely ruined and collapsed, and he had it built anew from
the ground to Christ and St Gregory, in the days of King EadꝠard, and in the days of
Earl Tosti ✠'. The abbreviations are: SC̄S, SCS = SANCTUS; XꝢE = CHRISTO
(probably with an OE dative inflexion -*e*); CN̄G = CYNING; N = IN. None of the
personal names in an oblique case is inflected. Two of the people mentioned can be
identified, and these identifications provide the dating; they are King Edward the
Confessor (A.D. 1042–66) and Tosti Earl of Northumbria (A.D. 1055–65). Orm is
probably the Orm who held *TRE* twelve Yorkshire manors including Kirkdale.[1]
The church retains the dedication to St Gregory.

Text ii reads: ✠ ꝐIS [:] IS [:] DÆGES : SOLMERCA ✠ ÆT ILCVM [:] TIDE ✠,
'✠This is the day's sun-marker ✠ at every hour ✠'. This text, which refers to the
sun-dial, has confusion between OE *aelc* 'each' and *ilca* 'same'. Text iii reads:
✠ ꝋ HAꝠARÐ [:] ME ꝠROHTE : ꝋ BRAND PR̄S, '✠And HaꝠarð made me and Brand
the priest', where PR̄S = PRESBYTER, though PRESBYTERI is also possible. All
the texts show a fairly strong ON element; all the names, with the exception
of ĒADWEARD, are of recorded ON origin, but none of them except Tosti and
possibly Orm can be identified. The texts also all show a late lack and confusion of
inflexions.

65 Knells

Knells, Cumberland. Lost.

First mentioned 1911, at Knells, possibly from Carlisle. 106·7 × 35·6 × 10·2 cm.
Probably complete carved stone slab, with incomplete and highly deteriorated text

1 DB Yorkshire fo. 327.

set in panel at top of face, upside down with respect to carving.[1] Probably OE text, possibly personal name. AS capitals. Possibly eighth to ninth century.

Collingwood, W. G. *et al.* (1911), 482–3 & fig.; Collingwood, W. G. (1923), 230.

[..]*MVN*[..] |

Collingwood read the text as -MVNDI.[2] From the photograph, this is a fairly likely reading, possibly the recorded second element of a name, -MUND.

66   Lancashire

Now in the British Museum, London, no. SL 64 (catalogued under 'rings, etc.'), ring cat. no. 181.

First mentioned 1705, in possession of Hans Sloane, Esq. Diam. *c.* 2·2 cm. Decorated gold ring, outside of hoop nielloed with legible text in gold lettering set right round it. OE maker and owner formulae. AS capitals, insular majuscule and runes. Probably ninth century.

Hickes (1705), I, xiii & figs.; Magnuson (1820), 351; Hamper (1821), 381; Magnuson (1822), 140–1 & fig.; Kemble (1840), 348; Waterton (1862), 327 & fig.; Cuming (1863), 216; Stephens (1866–7), xxxiv, 463 & figs.; Evans (1873), 332; Jones (1877), 58; Stephens (1884*b*), 139 & fig.; Sweet (1885), 130; Payne (1893), 112; Stephens (1894), 30; Searle (1897), 46, 210; Earle (1901), 154–6 & fig.; Smith, R. A. (1901), 233; (—) (1901*a*), 13; (—) (1901*b*), 215 & fig.; Bugge (1908), 176; Smith, H. C. (1908), 72; Dalton (1912), no. 181, p. 30 & figs.; Smith, R. A. (1923), 115–16 & fig.; Chamot (1930), 2; Oman (1931), 107 & fig.; Harder (1932), 37 & fig.; Bennett (1946–53), 273; Jessup (1950), 132 & figs.; Moss (1952–4), 59–61; Moss (1953), 76; Ploss (1958), 34 n.; Page, R. I. (1964), 75–7; Wilson, D. M. (1964), no. 30, pp. 1, 23, 27, 141 & figs.; Schneider (1968), 49–52 & fig; Swanton (1970), 66n.

✠æDREDMECAHEAnREDMECagROf |

The text reads: ✠ÆDRED MEC AH EANRED MEC AGROF, '✠Ædred owns me, Eanred engraved me'. The inverted T between the last and first letters (see Plate 66*d*) is presumably decorative. ĒANRǢD is a recorded name, and ÆDRED is probably a form of one of the recorded names AEÐRǢD, ǢEDRǢD.

67   Lancaster I

St Mary's Priory Church, Lancaster.

Found 1903, in inside fabric of church. *c.* 25·4 × 20·3 × 10·2 cm. Incomplete carved stone cross-shaft, with incomplete legible text set without framing lines but in panel on one face. Latin memorial formula. AS capitals. Probably ninth century.

[1] The description, etc., is from Collingwood, W. G. (1911), 482–3 & fig.
[2] Collingwood, W. G. (1911), 482.

Collingwood, W. G. (1903), 257–9 & figs.; Taylor, H. (1903), 49–50 & figs.; Garstang (1906), 266; Taylor, H. (1906), 341–3 & figs.; Collingwood, W. G. (1927), 59, index & fig.; Colling-wood, W. G. (1932), 40; Edwards *et al.* (1966), 148–9; Pevsner (1969), 154.

✠ OR/A/T/E | PANIM | A:H/A/RD | —

The text reads: ✠ ORATE P ANIMA : HARD —, '✠ Pray for the soul of Hard-'. The letter P = PRO does not seem to have an abbreviation sign. HARD- is a frequent first name-element.

68   Lancaster II

On loan to Lancaster City Museum from St Mary's Priory Church, Lancaster.

Found June 1965, in Roman well on site of new vicarage. 43·8 × 26 × c. 14 cm. Incomplete carved stone cross-shaft with incomplete rather deteriorated text set without framing lines on each face, faces reading anti-clockwise. Latin memorial formula. AS capitals. Probably ninth century.

Edwards *et al.* (1966), 146–9 & figs.; Pevsner (1969), 154.

[✠]ORA[T.] | P̄ANIM[.] | [..DED] | CYNIB/A[.] |
[...] | HOC | OPV[.] |
[..E]RF[...] | [.]ERPE | [..AR]AT |
[.]DG | LOR[I] | ĀDN̄[I] |

The text can be read: [✠] ORA[TE] P̄ ANIM[A...] CYNIBA[. ...] HOC OPV[S ... P]-ERPE[TUAR]AT [A]D GLOR[I]Ā DN̄[I], '[✠] Pray for the soul of Cynib[.] [?who] had promised this work [...] to the glory of the Lord'. The first lacuna may have contained QUI, and Edwards read PER FILI(UM) in the second.[1] The third line on the first side is an inset, possibly the later insertion of another name. The abbreviations are: P̄ = PRO, GLOR[I]Ā = GLORIAM and DN̄[I] = DOMINI. CYNI- is a recorded name element, and the name may be a form of the unrecorded *CYNEBAD, or an abbreviated form of CYNEBALD.

69   Lanteglos

Parish churchyard, Lanteglos by Camelford, Cornwall.

Found pre 1858, at Castlegoff Farm, possibly from nearby earthworks; possibly identical with stone mentioned 1753 by Borlase, 'about a mile west of Camelford, in the highroad'.[2] c. 198 × 41·9 × c. 20·3 cm. Tenoned stone shaft, possibly ori-

---

1 Edwards *et al.* (1966), 148, where the bracketed letters are an expanded abbreviation. Other readings for [P]ERPE[TUAR]AT are also given here.
2 Iago (1890–1), 188–9, quoting Dr Borlase's Manuscripts *Inscriptions*, p. 89.

ginally in a base, with text set on one face, except for third line set on left side; highly deteriorated text set without framing lines with letters facing left. OE or early ME text, probably memorial formula. Capitals. Probably eleventh century or post-Conquest.

Blight (1858), 126 & fig.; Hübner (1876), no. 16 & add., pp. 5–6, 89 & fig.; Maclean, J. (1876), 281–2 & fig.; Smith, W. and Cheetham (1880), 1978; Allen (1889), 221; Iago (1890–1), 188–9; Langdon and Allen (1895), 51, 58, 60 & fig.; Iago (1896), 148 & fig.; Stephens (1901), 101–2 & figs.; Langdon (1906), 416 & figs.; Macalister (1929), 184; Hencken (1932), 265; Pevsner (1951), 79.

✠ÆLSEL[..G]ENE[RE.] | [.]O[H]TEꝜYS[N]E[S]YB[.TE.] |
FORÆLꝜYNESS[.UL..]ORHE[.] |
[.EL] |

In July 1964 the text read as above: ✠ÆLSEL[Ð 7 G]ENE[REÐ Ꝝ]O[H]TE ꝜYS[N]E [S]YB[STEL] FOR ÆLꝜYNES S[OUL 7 F]OR HE[YSEL]. However by September 1965 it had noticeably deteriorated and then read: ✠ÆLSEL[Ð 7 G]ENE[REÐ Ꝝ]O[H]TE ꝜYS[N ...]FOR ÆLꝜYNES —. Nineteenth-century drawings suggest that it then read: ✠ÆLSELÐ 7 GENEREÐ ꝜOHTE ꝜYSNE SYBSTEL FOR ÆLꝜYNEYS SOUL 7 FOR HEYSEL; this can be translated, '✠ Ælselð and Genereð made this family-place (*or* place of peace) for Ælꝝyn's soul and for themselves (*or* for Heysel)', but there is evidence to suggest that these readings are not entirely trustworthy. Though in these forms unrecorded and rather odd, the names can be explained (see Index v), but the original text cannot now be ascertained. The script, though in capitals, resembles Cornish vernacular script, and the language (if post-Conquest) may preserve some early dialectal forms.

70 Laverstock

Laverstock, Wiltshire. Now in the British Museum, London, no. 1829.11–14.1, ring cat. no. 179.

Found 'about August 1780',[1] in field near Laverstock. Diam. *c.* 2·7 cm., ht. of bezel *c.* 3·2 cm. Decorated gold ring with legible text of nielloed letters set in panel on outside of hoop beneath bezel. OE personal name. AS capitals. *c.* A.D. 828–58.

Radnor (1785), 421 & figs.; Way (1846a), 163 & fig.; Akerman (1847), 144 & figs.; de Laborde (1852), 32; Labarte (1855), xxiv, 126 & fig.; Shaw, H. (1858), pl. 1, text & figs. (no pagination); Waterton (1862), 327 & fig.; Cuming (1863), 216; Fairholt (1871), 101–2 & fig.; Franks (1873–6), 307; Hübner (1876), no. 223a, p. 81; Jones (1877), 54–7 & fig.; Allen (1889), 246; Robson (1899), 202; Earle (1901), 149–50 & figs.; (—) (1901a), 13; Leclercq (1907b), col. 2205; Smith, H. C. (1908), 72 & fig.; Jackson, C. J. (1911), 54 & fig.; Dalton (1912), no. 179, pp. 29–30 & fig.; Brown, G. B. (1916), 178 & fig.; Smith, R. A. (1923), 90, 114 & fig.; Brøndsted (1924), 133 & fig.; Chamot (1930), 2; Leclercq (1930), col. 2402 & fig.; Oman (1931), 105 &

---

[1] Radnor (1785), 421.

fig.; Kendrick (1938), 183–4 & fig.; Jessup (1950), 130–1 & figs.; Maryon (1950), 178 & fig.; Hodgkin, R. H. (1952), II, ix & fig.; Moss (1952–4), 59–61; Moss (1953), 76; Stone (1955a), 36–7 & fig.; Wilson, D. M. and Blunt (1961), 107; Godfrey, J. (1962), 374; Page, R. I. (1964), 79, 80, 82; Wilson, D. M. (1964), no. 31, pp. 2, 5, 6, 22–3, 27, 29, 34, 56, 141–2 & figs.; Page, R. I. (1968), 18.

✠ETH/ELVVLFR/X: |

The text reads: ✠ ETHELVVLF RX:, '✠ King Ethelvvlf', where RX: = REX, or possibly RX = REX with a word-division sign used to fill up space, and where the letter T is upside down. ETHELVVULF is King Ethelwulf the father of Alfred the Great. The ring is dated to between the date of the first charter signed by Ethelwulf as king and the date of his death.

71 Leake I

Set into the south wall of the chancel, above the doorway, of Leake parish church, NR Yorkshire.

First mentioned 1914, in present *situs*. Diam. *c.* 30·5 cm. Carved stone circular sun-dial on visible face, possibly with illegible text set round perimeter of lower half of dial. Language, formula, script and date uncertain.

Green, A. R. (1928), 514–15; Morris (1931), 238.

It is not certain whether the remaining traces formed part of the decoration or were lettering. The lack of traces in the upper half of the dial suggests that a text is likely, but if so it is now illegible.

72 Leake II

Set in the south wall of the south aisle of Leake parish church, NR Yorkshire.

First mentioned 1913, in present *situs*. Diam. *c.* 40·6 cm. Probably uncarved, probably semi-circular sun-dial with possible traces of now illegible text set at top left side of dial. Language, formula, script and date uncertain.

Thompson, A. H. (1913), 233; Green, A. R. (1928), 504–5 & fig.; Morris (1931), 238; Zinner (1964), 117–18.

The text is now illegible though Green read A at one side.[1]

73 Lincoln I

Set into the west wall of the tower of St Mary-le-Wigford parish church, Lincoln.

First mentioned 1724, in present *situs* and possibly *in situ*. 139·7 × 91·4 cm. Stone slab, consisting of rectangular part containing RB text,[2] with triangular part above;

---

[1] Green, A. R. (1928), 505.   [2] The text is given in Collingwood, R. G. and Wright, R. P. (1965), 87.

highly deteriorated text set from base to apex in triangular part of visible face. Probably OE dedication formula. AS capitals. Probably late eleventh century.

Stukeley (1724), 85–6; Horsley (1732), 319; Stukeley (1776), 91 & fig. 64; Gough (1780), 520 & fig.; Johnson M. (1781), 70 & fig.; Gough (1806), II, 374 & fig. opp. p. 342; Trollope, E. & Trollope, A. (1860), 14–16 & fig.; Hübner (1876), no. 170, p. 62 & fig.; (—) (1877), 132–3; Wordsworth (1879), 16–17 & fig.; Sympson (1906), 331–2; Brown, G. B. (1925), 466–7; Smith, A. (1929), 8–9 & fig.; Lambert and Sprague (1933), 172–3; Dickins (1946), 163–5 & fig.; Hill, J. W. F. (1948), 136–8; (—) (?1953), 6–8 & fig.; Fisher (1962), 284–5 & fig.; Pevsner & Harris (1964), 144; Collingwood, R. G. and Wright, R. P. (1965), no. 262, pp. 87–8 & fig.; Taylor, H. M. and Taylor, J. (1965), 391–4; (—) (19 a), 4–5 and fig.

[. . .]TI[. . .]E[L]ET[V]I[. . .] | [A. .]FI[. . . .TO. .] | N[C]RISTETO[L] | O[F]E[.]SC̄E | M[. .]IE |

The first two lines of text are now illegible, but the rest reads: — [C]RISTE TO [L]O[F]E [7] SC̄E M[AR]IE, where SC̄E = SANCTAE, the inflexion agreeing with M[AR]IE. Earlier drawings and readings suggest that the first two lines read: EIRTIG ME LET VIRCE[A]N 7 FIOS GODIAN.[1] The text can then be translated, 'Eirtig had me made and endowed with possessions to the glory of Christ and St Mary', where *EIRTIG is an unrecorded name, though it could perhaps be explained as of ON origin. The OE text is not primary. The church retains the dedication to St Mary.

LINDISFARNE STONES, BIBLIOGRAPHY[2]

(—) (1887–8), 403–4	(I)
Crossman (1887–9), 412–14	(I)
Hall, G. R. (1889), 266–7 & fig.	(I)
Stephens (1891–2), 189–90 & fig.	(I)
Hodges (1893), 80	(I)
Stephens (1894), 51	(I)
Stephens (1901), 45–7	(I)
Peers et al. (1914–15), 132–7 & figs.	(I, II, VI)
Peers (1915–16), 53	(II)
Browne (1916), 79–81 & fig.	(II)
Brown, G. B. (1919), 202–4 & figs.	(I, II, VI)
Brown, G. B. (1921), 67–9 & figs.	(I, II, VI)
Peers (1925), 255–70 & figs.	(General)
Collingwood, W. G. (1927), 10–13, index & figs.	(General; figs. of II, VI)
Clapham (1930), 74–5 & fig.	(General; fig. of III)
Kendrick and Hawkes (1932), 343 & fig.	(General; fig. of II)
Friesen (1933), 52	(II)

---

[1] The last N is in fact on the third line.   [2] None of the works mentions Lindisfarne O.

Ross (1935–6), 36–9   (IV, V, VII)
Dahl (1938), 10, 188   (VII)
Henry (1940), 76 & fig.   (General; fig. of II)
Bæksted (1943), 44–5   (II)
Hodgkin, R. H. (1952), 1, 296 & figs.   (I, II)

74 Lindisfarne O

Lindisfarne Priory Museum, Northumberland.[1]

Found 1957, in Sanctuary Close, field east of Priory, during controlled excavation.[2] *c.* 19·1 × *c.* 17·8 × *c.* 3·8 cm. Incomplete stone slab, probably uncarved, with illegible text set without framing lines on one face. Language, formula and script uncertain. Probably eighth century.

Unpublished.

The text is now illegible. All the Lindisfarne stones probably pre-date the abandonment of Lindisfarne, A.D. 875, less likely the sacking by the Danes, A.D. 793.

75 Lindisfarne I[3]

Lindisfarne parish church, Northumberland.

Found 1888, below ground in churchyard, during controlled excavation. *c.* 21 × *c.* 16·2 × *c.* 2·5 cm. Carved red sandstone slab with rounded head; slightly deteriorated text set without framing lines in lower quadrants of cross on face. OE personal name. AS capitals. Probably eighth century.

For Bibliography, see *Lindisfarne Stones, Bibliography*.

A[ED] | BE | RE | C[H]T |

The text reads: A[ED]BEREC[H]T, a form of one of the recorded names AEÐBEORHT, ĀEDBEORHT. The letter H is smaller than the others and is inserted between C and T.

76 Lindisfarne II

Lindisfarne Priory Museum, Northumberland.

Found February 1915, in north transept of priory church, during controlled excavation. 21·6 × 15·2 × *c.* 3·8 cm. Incomplete carved red sandstone slab with rounded head; legible text set without framing lines in lower quadrants of cross on face,

---

[1] None of the Lindisfarne stones, all of which are preserved in the Lindisfarne Priory Museum, has acquisition numbers.

[2] Although all the stones were found during controlled excavations, adequate reports and find-lists were unfortunately not kept.

[3] The stones are numbered according to Peers (1925), 255–70.

with identical runic text in upper quadrants. OE personal name. AS capitals. Probably eighth century.

For Bibliography, see *Lindisfarne Stones, Bibliography*.

✠ OS | GYÐ |

The text reads, ✠ OSGYÐ, and the runic text: OSGYÞ, forms of the recorded feminine name ŌSGȲÐ.

77 Lindisfarne III

Lindisfarne Priory Museum, Northumberland.

Found 1920–5, during controlled excavation. 29·2 × 19.1 × *c.* 4·4 cm. Incomplete stone slab with rounded head; rather deteriorated text set without framing lines in lower quadrants of cross on face, with incomplete runic text in upper left quadrant. Language and formula uncertain. AS capitals. Probably eighth century.

For Bibliography, see *Lindisfarne Stones, Bibliography*.

B/EAN | N*A[H.]* | [.*A]VSI[.]* |

The text reads: BEANNA [H..A]VSI[.], perhaps with a cross above the H. Peers read this as: BEANNA HIC PAUSIL (= PAUSAT),[1] but the text is more likely to consist of one or more personal names of uncertain form. The runic text reads: — OIN[.], which Page suggested could also be a name, possibly [C]OIN[A] = COENA.[2]

78 Lindisfarne IV

Lindisfarne Priory Museum, Northumberland.

Found probably 1920, below ground in doorway of south wall of priory church, during controlled excavation. 17·8 × 15·9 × 4·1 cm. Incomplete carved stone slab in two pieces with rounded head; incomplete rather deteriorated text set without framing lines in remaining lower quadrant of cross on face, with runic text in remaining upper quadrant. Language, formula and script uncertain. Probably eighth century.

For Bibliography, see *Lindisfarne Stones, Bibliography*.

[.*A*] —

The text reads: [HA] — or [BA] —, and the runic text, H[.] —. They were probably one or more personal names, of uncertain form.

[1] Peers (1925), 260.   [2] R. I. Page, in a personal communication.

79   Lindisfarne VI[1]

Lindisfarne Priory Museum, Northumberland.

Found March–June 1915, possibly in nave of priory church during the controlled excavations there. 16·5 × c. 15·2 × 3·8 cm. Incomplete carved stone slab with rounded head; incomplete illegible text set without framing lines in remaining lower quadrants of cross on face. Language, formula and script uncertain. Probably eighth century.

For Bibliography, see *Lindisfarne Stones, Bibliography*.

The text is now illegible.

80   Lindisfarne VII

Lindisfarne Priory Museum, Northumberland.

Found 1920–5, during controlled excavation. 23·5 × 19·1 × 3·8 cm. Incomplete carved stone slab with rounded head; incomplete rather deteriorated text set without framing lines in lower quadrants of cross on face, with runic text in upper quadrants. Probably OE personal name. AS capitals. Probably eighth century.

For Bibliography, see *Lindisfarne Stones, Bibliography*.

— [. .] | [U]*INI* |

The text reads: — [. . U]INI, and the runic text: [.]AMᚹINI, probably two personal names with the same recorded second element -WINE.

81   Lindisfarne VIII

Lindisfarne Priory Museum, Northumberland.

Found May and August 1924, on shore of St Cuthbert's island, c. 183 m. from main island. 30·5 × 21·6 × c. 5·1 cm. Incomplete carved stone slab with rounded head, in two pieces; highly deteriorated text set without framing lines in quadrants of cross on face, with runic text in lower left quadrant. Possibly OE personal name. Probably AS capitals. Probably eighth century.

For Bibliography, see *Lindisfarne Stones, Bibliography*.

[...] | [P. .] | [. .*INI* | —

The text reads: — [P. . . .INI] —, and may be a personal name. However Page was uncertain how much of the text was runic and tentatively read runic texts, ᚹI —, and NA — or NO —, in two lines in the lower left quadrant.[2]

---

1 Lindisfarne V has runic texts reading: AUD — and — LAC.   2 R. I. Page, in a personal communication.

82   Lindisfarne IX

Lindisfarne Priory Museum, Northumberland.

Found February 1923, in priory grounds during controlled excavation. 24·8×
19·1× c. 3 cm. Incomplete carved stone slab with rounded head; illegible text set
without framing lines in quadrants of cross on face. Language, formula and script
uncertain. Probably eighth century.

For Bibliography, see *Lindisfarne Stones, Bibliography*.

The text is now illegible.

83   Lindisfarne X

Lindisfarne Priory Museum, Northumberland.

Found 1920–5, during controlled excavation. 15·9× 20·3× 3·8 cm. Incomplete
carved stone slab; rather deteriorated text set without framing lines in remaining
lower quadrants of cross on face. Probably OE personal name. AS capitals. Probably
eighth century.

For Bibliography, see *Lindisfarne Stones, Bibliography*.

[E.] | [..] | HA | [R]D |

The text reads: [E...]HA[R]D, probably a personal name, possibly a form of
AEÐELHEARD. The lost upper quadrants may also have been inscribed.

84   Lindisfarne XIV

Lindisfarne Priory Museum, Northumberland.

Found 1920–5, during controlled excavation. 16·5× 13·7× 5·1 cm. Incomplete
carved stone, possibly once circular, of diam. c. 35·6 cm.; illegible text set without
framing lines inside carving on face. Language, formula and script uncertain. Probably eighth century.

For Bibliography, see *Lindisfarne Stones, Bibliography*.

The text is now illegible.

85   Little Billing

Little Billing parish church, Northamptonshire.

First mentioned 1822–30, in church, possibly *in situ*, possibly in present *situs*.
Ht. c. 91·5 cm., perimeter c. 234 cm. Sandstone barrel-shaped font, with incomplete but legible text set without framing lines round it, half way up; traces of red

paint occur on text. Latin maker formula. Capitals. Probably eleventh century or post-Conquest.

Baker (1822–30), 30 & fig.; Paley (1844), & fig. (no pagination, first illustration); Allen (1887), 252; Searle (1897), 487; Allen (1906b), 187–8; Bond (1908), 37, 107, 113, 127 & fig.; Tyrrell-Green (1928), 149, 160; Page, W. et al. (1937), 76 & fig.; Clapham (1948a), 7; Fisher (1959), 95–6 & fig.; Pevsner (1961a), 280; Okasha (1967), 250.

WIGBERHTVSARTIFEXATQ: CEMENT*ARIVSH*VICFABRICAVIT[...]|
QVISQVISSVVMVENITMERGERECORPVSPROCVLDVBIOCAEIT —

The text reads: WIGBERHTVS ARTIFEX ATQ: CEMENTARIVS HVIC FABRICAVIT [...] QVISQVIS SVVM VENIT MERGERE CORPVS PROCVL DVBIO CAEIT —, 'Wigberht craftsman and mason constructed for this [...] whoever comes to immerse his body without doubt —'. WĪGBEORHT is a recorded name and ATQ: = ATQUE. CAEIT is inexplicable: it may contain an error or have a letter omitted. If the text originally continued right round, about 19 to 22 letters are lost from each line, where the font has been mended with mortar. Other letters also occur, though they are larger and may have been differently formed: A after FABRICAVIT and AV*L*A below the mortar. The date of the paint and the mortar are both uncertain; when found, the font was covered with white-wash.[1] It has been dated to both the Anglo-Saxon and the Norman periods, but there is no certain evidence for either.

86 Llysfaen

Llysfaen, Caernarvonshire, Wales. Now in the Victoria and Albert Museum, London, no. 627–1871.

Found probably 1753, certainly pre-July 1771, on common. Diam. 2·9 cm. Decorated gold ring, consisting of four circular pellets alternating with four lozenges; legible text set in panels on outside of pellets, letters gold on niello. OE personal name. AS capitals and rune. Ninth century.

Pegge (1777), 47–68 & figs.; Gough (1806), III, 192 & figs. opp. p. 172; Hanshall (1823), 483–4 & figs.; Way (1846a), 163–4; de Laborde (1852), 32; Braybrooke (1856), 14; Waring (1858), in 'Vitreous Art: Enamel' pt. 1, & figs. (no pagination); Waterton (1859), 194; Waterton (1859–61a), 107; Waterton (1859–61b), 277; Waterton (1862), 327 & figs.; Cuming (1863), 216; French (1863), 497 & figs.; Waterton (1863), 226 & figs.; Fowler (1869–70), 159, 161–2; Fairholt (1871), 102–3 & figs.; Jones (1877), 62–3 & figs.; Smith, W. and Cheetham (1880), 1804 n.; Earle (1901), 147–9; Leclercq (1907b), col. 2205 & fig.; Smith, H. C. (1908), 71–2 & fig.; Jackson, C. J. (1911), 54–5 & figs.; Brown, G. B. (1916), 178 & figs.; Brøndsted (1924), 133–4 & figs.; Oman (1930), no. 227, pp. 63–4 & figs.; (—) (1930a), no. 49, p. 11; Oman (1931), 105 & fig.; Jessup (1950), 133 & fig.; Bruce-Mitford (1956), 193; Wilson, D. M. and

---

[1] Baker (1822–30), 30.

Blunt (1961), 107; Page, R. I. (1964), 75, 76; Wilson, D. M. (1964), 23, 31; Page, R. I. (1968), 18.

⊹A |
LH |
ST |
An |

The text reads: ⊹ ALHSTAN, '⊹ Alhstan', a recorded name. The rune, ᛉ, 'n', provides symmetry of design between the last and the first pellets.

87 London I

All Hallows church, Barking-by-the-Tower, London.

Found December 1951, beneath eleventh century pillar of nave. Diam *c.* 61 cm. Incomplete carved sandstone wheel-headed cross, with incomplete rather deteriorated text set round perimeter on one face, letters facing inwards, traces of original paint remaining on stone and letters. OE memorial formula. AS capitals. Tenth to eleventh century.

(—) (1951), 7 & fig.; (—) (1952b), 88 & fig.; Pevsner (1962), 134; Okasha (1967), 249–51 & figs.

— STANᚠELV[.]RLETSE[......F]ERH/ERE —

The text probably reads: — STAN ᚠELV[A]R LET SE[... OF]ER HERE —, '— ᚠelv-[a]r had (this) stone set up over Here- ', where the verb is presumably SE[TTE]. Alternative but less likely readings of the first words are: STANᚠEL V[A]R, or: STANᚠEL V[A]RLET, with STANᚠEL in the unrecorded sense 'standing-stone'; though explicable, none of these possible personal names is recorded. The stone may have been decorated with paint rather than sculpture. It appears to have been re-used in medieval building.

88 London II

All Hallows church, Barking-by-the-Tower, London.

Found 1941, in church fabric. *c.* 40·6 × *c.* 30·5 × *c.* 30·5 cm. Incomplete carved stone cross-shaft in nine pieces; slightly deteriorated, possibly incomplete text set without framing lines between carving on one face, text contained on two pieces. Traces of original paint remain on stone. Possibly OE personal name, or OE descriptive formula. AS capitals. Probably eleventh century.

7-2

Kendrick and Radford (1943), 14–18 & figs.; Kent (1947), 95 & figs.; Kendrick (1949), 83–6 & figs.; Rice (1952), 143; Clayton (?1960), 6–7; Radford (?1960), 13–16 & figs.; Pevsner (1962), 134; Okasha (1967), 249–50.

[.]ERH[E.] | ϷORRD |

The text probably reads: [.]ERH[E.]ϷORRD, though some letters may also be lost from the beginning of the second line. The text is either an unrecorded personal name, or a descriptive text where ϷORRD might refer to the word of God.

89 Manchester

Set in the west face of the north interior wall of the Chancel screen of Manchester Cathedral, Lancashire.

Found February 1871, in cathedral fabric. 22·2 × c. 33 × 3·8 cm. Probably complete, carved red sandstone slab, with probably complete rather deteriorated text set without framing lines on visible face. Latin text, memorial formula, or possibly descriptive formula, type c. Probably AS capitals. Possibly ninth century.

Crowther (1893), 7–8 & fig.; Taylor, H. (1904), 80 & fig.; Axon (1905), 169–71 & fig.; Phelps (1905), 172–98 & figs.; Garstang (1906), 264; Taylor, H. (1906), 410 & fig.; Rice (1952), 94–5.

INMA/NVST | VASD[MĒ]CO | MMĒDO[SP] |

The text reads: IN MANVS TVAS D[MĒ] COMMĒDO [SP], probably 'Into thy hands, O Lord, I commend (?my) spirit'. This is similar to the Vulgate versions of Psalm XXX 6, and Luke XXIII 46, both of which read: 'in manus tuas commendo spiritum meum'. In this case the abbreviations would be D[MĒ] = DOMINE, COMMĒDO = COMMENDO, and [SP] = SPIRITUM. The text may not be primary. The script is rather odd and could perhaps be post-Conquest, though the carving is earlier.

90 Mildenhall

Mildenhall, Suffolk. Now in the Museum of Archaeology and Ethnology, Cambridge, no. 1904.158.

Found 1903, near Mildenhall. 5·4 × 3·8 × c. 0·3 cm. Concave decorated bronze object, perhaps strap-end covering, with incomplete slightly deteriorated text set in panel on face, letters facing left. Language and formula uncertain. Some letters possibly AS capitals, some possibly runes. Date uncertain.

Page, R. I. (1964), 89 & fig.

[.]IOB[...] |

The sixth letter may be P or ϸ, and the seventh R. The meaning of the text is quite uncertain; it may be an illiterate copying for purposes of decoration.

91   Monkwearmouth I

Monkwearmouth, Sunderland, Durham. Now in Sunderland Museum, no. 205–1969.

Found 1961, during controlled excavation, amongst disturbed Saxon and medieval building debris. 10·2 × 5·7 × 1·3 cm. Incomplete carved red calcareous silt-stone slab, with incomplete rather deteriorated text set without framing lines in remaining lower quadrant of cross on face, with runic text in upper quadrant. Probably OE personal name. AS capitals. Possibly eighth to ninth century.

Cramp (1964), 294–8 & fig.; Colgrave, B. and Cramp (1965), 23; Cramp (1965b), 4.

A[LD] —

The text probably reads, A[LD] —, presumably the recorded first element of a personal name. The runic text reads, EO —, and is probably the first element of a different name. The stone has been re-used in building.

92   Monkwearmouth II

Monkwearmouth parish church, Sunderland, Durham.

Found September 1866, during controlled excavation, face downwards below ground, above medieval coffin in west porch. c. 104 × c. 53·3 × c. 17·8 cm. Incomplete carved stone slab containing traces of red paint; legible text set without framing lines in quadrants of cross on face. Latin memorial formula. AS capitals. Probably ninth to eleventh century, possibly pre A.D. 875.

(—) (1862–8), 142–3 & fig.; Johnson, R. J. (1866), 364; Greenwell and Westwood (1869), 282–3; Haigh (1869–70), 216; Hübner (1876), no. 197, p. 71 & fig.; Bloxam (1877), 298–300 & fig.; Browne (1884–8), 11–14 & fig.; Boyle (1886), 51 & fig.; Browne (1886), 30–2; Browne (?1886), 11–13 & fig.; Allen (1889), 220, 221, 222; Hodges (1893), 147 & fig.; Hodges (1905), 234 & fig.; Howorth (1917), II, 286 & fig.; Brown, G. B. (1921), 70 & fig.; Levison (1943), 121 & fig.; Hodgkin, R. H. (1952), II, 296 & fig.; Radford (1954b), 211; Hyslop (1960), 32 & fig.; Colgrave, B. and Cramp (1965), 23 & fig.; Taylor, H. M. and Taylor, J. (1965), 444.

HIC | INSE | PUL | CRO | REQV | IESCIT | COR | PORE | HERE |
  BERI | CHT | PR̄B: |

The text reads: HIC IN SEPULCRO REQVIESCIT CORPORE HEREBERICHT PR̄B:, 'Here in the tomb rests Herebericht the priest in his bodily form', where PR̄B or PR̄B: = PRESBYTER. The name is recorded. Traces of illegible lettering may exist in the lower right quadrant, supporting Browne's view that the gravestone was re-used.[1] Further supporting evidence is the slightly smaller size of the letters of the last two words.

[1] Browne (1886), 30.

93   Mortain

Mortain Collegiate Church, Normandy, France.

First mentioned 1864, in church. *c.* 12 × *c.* 13·5 × *c.* 5 cm. Decorated wooden casket with roofed top, covered with gilded copper; legible texts in relief set vertically in panels between figures on back, with runic text on roof.[1] Latin descriptive formula, type b. AS capitals. Probably eighth to ninth century.

Le Cordier (1865), 182–4; Moulin (1865), 75–7; Vasseur (1871), 229–30 & fig.; Pigeon (1888), 245–6; Laveille (1899), 306 & fig.; Moulin (1923), 13–15; Cahen and Olsen (1930), *passim* & figs.; Leclercq (1935), cols. 52–6 & figs.; Blouet (?1954), *passim* & figs.; Taralon (1958), 83–93 & figs.; Page, R. I. (1961), 78.

i: SCSM*I*H |
ii: SCSGAB |

The texts read: scs mih and scs gab, 'St Michael' and 'St Gabriel' where scs = sanctus. The texts refer to the decoration. The runic text reads, ⊕ good helpe : Æadan þiiosne ciismeel geᚹarahtæ, '⊕ May God help Æadan (who) made this casket'.

94   Newent

Newent parish church, Gloucestershire.

Found 1912, with bones below ground to north of church, possibly *in situ* and possibly as pillow stone.[2] 20·3 × 16·5 × 3·2 cm. Carved sandstone slab with text i legible set above carving on face, ii slightly deteriorated set round edges of stone; lettering of both texts in relief and without framing lines, letters of ii face backwards and read clockwise. i OE personal name, ii Latin descriptive formula, type c. AS capitals. Probably late tenth to early eleventh century.

Condor *et al.* (1911–12), 323–6 & figs.; Dobson (1933), 272–3 & figs.; (—) (1934), 19–20; Willmore (1939), 146; Rice (1952), 143; Zarnecki (1953), 49–55 & figs.; Gray (1962), 5 & fig.; Mee (1966), 215–16.

i: EDRED |
ii: ⊕MARCVS |
     ⊕LVCAS ⊕*I*O [..] |
     NNES ⊕EDRE |
     D ⊕*M*ATHEUS ⊕ |

Text i reads: edred, probably a form of one of the recorded names āedrāed or ēadrāed. It may not be primary. Text ii reads ⊕ marcvs ⊕ lvcas

---

[1] The description, etc., is taken from published accounts.   [2] Condor *et al.* (1911–12), 324.

✠ IO[HA]NNES ✠ EDRED ✠ MATHEUS ✠. EDRED is presumably the deceased commemorated and the subjects carved and the evangelists' names also suggest a funeral monument. The order of text ii suggests that it was copied from an exemplum. Rice thought the stone reminiscent of metalwork.[1]

95 Norham I

Norham, Northumberland. Lost, after 1778.

Found pre 1774, below ground in foundations of buildings to east of church. Dimensions uncertain. Incomplete carved stone slab, with probably incomplete probably legible text set above carving on visible face.[2] Probably Latin descriptive formula, type b. AS capitals. Date uncertain.

Lambe (1774), *Notes* p. 39; Hutchinson (1778), 24–7 & fig.; Raine, James the elder (1852), 259; Langlands (1856–62), 121; Stuart (1867), 20–1; Page, R. I. (1969), 47.

I[M ...] | IHS:INCACIZ[O] —

The meaning of the text is uncertain. Raine read it as IHS NAZARAIOS, where IHS is the *nomen sacrum*; this seems possible, though he gave no figure.[3] There may have been traces of a runic text on the back of the stone. The stone was lost by 1852, and is therefore unlikely to have formed part of the 'pillar' of carved stone fragments fitted together 1852–6 and preserved in the church.

96 Norham II

Norham, Northumberland. Lost.

Found 1833, during controlled excavation, in foundations of building to east of church. Dimensions uncertain. Incomplete stone slab, with incomplete but legible text set in panel on visible face.[4] Probably Latin memorial formula. AS capitals. Date uncertain.

Raine, James the elder (1852), 259; Langlands (1856–62), 121–2 & fig. opp. p. 219; Stuart (1867), 20–1; Hodges (1893), 85; Graham (1920), 46.

PANIM | A✠AI: | [C] —

The text reads: P ANIMA ✠ AI : [C] —, presumably 'For the soul of —', where P = PRO. This reading of the text is from Allen's drawing.[5] In the church is preserved a drawing copied from a published figure, showing an abbreviation mark

---

[1] Rice (1952), 143.   [2] The description, etc., is taken from published accounts and figures.
[3] Raine, James the elder (1852), 259.
[4] The description, etc., is taken from published accounts and existing drawings.
[5] J. R. Allen, BM Add. MS 37580, entry 614.

over the first A (presumably intended for the P) and the name as ÆIC[A.] —.[1] The stone is said to have been built into the 'pillar' of carved stone fragments formed 1852–6 and preserved in the church. If this is so, however, the text must have been placed inwards or have now deteriorated completely.

97 North Elmham

North Elmham, Norfolk. Now in the Museum of Archaeology and Ethnology, Cambridge, no. z. 15154.

Found 1847, in Cambridgeshire (Maskell), but cf. Longhurst: 'there seems to be more evidence in favour of the Elmham provenance'.[2] 10·2 × c. 6·4 × c. 0·3 cm. Carved walrus ivory panel with texts on face; text i legible, set without framing lines above carving, ii rather deteriorated, set round upper mandorla, letters facing inwards. Latin descriptive formulae, type b. AS capitals. Tenth to eleventh century.

Westwood (1868), 150; Maskell (1872), 164–5; Westwood (1876), no. 304, p. 138; Allen (1889), 247; Longhurst (1923), no. 74, p. 60; Goldschmidt (1926), no. 2, p. 9 & fig.; Longhurst (1926), 6–7, 71–2 & fig.; (—) (1930a), no. 80, pp. 16–17; Rice (1952), 163 & fig.

i: S̄C̄AMA/R/IA | S̄C̄PETRVS |
ii: OUOSOMS:UI[..] | [.]EMANUSETP[.] |

Text i reads: S̄CA MARIA S̄C̄ PETRVS, 'St Mary, St Peter', where S̄CA = SANCTA, S̄C̄ = SANCTUS, and the names refer to the carving. Text ii probably reads: O UOS OMS: UI[DET]E MANUS ET P[.], 'O you all, observe (my) hands and feet', where OMS: or OMS = OMNES and P[.] is the beginning, or an abbreviation, of PEDES. The reference is presumably to Luke XXIV 39, in the Vulgate, 'Videte manus meas, et pedes, quia ego ipse sum'. Traces of other letters may exist on the lower mandorla. Longhurst compared MS drawings of the Winchester school, and suggested that this one may have been associated with a church dedicated to the Virgin and St Peter.[3]

98 Old Byland

Set upside down in the east face of the tower of Old Byland parish church, NR Yorkshire.

Found 1846, in present *situs*. c. 28 × c. 43 × c. 18 cm. Carved stone sun-dial on visible face with illegible text set above horizontal diameter and to left of dial. Language and formula uncertain. Possibly AS capitals. Possibly eleventh century.

[1] Rev. Canon J. A. Little, formerly vicar of Norham, in a personal communication of 9 September 1964 to Mrs K. Salisbury, Norham, said the drawing was copied from one of the Histories of Northumberland. I cannot find any published illustrations of this stone.
[2] Maskell (1872), 164; Longhurst (1926), 71. I can find no evidence one way or the other.
[3] Longhurst (1926), 6–7.

Haigh (1857), 179; Way and Noyer (1868), 211; Hübner (1876), no. 179, p. 65 & fig.; Haigh (1879), 141–4, 205; Taylor, R. V. (1881), 147; Frank (1888), 114–16; Gatty (1900), 56 & fig.; Collingwood, W. G. (1907), 379 & fig.; Leclercq (1910b), col. 1545 & fig.; Collingwood, W. G. (1912), 122, 126; Collingwood, W. G. (1915a), 288, 289; Curtis (1923), 4 & fig.; Green, A. R. (1928), 507–8 & fig.; Cooper (?1964), no pagination; Zinner (1964), 3, 150; Okasha (1969), 29.

Haigh read: ✠ SVMARLEÐAN HVSCARL ME FECIT,[1] probably '✠ Svmarleði's house-servant made me'. Rubbings preserved in the British Museum show very faintly, SVMAR[...]ARL.[2] However the text is now illegible, and it is even uncertain which way up the letters were with respect to the dial.

99 Orpington

Set (incorrectly positioned) in an interior pillar of All Saints' parish church, Orpington, Kent.

Found August 1958, in church fabric. 43·2 × c. 61 × 7·6 cm., diam. c. 61 cm. Incomplete carved stone circular sun-dial on square base;[3] three incomplete texts on visible face, i, iii legible, set with letters facing inwards, ii slightly deteriorated, with letters facing outwards; i, ii set without framing lines but in panels round perimeter, iii and runic text set between *tid*-marks. Texts i, ii OE descriptive formulae, type a, iii Latin descriptive formula, type a. AS capitals. Date uncertain.

(—) (1962), 9. Page, R. I. (1964), 70; Taylor, H. M. and Taylor, J. (1965), 476–8 & fig.; Taylor, J. and Taylor, H. M. (1966), 23–5 & fig.; Bowen (1967), 287–9 & fig.; Page, R. I. (1967), 289–91; Okasha (1969), 29.

i: — [.]/ECÐÐANÐESECANCAN/HV✠ |
ii: — [.]ELTE[LL]AN7H/EALDAN |
iii: OR[....]VM |

Text i reads: — ECÐ ÐAN ÐE SECAN CAN HV ✠, '— for him who knows how to seek (it) ✠'. Text ii reads: — EL TE[LL]AN 7 HEALDAN, '— to tell (*or* to count) and to hold'.[4] Text iii reads: OR[...]VM, presumably a form of [H]OROLOGIVM, 'clock'. Certainly text iii, and possibly also i, ii refer to the dial and its function; it is possible that texts i, ii were part of the same text. The runic text consists of three characters, 'o', 'œ' and 'æ', but it has not been interpreted.[5]

[1] Haigh (1879), 141.
[2] BM Add MS. 37581.31, 32.
[3] The stone has been identified as Upper Greensand, Reigate, Merstham or Gatton stone; Bowen (1967), 288.
[4] The cross could belong to the end of either text i or ii, but its shape suggests the former.
[5] See Page, R. I. (1967), 289–91.

100 Pershore

Pershore, Worcestershire. Now in the British Museum, London, no. 1960.7–7.1.

Found possibly 1759–69, certainly pre 1779, below ground. Ht. 10·2, base 6 × 5·4 cm. Decorated tower-shaped bronze censer-cover, with legible text set without framing lines along base of one gable, with last letter on side of animal head. OE maker formula. AS capitals and insular minuscule. Tenth to eleventh century.

(—) (1779), 535–6 & fig.; Pegge (1780), 75; (—) (1780), 128; Brassington (?1895), 108 & fig.; Smith, R. A. (1901), 232–3; (—) (1905), 3; Allen (1906 a), 50–3 & figs.; Peers et al. (1906–7), 52–9 & figs.; Jackson, C. J. (1911), 87–8 & fig.; Brøndsted (1924), 263–5 & fig.; Tonnochy (1932), 2; Tonnochy (1937), 54; Rice (1952), 233 & fig.; Arbman (1958), 189–90; (—) (1960), 8–9 & fig.; Godfrey, J. (1962), 374 & fig.; Page, R. I. (1964), 84, 88; Wilson, D. M. (1964), no. 56, pp. 44, 47, 53, 157–8 & figs.; Page, R. I. (1968), 16.

✠ GODRICMEᚹVORH |

T |

The text reads: ✠ GODRIC ME ᚹVORHT, '✠ Godric made me', where GODRĪC is a recorded name. The text contains the grammatically incorrect ᚹVORHT = ᚹORHTE, perhaps due to lack of space, accentuated by ᚹV = w. The censer-cover resembles in shape the unique Anglo-Saxon church tower of Sompting, Sussex, which Taylor and Taylor date to A.D. 1050–1100.[1]

101 Plymstock

Fastened to a wall in the grounds of the Telephone Exchange, Stentaway Road, Plymstock, Plymouth, Devon. National Grid reference SX 518 536.

First mentioned 1939, in field off Plymstock to Billacombe road. 142·2 × 43·2 × 16·5 cm. Incomplete carved wheel-headed cross, with legible, probably complete text set in panel at foot of one face. Probably OE personal name. AS capitals. Probably tenth to eleventh century.

Phillips (1939), 232 & fig.; Phillips (1950), 105–6; Phillips (1954), 184–5 & figs.

ELEᚹ |

The text may be a personal name, ELEWYNN or ELEWYN; such a name is unrecorded though both elements occur. In this case, it would be abbreviated, incomplete, or with ᚹ representing its rune-name.

---

[1] Taylor, H. M. and Taylor, J. (1965), 558.

102 Ripon

Ripon, WR Yorkshire. Now in the Yorkshire Museum, York, no. 13.

First mentioned 1872, from near site of Ripon old monastery. 33 × *c*. 15·2 × 8·3 cm. Incomplete stone carved cross; rather deteriorated, probably complete text, set in panels but without framing lines on face of shaft. OE personal name. AS capitals. Possibly eighth to ninth century.

(—) (1872), 9; Hübner (1876), no. 178, p. 65; Wellbeloved (1881), no. 13, p. 69; Allen (1889), 213, 221; Allen (1890), 298; Allen (1891), 229; Browne (1897), 283–4; Collingwood, W. G. (1909), 185 & fig.; Collingwood, W. G. (1912), 110, 130 & fig.; Collingwood, W. G. (1915*a*), 289; Collingwood, W. G. (1927), 94, index & fig.; Collingwood, W. G. (1932), 51; Elgee, F. and Elgee, H. W. (1933), 193; Dahl (1938), 15–16; Page, R. I. (1964), 83.

✠*A*DH | [.]SE | [..]*B̄* |

The text reads: ✠ ADH[Y]SE [PR]B̄, '✠ Adh[y]se the priest' where [PR]B̄ = PRESBYTER. The name is probably a form of ĒADHYSE, recorded elsewhere only in *LV* 278, ADHYSI.

103 Rome I

Rome, Italy. Now in the Victoria and Albert Museum, London, no. 629–1871.

First mentioned January 1859: 'found near Rome some years ago, with a considerable number of coins of Alfred the Great'.[1] No such coin-hoard is known, though two containing non-Alfredian coins fit the date mentioned. Diam. *c*. 2·2 cm. Decorated gold ring with seal-face containing human bust, with legible text set without framing lines, first line on left of bust reading up, second on right reading down, letters laterally displaced and facing inwards. OE personal name. AS capitals. Date uncertain, possibly ninth century.

Waterton (1859), 194; Waterton (1859–61*a*), 107; Waterton (1859–61*b*), 277; French (1863), 496; Smith, W. and Cheetham (1880), 1800; Oman (1930), no. 228, p. 64 & fig.; (—) (1930*a*), no. 51, p. 11; Oman (1931), 107 & fig.; Jessup (1950), 134–5 & fig.

✠ A[*V*]F | RET |

The text reads: ✠ A[V]FRET, or possibly, ✠ A[L]FRET, a personal name with various possible etymologies; the first element may be A[V]-, A[V]F-, or A[L]- = AELF-, AEÐEL- etc., while the second could be -RET = -RĀED, or -FRET = -FRIÐ. Alternatively the name could be Cont Gmc, with the recorded elements AV- and -FRIÐ.[2] The ring may be a signet-ring, and/or its face a coin-copy. Dolley did not

---

[1] Waterton (1859), 194.

[2] See Förstemann (1913), cols. 290–4, 950; and Förstemann (1916), cols. 893, 1218.

reject the mid ninth century date which would be consistent with the date of the allegedly associated coin-hoard.[1]

104 Rome II

Rome, Italy. Now in the British Museum, London, no. 1951.2–6.1.

Found Villa Wolkonsky gardens, Rome, c. 1928; previously attributed to coin-hoard from near Rome, dispersed 1929–30.[2] Diam. c. 3·8 cm. Circular silver decorated coin-brooch, with legible texts in relief and laterally displaced; letters face inward and read anti-clockwise. Text i set right round bust on face, ii without framing lines on back. OE personal names. AS capitals. Early tenth century.

Spink (1949–51), 234 & figs.; Bruce-Mitford (1956), 200; Wilson, D. M. (1964), no. 64, pp. 8, 35–6, 52, 163 & figs.

i: ⚔ EADVVEARDREX |
ii: FRA[M]V VIS[M̄]: |

Text i reads: ⚔ EADVVEARD REX, '⚔ King Eadvveard' where x and ⚔ are identical in form. Text ii reads: FRA[M]VVIS [M̄] :, 'Fra[m]vvis the moneyer' where M̄, M̄ :, or M̄O = MONETARIUS. The coin is likely to be one of Edward the Elder, A.D. 899–924, and other coins of his with this moneyer exist, though from different dies.[3] On coin evidence, Dolley dated this contemporary copy to the end of the first quarter of the tenth century.[4]

105 Ruthwell

Ruthwell parish church, Dumfriesshire, Scotland.

First mentioned c. 1600, in church;[5] presumably identical with monument mentioned 1642 in church.[6] c. 549 × c. 50 × c. 34 cm. New red sandstone carved cross, originally in two pieces, now in six plus modern additions, probably with shaft tenoned at base. Texts N i–v set on present north face, S i–v on south face, all texts set round carvings from top to bottom within panels but without framing lines. Text N ii incomplete and slightly deteriorated, set to left of and below John the Baptist; N iii rather deteriorated set above, to left and right of Christ in glory; N iv

---

1 M. Dolley, in a personal communication.
2 This information is contained in Wilson, D. M. (1964), 163, with reference to confidential documents in the British Museum. I have not been able to see these documents.
3 E.g. Grueber and Keary (1893), 95; BMC. nos. 79, 80. I am most grateful to Miss M. A. O'Donovan, University of Exeter, for her help with this.   4 M. Dolley, in a personal communication.
5 BM MS Cotton Julius F VI, fo. 352. Page (1959 b) 285–8.
6 Minutes of the General Assembly of the Church of Scotland, 30/7/1642, S.R.O. CH 1/1/9, page 15: 'Anent the report of idolatrous monuments in the Kirk of Ruthwa[ll] the Assemblie finds that the monument therin mentioned is idolatrous, and therefore recõmends to the Presbytrie that they careful[l]y urge the order prescrived be the act of Parliament anent the abolishing of these monuments, to be put to execution.'

incomplete and slightly deteriorated, set above, to left and right of Paul and Anthony; N v incomplete and rather deteriorated, remaining text above and to left of flight to Egypt; S i illegible set round cross-head top; S ii illegible set above, to left and right of Visitation; S iii rather deteriorated set above, round and below Mary Magdalene; S iv incomplete and rather deteriorated, set to left and right of blind man; S v incomplete and rather deteriorated, remaining text above and to left of Annunciation. Text N i and texts on sides of cross are runic. Latin descriptive formulae, type b. AS capitals and insular minuscule. Early eighth century.

Gibson, E. (1695), col. 910; Hickes (1705), I, pt. 3, p. 5; II, tab. iv; Gordon (1726), 160–1 & figs.; Pennant (1774), 85–6; (—) (1789), pls. LIV, LV & following pp. 1–3; Craig (1794), 226–7; Gough (1806), IV, 60–1; Kemble (1840), 349–60 & figs.; (—) (1845), 221–7 & figs.; Duncan (1857), 313–26 & figs.; Scarth (1860), 122–5; Dietrich (1865), passim & figs.; Stephens (1866–7), xxx–xxxi, 405–48 & figs.; Stuart (1867), xcv, 12–16 & pls. xix, xx; Smith, W. and Cheetham (1875), 850; Anderson (1881), 233–46 & figs.; Stephens (1884b), 130–2 & figs.; Allen and Browne (1885), 340, 343; Browne (1885a), 78–9 & figs.; (—) (1888), 85–8 & fig.; Allen (1889), 209–11; Browne (1890), 170–1; MacLean (1893), xxviii–xxix, 2–4; Stephens (1894), 12; Viëtor (1895), 2–13 & figs.; Browne (1897), 235–54 & figs.; Browne (1899–1901), 167–9 & figs.; Cook (1902), 367–90; Nicolson (1902), 195–6; Rousseau (1902), 53–71 & figs.; Stevens (1904), 46; Cook (1905), ix–xvii, 3–5; Dalton (1911), 103, 236 & fig.; Cook (1912), 213–361 & figs.; Lethaby (1912), 145–6 & fig.; Rivoira (1912), 24–5 & figs.; Brown, G. B. and Lethaby (1913), 43–9; Lethaby (1913), 145–61 & figs.; Hewison (1914), passim & figs.; Howorth (1914), 45–64; Browne (1916), passim & figs.; Collingwood, W. G. (1916–18), 34–84 & figs.; Brandl (1917), 150–1; Howorth (1917), III, 269–78, 304–20 & fig.; (—) (1920), 219–86 & figs.; Brown, G. B. (1921), 102–317 & figs.; Brøndsted (1924), 38–42, 74–9 & figs.; Collingwood, W. G. (1927), 84–5, 119, index, passim & figs.; Dinwiddie (1927), passim & figs.; Clapham (1930), 56–7, 60, 63–4 & figs.; Porter (1931), 99–104 & figs.; Collingwood, W. G. (1932), 46 & figs.; Saunders (1932), 12–16 & fig.; Rivoira (1933), 151, 209 & fig.; Bütow (1935), 173–5 & passim; Dahl (1938), 4–7; Kendrick (1938), 128–30 & figs.; Dobbie (1942), cxviii–cxxiii, clxxv–clxxvi, 115, 204 & figs.; Saxl (1943), 1–19 & figs.; Schapiro (1944), 232–45 & figs.; Bennett (1946–53), 276–82; Saxl and Wittkower (1948), 15–16 & figs.; Dickins and Ross (1954), 1–13, 25–9 & figs.; Elliott (1959), 90–6, passim & figs.; Page, R. I. (1959 b), 285–8 and fig.; Wilson, D. M. (1960), 152–3, 220 & figs.; Godfrey, J. (1962), 179–80; Cramp (1965a), no. 1, p. 2; Cramp (1965b), 8–10 & figs.; Thomas (1965), 253 & fig.; Stoll (1967), 307 & fig.; Burlin (1968), 23–43; (—) (1968), 415 & fig; Swanton (1970), 9–42, 90, 92, passim and figs.

In the following texts, there are c. 38 letters lost in the lacuna in N iv, c. 16 at the end of N v, and c. 16, c. 20 and c. 36 respectively in S iv.

N ii:　— DORAMVS | [...] |

N iii:　[.]IHSX[.S] | IVD[.]X[:.]EQV[IT]A[TI]S: | BESTIAE:ET:
　　　　DRACON[ES]:COGNOUERVNT:INDE: | SERTO:
　　　　SALVA[.O]REM:MVNDI: |

N iv: ✠ SCS:PAVLVS: | ET:A[...] | FREGER[..T]:PANEMINDESERTO: |

N v: ✠ MARIA:ETIO[.. ...] | T V[O ...] |

S iii: ✠ A[..V.......]B[.] | STRVM:V[NGVE]NTI:
&S[T]AN[S R]E[T R]OSECVSPEDES: | EIVSLACRIMIS:
C/OEPITRIGARE:PEDESEIVS: &CAPILLIS: |
CAPITISSVITERGEBAT |

S iv: ✠ ETPRAETERIENS:VIDI[...]T[...]R[. ...] |
ANATIBITATE:ETS[...] |

S v: INGRESSVSA[NG] —

Early drawings suggest that more of the texts was once visible than now is. They now read:

N ii: possibly, — [A]DORAMVS —, '— we worship —'.

N iii: [✠] IHS X[PS] IVD[E]X [: A]EQV[IT]A[TI]S : BESTIAE : ET : DRACON[ES] : COGNOUERVNT : IN DE : SERTO : SALVA[TO]REM : MVNDI :, '[✠] Jesus Christ the judge of equity. The animals and the serpents recognised the Saviour of the world in the desert'. The first part presumably refers to the carving and has the abbreviations of the *nomina sacra*. Saxl suggested that the source was the Vulgate Acts XVII 31: 'iudicaturus est orbem in æquitate', though the same idea occurs in various psalms, for example, as suggested by Schapiro, Psalm LXVI 5: 'quoniam iudicas populos in æquitate'.[1] The source of the rest, which has wrong word-division in DE : SERTO, may be the Vulgate Isaiah XLIII 20: 'Glorificabit me bestia agri, dracones et struthiones: quia dedi in deserto aquas, flumina in invio, ut darem potum populo meo, electo meo.' But in view of the appearance of Paul and Anthony in N iv, cf. Jerome's *Vita S. Pauli* where the representative of the Fauns *et al.* says to Anthony: 'Precamur ut pro nobis communem Dominum depreceris, quem in salutem mundi olim venisse cognovimus' and Anthony replies: '...Bestiæ Christum loquuntur'.[2]

N iv: ✠ SCS : PAVLVS : ET : A[...] FREGER[VNT] : PANEM IN DESERTO :, '✠ St Paul and [?Anthony] broke bread in the desert' where SCS = SANCTUS or SANCTI. This is presumably a reference to Jerome's story of Paul and Anthony, referring to the carving: '...integrum panem ante ora mirantium deposuit. ...Hic vero quis frangeret panem oborta contentio, ...Tandem consilium fuit, ut apprehenso e regione pane, dum ad se quisque nititur, pars sua remaneret in manibus.'[3]

1 Saxl (1943), 1; Schapiro (1944), 233.
2 Jerome (1845), cols. 23, 24. I am most grateful to A. F. Walls, University of Aberdeen, for his help with this. Saxl (1943), 2, compared also Eusebius (1857), cols. 1155 ff.
3 Jerome (1845), col. 25. Cf. Saxl (1943), 3–4, who described the rite of *cofractio* in the Mass of the Irish Church.

N v: ⛭ MARIA : ET IO[...] TV[O] —, possibly '⛭ Mary and Joseph —' referring to the carving.

S iii: ⛭ A[..V...]B[.]STRVM : V[NGVE]NTI : & S[T]AN[S R]E[TR]O SECVS PEDES : EIVS LACRIMIS : COEPIT RIGARE : PEDES EIVS : & CAPILLIS : CAPITIS SVI TERGEBAT, where the last two letters are set one above the other. The source is the Vulgate Luke VII 37–8, from which the first words can be reconstructed, A[TTVLIT ALA]B[A]STRVM, and the whole translated: '⛭ She brought an alabaster box of oint-ment; and standing behind, (beside) his feet, she began to moisten his feet with tears, and with the hairs of her own head she wiped (them)'. This refers to the carving.

S iv: ⛭ ET PRAETERIENS : VIDI[...] A NATIBITATE : ET S —, '⛭ And passing [?he] saw [...] from birth—'. From the carving, this is likely to refer to the Vulgate John IX 1: 'Et præteriens Iesus vidit hominem cæcum a nativitate', where NATI-BITATE = NATIVITATE.

S v: INGRESSVS A[NG] —, 'The [?angel] coming in —'. The probable source of this text which describes the carving is the Vulgate Luke I 28: 'Et ingressus Angelus ad eam dixit'.

The runic texts read:

— ÆFAUŒÞO —, of uncertain meaning.

— M[.]R[.]A M[. ...]ER DOMINNAE —, possibly for MARIA MATER DOMINI, 'Mary, mother of the Lord'.

— DÆGISGÆF [.], of uncertain meaning.

The other runic text is poetic and related to the *Dream of the Rood*. The MS text of this poem has been used in the following reconstruction:

[⛭ .ND] GEREDÆ HINÆ ḠOD ALME3TTIG ÞA HE ƿALDE ON ḠALḠU GISTIḠA MODIG F[ORE ...] MEN [BUḠ ...], '— God almighty stripped himself when he wanted to ascend the cross, brave before men —'.

— IC RIICNÆ K̄YNINGC HEAFUNÆS H[L]AFARD HÆLDA IC NI DORSTÆ [B]IS-MÆRÆ[D]U UNGK̄ET MEN BA ÆT[Ḡ]AD[RE I]C [ƿÆS M]IÞ BLODÆ BIST[E]MI[D] BI —, '— I (bore) the noble King, the Lord of Heaven, I did not dare bow; men mocked us both together; I was smeared with blood —'.

[⛭] KRIS[T] ƿÆS ON RODI HƿEÞRÆ ÞER FUS[Æ] FEARRAN Kƿ[O]MU [Æ]ÞÞILÆ TIL ANUM IC ÞÆT AL BI[HEALD] SA[R ...] IC ƿ[Æ]S MI[Þ] S[OR]ḠU[M] GIDRŒ[F.]D H[N]AḠ —, '[⛭] Christ was on the cross; yet there eager noble men came from afar to him alone; I beheld all that; I was sorely troubled with sorrows —'.

[M]IÞ S[T]RE[L]UM GIꝼUNDAD ALEGDUN HIÆ HINÆ LIMꝼŒRIGNÆ
GISTODDU[N] HIM [... LI]CÆS [HEA]F[DU]M [BIH]EA[LD]U [H]I[Æ ÞE[R] —, 'They
laid him wounded with arrows, weary in limb; they stood at the head of his body,
they beheld there —'.

106 Sandford

Sandford, Oxfordshire. Now in the Ashmolean Museum, Oxford, no. 1891–10.

Found pre 1849, on site of Knights Templars' Preceptory, Sandford. *c.* 7·6 × 5·1 × *c.*
0·6 cm. Decorated bronze nonagon with curved sides and traces of gilding, probably
pyx; legible text set round thickness without framing lines, letters facing back.[1]
Latin descriptive formula, type c. AS capitals. Possibly late tenth to eleventh century.

Spiers (1849), 412 & figs.; (—) (1930*a*), no. 86, p. 18 & fig.; Swarzenski (1967), 49 & fig.

✠ IN |
TUS |
QVOD |
LAT |
ETCVNCTONOS |
CRI |
MINE LA |
X |
ET |

The text reads: ✠ INTUS QVOD LATET CVNCTO NOS CRIMINE LAXET, '✠ May
that which lies hidden within free us from all guilt', and is a leonine hexameter
verse. If it is a pyx, this presumably refers to the wafer.

107 Sherburn

Sherburn, WR Yorkshire. Now in the British Museum, London, no. AF 458, ring cat. no. 180.

Found *c.* 1870, in field between Aberford and Sherburn. Diam. *c.* 3·2 cm., ht. of
bezel 1·9 cm. Decorated gold ring consisting of hoop and bezel with legible texts;
text i set without framing lines in gold lettering on niello on face of bezel, ii incised
upside down on back of bezel. Text i, Latin descriptive formula, type b, ii OE
personal name. AS capitals. A.D. 853–88.

(—) (1873), 304; Franks (1873–6), 305–7 & figs.; Hübner (1876), no. 224, p. 81; Jones (1877),
55–7; Allen (1889), 246; Searle (1897), 53; Robson (1899), 202; Earle (1901), 151–3 & figs.;

---

1 For convenience the illustrations show the text reading from left to right.

(—) (1901*a*), 13; Smith, H. C. (1908), 71–2 & fig.; Dalton (1912), no. 180, p. 30 & figs.; Smith, R. A. (1912), 98–9 & figs.; Brown, G. B. (1916), 178 & fig.; Smith, R. A. (1923), 114 & figs.; Brøndsted (1924), 133 & figs.; Leclercq (1930), col. 2402 & figs.; Oman (1931), 105 & fig.; Elgee, F. and Elgee, H. W. (1933), 188 & figs.; Kendrick (1938), 183–4; Jessup (1950), 131–2 & figs.; Hodgkin, R. H. (1952), II, ix & fig.; Wilson, D. M. and Blunt (1961), 107; Godfrey, J. (1962), 374; Page, R. I. (1964), 80, 82–3; Wilson, D. M. (1964), no. 1, pp. 2, 6, 22–3, 56, 117–19 & figs.; Page, R. I. (1968), 18.

i: Ā | Đ |

ii: ✠ EA | ĐELSVIÐ | REGNA |

Text i reads: ĀĐ, and is presumably an odd abbreviation for AGNUS DEI, describing the decoration, the reference being to the Vulgate John I 29. Text ii reads: ✠ EAĐELSVIÐ REGNA, '✠ Queen Eaðelsvið' where REGNA = REGINA. The queen is Ethelswith, sister of Alfred the Great and wife of Burgred of Mercia. The ring is dated to between her marriage and her death. The state of text ii suggests that the ring was not worn much after its engraving, and it might therefore slightly post-date the ring.

108   Sinnington

Sinnington, WR Yorkshire. Probably lost.

Found pre 1879, in church fabric. Dimensions uncertain. Stone sun-dial, location of text uncertain. Possibly OE descriptive formula. Script and date uncertain.

Haigh (1879), 159 & fig. opp. p. 135; Taylor, R. V. (1881), 148; Frank (1888), 153–4; Gatty (1900), 59; Collingwood, W. G. (1907), 386; Green, A. R. (1928), 515; Morris (1931), 348–9; Zinner (1964), 183; Okasha (1969), 28.

Haigh described the sun-dial, and all other descriptions are derivative from him: 'It had an inscription, of which I can only distinguish faintly the last words, MERGEN ÆFERN, "morning—evening."'[1] A text recorded on the sole evidence of Haigh is of doubtful validity. Various Anglo-Saxon carved stones are built into the church fabric including a semi-circular dial, whose horizontal arms measure 13·7 cm. However this has no trace of any text and may not be the one referred to by Haigh.

109   Sittingbourne

Sittingbourne, Kent. Now in the British Museum, London, no. 1881.6–23.1.

Found pre 1871, below ground. 6 × 32·4 × 0·6 cm. Decorated iron knife consisting of blade and handle tang with legible texts set on both faces of blade; text i incised

---

[1] Haigh (1879), 159.

in panels of silver and bronze, ii set in panel in silver lettering on bronze. OE maker and owner formulae. AS capitals. Late ninth to early tenth century.

Evans (1873), 331–4 & figs.; Stephens (1884*a*), 160; Payne (1893), 111–14 & figs.; Searle (1897), 89, 418; Smith, R. A. (1908), 382–3; Smith, R. A. (1923), 94–6 & figs.; Brøndsted (1924), 129 & fig.; Jessup (1930), 237–8 & figs.; Leclercq (1930), cols. 2403–4 & figs.; Harder (1932), 37; Kendrick (1934), 398 & figs.; Himsworth (1953), 42 & fig.; Wilson, D. M. (1960), 112, 216 & fig.; Davidson (1962), 41, 80, 112 & figs.; Page, R. I. (1964), 86; Wilson, D. M. (1964), no. 80, pp. 38–43, 60, 172–3 & figs.; Evison (1967), 181; Swanton (1970), 66 n.

i: ✠ S GEBEREHT | MEAH |
ii: ✠ BIORHTELMMEƿORTE |

Text i reads: ✠ s[I]GEBEREHT ME AH, '✠ S[i]gebereht owns me', where the missing I is presumably an error. Text ii reads: ✠ BIORHTELM ME ƿORTE, '✠ Biorhtelm made me', where ƿORTE = ƿORHTE. The names are forms of the recorded SIGEBEORHT and BEORHTHELM.

110 Skelton

Skelton old church of All Saints, NR Yorkshire.

Found *c.* 1891, below ground in churchyard. 36·8 × 29·2 × *c.* 17·8 cm. Incomplete carved stone sun-dial, with incomplete slightly deteriorated text set in panel on face below dial; to the right is set ON runic text. Probably ON, formula uncertain. AS capitals. Probably eleventh to twelfth century.

Fallow (1892), 65–7 & figs.; (—) (1892), 55–6; Stephens (1894), 14–15; Fowler (1895), 189–90; Gatty (1900), 58–9 & fig.; Stephens (1901), 49–51 & fig.; Collingwood, W. G. (1907), 386; Collingwood, W. G. (1912), 122, 127; Collingwood, W. G. (1915*a*), 288, 290. Mackay (1923), 409–10; Ekwall (1924), 91; Zinner (1964), 183; Okasha (1969), 28–9.

— [.]S:[.*E*] T: | [...] *N*A:G[.]ERA | [...] [*O*]C:HƿA | [...] A:COMA: |

The text reads: — [.]s : [.E]T : [...]NA : G[.]ERA [... O]c : HƿA [...]A : COMA :, and may also be incomplete at the end. The meaning is uncertain. It is probably in ON, though the use of ƿ is odd; alternatively it may be in mixed OE and ON. The only certainly complete word, COMA, could be ON 'to come'.

111 Stratfield Mortimer

Set into the interior south wall of the chancel of Stratfield Mortimer parish church, Berkshire.

Found 1866, below floor of tower, during repairs. *c.* 204 × 54·6 × 11·4 cm. Tapering stone slab in two pieces, with slightly deteriorated text set round perimeter on visible face, with letters facing inwards. Latin maker and memorial formulae. AS capitals. Probably eleventh century.

Westwood (1885–7), 224–6; Westwood (1886–93), 293–5 & fig.; Cameron (1901), 71–3; Smith, R. A. (1906b), 248–9; Hollings (1923), 427; Feilitzen (1937), 222; Pevsner (1966), 229.

✠ VIII:KL̄:OCTB: | FVIT:POSITVS:ÆGELƷA[R]DVS:FILIVS:
KYPPINGVS:INISTOLOCO | :BEATV | S:SITOMO:QVI:ORAT:
PROANI[MA]:EIVS:✠TOKI:ME:SCRIPSIT: |

The text reads: ✠ VIII : KL̄ : OCTB : FVIT : POSITVS : ÆGELƷA[R]DVS : FILIVS : KYPPINGVS : IN ISTO LOCO : BEATVS : SIT OMO : QVI : ORAT : PRO ANI[MA] : EIVS : ✠ TOKI : ME : SCRIPSIT : , '✠ On 24 September Ægelƿa[r]d son of Kypping was put in this place. Blessed be the man who prays for his soul. ✠ Toki wrote me', where KL̄ = KALENDAS and OCTB = OCTOBRIS. TOKI is a recorded name of ON origin. The spelling ÆGELƷA[R]D = AEÐELWEARD occurs also in DB,[1] as does that of CYPPING; KYPPINGVS is here uninflected. In DB a church was mentioned at Stratfield Manor which was held TRE in paragio by the thegns Cheping and Eduin.[2] This Cheping may be of the same family as Kyppingvs. Judging by the shape of the stone, it may have been a grave or tomb cover.

112 Suffolk

Moyse's Hall Museum, Bury St Edmunds, no. K.132.

First mentioned 1911. Possibly identical with ring found in John of Beverley's coffin A.D. 1037.[3] Diam. c. 2·2 cm. Decorated silver alloy ring with texts set right round without framing lines; i legible, round inside, ii highly deteriorated, round outside. Text i Latin, possibly owner formula. AS capitals. Date uncertain.

Dugdale (1716), 55; Leland (1770), 102; Braybrooke (1856), 15; Waterton (1863), 225; Smith, W. and Cheetham (1880), 1804;[4] Smith, R. A. (1911), 349; (—) (1930a), no. 56, p. 12; Oman (1931), 107 & fig.

i: IOHNSE BEVERIYA/RCEB |
ii: [A.E.STA.]R[...]G[...]N |

Text i reads: IOHNSE BEVERIY ARCEB, possibly 'John of Beverley, Archbishop', though such a spelling of Beverley is unrecorded. Previously text ii was read as: ATHELSTAN.R.AN.GIFAN, 'Athelstan King of the English Giver' which fits the remaining traces.[5] For a full discussion of the interpretation of these texts, see

---

[1] Cf. Feilitzen (1937), 102–6, 188.   [2] DB Berkshire, fo. 62 v.   [3] Leland (1770), 102.
[4] The first five works refer only to the ring found in 1037.   [5] Oman (1931), 107, quoting M. Förster.

my forthcoming article.[1] The script suggests that the texts may be post-Conquest, but spectrographic analysis indicates that the ring is likely to be medieval.[2]

113 Sulgrave

Sulgrave, Northamptonshire. Now in the care of B. K. Davison, Royal Archaeological Institute.

Found September 1968, in floor of stone and timber tower building attached to manor of Sulgrave, during controlled excavation. Diam. *c.* 4·5 cm. Incomplete decorated circular bronze brooch, with incomplete highly deteriorated text set without framing lines round decoration on face; letters in relief and laterally displaced, first line facing inwards and reading anti-clockwise, second line reading clockwise and probably facing outwards. Possibly Latin descriptive formula, type b. AS capitals. Probably eleventh century.

Unpublished.

✠[A.] [.✠] —
D I V |

The text reads: ✠ [A..✠ ...]DIV, where the first lost letter is C, E, G, the second possibly E, and where there may be an abbreviation mark over the I. It is possible that the final V should be read upside down with the first line as A. The text does not appear to be a personal name and may be descriptive; it might be a form of AGNUS DEI, describing the decoration. The archaeological and historical contexts suggest a date *c.* A.D. 1010–30.[3] Dolley suggested that the brooch was directly copied from an abortive coinage associated with the early autumn of A.D. 1009.[4]

114 Sutton

Sutton, Cambridgeshire. Now in the British Museum, London, no. 1951.10–11.1.

Found *c.* 1694, below ground in field with jewellery and coins of William the Conqueror, surrounded by lead. Diam. *c.* 15.2 cm. Decorated circular silver disc brooch, with legible texts on back; text i set without framing lines right round perimeter, letters facing inwards, ii incomplete set on broken plate for pin. Text i OE owner formula and curse. Text i AS capitals, ii of uncertain script. Late tenth to early eleventh century.

Gibson, E. (1695), cols. 415–16; Hickes (1705), I, pt. iv, 186–8 & figs.; Gough (1806), II, 223–4 & fig. opp. p. 188; Lewis (1842), 258; Stephens (1866–7), 289–93 & figs.; Stephens (1867–8),

---

[1] To appear in *Anglo-Saxon England*.
[2] But cf. Smith, R. A. (1911), 349: 'the inscription does not inspire confidence'.
[3] B. K. Davison, in a personal communication.
[4] M. Dolley, in a personal communication, from material in press.

figs. *ad finem*; Stephens (1894), 20; Black (1898–9), 340 & fig.; Fox (1923), 300; Smith, R. A. (1925), 137–8 & figs.; Lethbridge (1938), 328; Bruce-Mitford (1952), 15–16 & fig.; Bruce-Mitford (1956), 193–8 & figs.; Thompson, J. D. A. (1956), 131; Wilson, D. M. (1958), 170; Thompson, J. D. A. (1959), 280; Wilson, D. M. (1960), 69, 162, 223 & figs.; Wilson, D. M. and Blunt (1961), 108; Page, R. I. (1964), 86–9; Wilson, D. M. (1964), no. 83, pp. 7, 48–50, 174–7 & figs.; Wilson, D. M. and Klindt-Jensen (1966), 142, 146 & fig.

i: ✠ÆDVƿEN MEAG AGEHYODRIHTEN DRIHTEN HINEAƿERIE ÐEMEHIREÆTFERIEBVTONHYOMESELLEHIREAGENES ƿILLES|[1]

Text i is in verse and reads:

✠ÆDVƿEN ME AG   AGE HYO DRIHTEN

DRIHTEN HINE AƿERIE   ÐE ME HIRE ÆTFERIE

BVTON HYO ME SELLE   HIRE AGENES ƿILLES

It is probably to be translated, ✠ Aedvƿen owns me, may the Lord own her. May the Lord curse him who takes me from her, unless she gives me voluntarily'. ÆDVƿEN is a feminine name, a form of either the recorded ĒADWYNN or the unrecorded *AEÐWYNN. The owner formula is followed by a Christian curse, as occurs in wills and charters. The first line appears to be alliterative, the second two rhyming. Text ii is uninterpreted; it consists of seven characters in a cryptic script, possibly based on the runic *fuþorc*.

115 Swindon

Swindon, Wiltshire. Now in the British Museum, London, ring cat. no. 183, not separately registered.

First mentioned 1912, in BM, found near Swindon. Diam. *c.* 2·2 cm. Decorated gold ring with legible text set right round outside of hoop, lettering plain on pounced background. OE personal name and descriptive formula, type c. AS capitals. Probably late ninth to tenth century.

Dalton (1912), no. 183, p. 31 & fig.; Smith, R. A. (1923), 116 & fig.; Page, R. I. (1964), 83–4; Wilson, D. M. (1964), no. 85, pp. 23, 27, 178 & figs.

✠BVREDRVÐ✠:ω:ꝩ: |

The text reads: ✠ BVREDRVÐ ✠ : ω : A :, '✠ Bvredrvð ✠ ω A' where ω and A represent *alpha* and *omega*, the reference being to the Vulgate Revelations XXII 13. The name is probably a form of the recorded BURGÐRȲÐ or the unrecorded *BUREÐRȲÐ.

---

[1] There may be other intentional spaces but flaws in the metal make them difficult to distinguish; cf. Bruce-Mitford (1956), 197, and Page, R. I. (1964), 86.

117

116 Thornhill

Thornhill parish church, WR Yorkshire.

Found *c.* 1876, near church. *c.* 15·2 × *c.* 26·7 × *c.* 7 cm. Incomplete sandstone slab in two pieces, with incomplete slightly deteriorated text set in panel but without framing lines on one face. OE text, probably memorial formula. AS capitals. Possibly eighth to ninth century.

Haigh (1877), 416, 420–7 & fig.; Browne (1880–4), cxxxiv–cxxxv; Stephens (1884*a*), 212 & fig.; Stephens (1884*b*), 150 & fig.; Allen and Browne (1885), 341, 343; Browne (1885*a*), 80; Frank (1888), 45; Allen (1889), 222; Allen (1890), 297–8; Allen (1891), 232–3; Stephens (1894), 12–13; Collingwood, W. G. (1912), 131; Collingwood, W. G. (1915*a*), 243–8, 285, 289 & fig.; Collingwood, W. G. (1927), 17, index & fig.; Collingwood, W. G. (1929), 33–6 & fig.; Elgee, F. and Elgee, H. W. (1933), 196; Dahl (1938), 16, 193; Page, R. I. (1958), 149; Nuttall (?1963), 5; Pevsner (1967*b*), 511.

— [.]A[E]F[T] | [..]OSBER | [.....]BEC | [.........] —

By comparison with other memorial formulae the text can be partially reconstructed: — A[E]F[TER] OSBER[...] BEC[UN] —, '— in memory of Osber-, a monument —', where ōs- is a recorded name element.

117 Wallingford I

Wallingford, Berkshire. Now in the British Museum, London, no. 1881.4–4.1.

Found August 1879, below ground in garden on west side of market place. Ht. 8·3 cm., diam. of circle *c.* 4·1 cm. Decorated ivory seal-die consisting of oval piece above circular piece; legible texts, with letters laterally displaced facing inwards and reading anti-clockwise, set right round circular piece, i on face, ii on back. Latin descriptive formulae, type a. AS capitals. Probably tenth and eleventh centuries.

Franks (1879–81), 468–70 & figs.; Hedges (1881), 183–5 & figs.; Allen (1889), 248; Searle (1897), 261, 264; Read (1903), 412 & fig.; Smith, R. A. (1906*b*), 244–6 & figs.; Dalton (1909), no. 31, pp. 32–3 & figs.; Stevenson (1912), 6 n.; Smith, R. A. (1923), 111–12 & figs.; Dalton (1925), 69; Goldschmidt (1926), no. 59, pp. 19–20 & figs.; Longhurst (1926), 10, 74–5 & fig.; Casson (1933), 31 & fig.; Rice (1947), 7–8; Tonnochy (1952), no. 2, pp. xviii, 1–2 & figs.; Gilbert (1954), 112 & fig.

i: ✠SIGILLVM8GODƷINIMINISTRI |

ii: ✠SIGILLVMGODGYÐEMONACHEDŌDATE |

Text i reads: ✠ SIGILLVM 8 GODƷINI MINISTRI, '✠ The seal of Godƿine the priest (*or* the thane)'. Smith suggested that the letter following SIGILLVM was B = BEATI,[1] but it could also be decoration or an error, especially in view of the

[1] Smith, R. A. (1923), 112.

lack of space at the end of the text. Text ii reads: ✠ SIGILLVM GODGYÐE MONACHE DŌ DATE, '✠The seal of Godgyð, a nun given to God', where DŌ = DEO. GODWINE and GODGȲÐ (feminine) are names too common to be identified, but they could have belonged to relatives. Dolley, on numismatic parallels, believed the back to be the earlier and to date from the beginning of the last quarter of the tenth century, while the face represented secondary use in the middle of the eleventh century.[1] It is possible, therefore, that text i might not be primary.

118 Wallingford II

Wallingford, Berkshire. Now in Reading Museum and Art Gallery, no. $\frac{170:66}{3}$.

Found August 1966, during controlled excavation, in destruction level of house (c. 1150) in original north street, immediately within borough ramparts. c. 5·1 × c. 21 × c. 0·6 cm. Incomplete whale-bone implement, probably weavers' sword, in three pieces, one lost; incomplete texts set without framing lines on one face, i slightly deteriorated, ii rather deteriorated. OE texts, owner formula. AS capitals. Tenth to eleventh century.

Unpublished.[2]

i: ✠EADBVRHMECAH*A*[.....]✠ Æ[.......] —
ii: ✠ *EADBVRH*[*M*]*ECAH*[*AH* :]*E*[...]✠*Æ*[....] —

Text i reads: ✠ EADBVRH MEC AH —, '✠ Eadbvrh owns me —'. Text ii reads: ✠ EADBVRH [M]EC AH [AH :] —, '✠Eadbvrh owns me —'. The meaning of the rest of either text is uncertain. Text ii seems to be a less skilful copy of text i, although it is possible that text ii is the original, text i the copy, or that both are original. The feminine name ĒADBURG is recorded.

119 Weeke

Weeke, Hampshire. Now in the British Museum, London, no. 1832.5–12.2.

Found March 1832, in bank beside Winchester to Stockbridge road. Diam. c. 4·1 cm. Decorated circular bronze seal-die; legible text set right round face, with letters laterally displaced, facing inwards and reading anti-clockwise. Latin descriptive formula, type a. AS capitals. Late tenth to eleventh century.

Barnes (1832), 359–61 & figs.; Madden (1856), 370; Birch (1887), no. 4, p. 2; Smith, R. A. (1900), 397–8 & figs.; Smith, R. A. (1909–11), 305–6; Stevenson (1912), 6 n.; Smith, R. A. (1923), 110; Brøndsted (1924), 255 & fig.; Rice (1952), 235; Tonnochy (1952), no. 3, pp. xviii, 2–3 & figs.; Page, R. I. (1964), 81–2; Wilson, D. M. (1964), no. 104, pp. 5, 43, 60, 191 & figs.

[1] M. Dolley, in a personal communication.   [2] To be published by N. P. Brooks.

✠SIGILLVMÆLFRICIⱭ |

The text reads: ✠ SIGILLVM ÆLFRICI Ɑ, '✠The seal of Ælfric'. The final letter may represent *alpha* or *alpha* and *omega*, since A is not meaningful. Aelfric has been identified as he who commanded Ethelred's fleet and died A.D. 1016, but the name is common and the identification far from certain. Dolley suggested, on the analogy of coins, a date early in the last quarter of the tenth century, pointing out that the 'aigrette' treatment of the ties of the cloak can be exactly paralleled only on the earliest coins of Ethelred II.[1]

120 Wensley I

Set in the interior north wall of the nave, Wensley parish church, NR Yorkshire.

First mentioned 1789, found below ground in churchyard. 40·6 × 22·9 cm. Incomplete carved sandstone slab with rather deteriorated text set in relief lettering in panel below cross on visible face. OE personal name. AS capitals. Possibly eighth to ninth century.

Gough (1806), III, 334 & fig. opp. p. 311; Whitaker (1823), 371–2 & fig.; Gough (1838), 145 & fig.; Haigh (1846a), 196 & fig.; Archer (1849), 289; Haigh (1852), 75–6 & fig.; Hübner (1876), no. 20*, p. 86; Haigh (1881), 45–6; Allen (1887), 123–4 & fig.; Pettigrew (1888), 34–6 & fig.; Allen (1889), 216, 221; Hall, G. R. (1889), 261; Searle (1897), 168; Hodgson, J. F. (1902), 109; Collingwood, W. G. (1907), 407 & fig.; Collingwood, W. G. (1912), 111, 128; Collingwood, W. G. (1915a), 285, 289; Brown, G. B. (1921), 69–70 & fig.; Collingwood, W. G. (1927), 12, index & fig.; Morris (1931), 396–7; Zarnecki (1953), 54–5 & fig.

DONFR[..] |

From early drawings, the text appears to have read: DONFRID, though now it reads: DONFR[..]. This is perhaps a variant of the recorded name DŌMFRIÞ.

121 Wensley II

Set in the interior north wall of the nave, Wensley parish church, NR Yorkshire.

Found May 1846, in path in churchyard. 34·9 × 33 cm. Incomplete carved sandstone slab with rather deteriorated text set in relief lettering without framing lines in quadrants of cross on visible face. OE personal name. AS capitals. Possibly eighth to ninth century.

Haigh (1852), 75–6 & fig.; Haigh (1861), 42; Hübner (1876), no. 177, p. 64; Haigh (1881), 45–6 & fig.; Frank (1888), 45; Pettigrew (1888), 34–6 & fig.; Allen (1889), 216, 221; Hall, G. R. (1889), 261–2; Browne (1897), 289–90; Collingwood, W. G. (1907), 408 & fig.; Collingwood,

[1] M. Dolley, in a personal communication.

W. G. (1912), 128; Collingwood, W. G. (1915*a*), 285, 289; Howorth (1917), II, 503; Brown, G. B. (1921), 69–70; Collingwood, W. G. (1927), 12, index & fig.; Morris (1931), 396–7; Dahl (1938), 10, 188; Zarnecki (1953), 54–5.

EAT | BER | EH | [.T] |

The text reads: EATBEREH[CT], a variant of the recorded name ĒADBEORHT. Haigh on one occasion read, EATBEREHT ET ARUINI, but it is unlikely that there was ever any more text than is now visible.[1]

122   Whitby O

Whitby Abbey, NR Yorkshire.

Found probably 1920–5, at abbey during controlled excavation.[2] 25·4 × 26·7 × 15·2 cm. Incomplete stone cross, with incomplete but legible text set without framing lines on one face. Language, formula and script uncertain. Eighth to ninth century.

Unpublished.

— *N* —

The text can be read as: — N —, or: — H —, and is too fragmentary to be meaningful. It can be compared with 130 Whitby XI which has three letters on one remaining cross-arm.

123   Whitby II[3]

Whitby, NR Yorkshire. Now in the British Museum, London, no. W 2.

Found pre 1911, at abbey. 45·1 × 29·2 × 12·7 cm. Incomplete micaceous red sandstone cross, with traces of illegible text in panel on one face, letters facing right. Language, formula and script uncertain. Eighth to ninth century.

Collingwood, W. G. (1911), 302 & fig.; Collingwood, W. G. (1915*a*), 290; Brown, G. B. (1937), 100 & fig.; Peers and Radford (1943), 27–47 & figs. (General article); Page, R. I. (1969), 43–4.

The text is now illegible; it is possible that it was in runic script.

124   Whitby III

Whitby, NR Yorkshire. Now in the British Museum, London, no. W 3.

Found December 1924, at abbey during controlled excavation. *c*. 24·1 × *c*. 18·4 × *c*. 10·8 cm. Incomplete micaceous red sandstone cross with incomplete rather

[1] Haigh (1881), 45–6; Dahl (1938), 10, mistakenly took this as the text of another stone.
[2] This investigation does not appear to have been very scientific and the reports produced not always accurate.
[3] The numbering of stones 123–34 corresponds to the BM numbers which are taken from the Whitby Loan Register; the stones are on permanent loan to the British Museum from Mrs Strickland, Whitby.

deteriorated text set without framing lines on one face. Latin text, possibly memorial formula. AS capitals. Eighth to ninth century.

Peers and Radford (1943), 27–47 & figs. (General article).

HICRE[...] | [*P*]*V* —

The text reads: HIC RE[...] [P]V —, and may have originally begun: HIC RE[QUIESCIT] —, 'Here rests —'.

125 Whitby IV

Whitby, NR Yorkshire. Now in the British Museum, London, no. W4.

Found December 1924, at abbey during controlled excavation. *c.* 30·5 × *c.* 43·2 × *c.* 10·2 cm. Incomplete micaceous red sandstone cross, possibly with traces of original paint; legible text set without framing lines on one face. OE personal name. Insular majuscule. Eighth to ninth century.

Peers and Radford (1943), 27–47 & figs. (General article); Clapham (1948 *a*), 10.

✠ A[BB]A E✠ |

The text reads either: ✠ ABBAE ✠ or ✠AHHAE ✠. ABBE is a recorded feminine name, while AHHAE could be a form of AEHCHA, ECHHA etc., variants of a possible but unrecorded *EAHHA.[1] The inflexion could be OE or Latin.

126 Whitby V

Whitby, NR Yorkshire. Now in the British Museum, London, no. W5.

Found December 1924, at abbey during controlled excavation. *c.* 47 × *c.* 38·1 × *c.* 15·9 cm. Incomplete micaceous red sandstone cross, with highly deteriorated text set without framing lines on one face. Language and formula uncertain. AS capitals. Eighth to ninth century.

Peers and Radford (1943), 27–47 & figs. (General article).

[. .]*HI*[*E.*]*REN*[*.E*]*O*[*Þ*] | [*.*]*A*[. . . . .]*R*[*.*]*AE*[*. ...*] | [...] | —

The text is now too illegible to be meaningful, though Peers & Radford read it as: [HIC R]EQUIESCENT COR[PORA] —.[2] For this reading to be tenable, however, the text must have greatly deteriorated, and somewhat altered, in the last thirty years.

[1] Cf. Redin (1919), 94–5.
[2] Peers and Radford (1943), 46.

127 Whitby VI

Whitby, NR Yorkshire. Now in the British Museum, London, no. W 6.

Found January 1924, in north-west external angle of abbey chancel, during controlled excavation. *c.* 16·5 × *c.* 17·8 × *c.* 7·3 cm. Incomplete micaceous red sandstone cross, with highly deteriorated text set without framing lines on one face. Language and formula uncertain. AS capitals. Eighth to ninth century.

Peers and Radford (1943), 27–47 & figs. (General article); Page, R. I. (1969), 43–4.

— [.]*VG[C. .H. N]R[. . . .]* | [... . .]*E[G]E[. . . . .]* | —

The text is now too illegible to be meaningful.

128 Whitby VII

Whitby, NR Yorkshire. Now in the British Museum, London, no. W 7.

Found March 1924, in north side of north transept of abbey, during controlled excavation. *c.* 21·6 × *c.* 19·1 × *c.* 9·5 cm. Incomplete micaceous red sandstone cross, with rather deteriorated text set without framing lines but probably in panel on one face. Probably OE personal name. AS capitals or insular majuscule. Eighth to ninth century.

Peers and Radford (1943), 27–47 & figs. (General article).

E *O*[. .]*ND* |

The text reads: E O[. .]N D, probably a personal name, possibly E O[M V]N D, which is a recorded name. The script may be AS capitals with insular D, E, or insular majuscule with capital N.

129 Whitby VIII

Whitby, NR Yorkshire. Now in the British Museum, London, no. W 8.

Found December 1923, north of abbey chancel, during controlled excavation. *c.* 22·9 × *c.* 22·9 × *c.* 8·9 cm. Incomplete carved micaceous red sandstone cross with incomplete illegible text set probably in panel on one face. Language, formula and script uncertain. Eighth to ninth century.

Peers and Radford (1943), 27–47 & figs. (General article); Page, R. I. (1969), 43–4.

The text is now illegible. Peers and Radford considered it to have been runic, but Page was less certain.[1]

[1] Peers and Radford (1943), 39; Page, R. I. (1969), 44.

130 Whitby XI

Whitby, NR Yorkshire. Now in the British Museum, London, no. W 11.

Found December 1924, at abbey during controlled excavation. 19·7 × 22·9 × c. 8·9 cm. Incomplete micaceous red sandstone cross, with incomplete but legible text set without framing lines on one face. Language and formula uncertain. AS capitals. Eighth to ninth century.

Peers and Radford (1943), 27–47 & figs. (General article).

— RHT —

The text reads: — RHT —, but is too fragmentary to be meaningful.

131 Whitby XII

Whitby, NR Yorkshire. Now in the British Museum, London, no. W 12.

Found February 1924, in north side of abbey chancel, during controlled excavation. Inscribed piece: c. 19·1 × c. 24·1 × c. 8·6 cm. Incomplete micaceous red sandstone slab in two pieces, one uninscribed (no. W 15); incomplete but legible text set without framing lines on one face. Language and formula uncertain. AS capitals. Eighth to ninth century.

Peers and Radford (1943), 27–47 & figs. (General article).

— SU —

The text reads: — SU —, or possibly upside down: — HS —; in either case it is too fragmentary to be meaningful.

132 Whitby XIV

Whitby, NR Yorkshire. Now in the British Museum, London, no. W 14.

Found March 1924, in north side of north transept of abbey, during controlled excavation. c. 39·4 × c. 50·8 × c. 8·9 cm. Incomplete carved micaceous red sandstone slab with legible text set without framing lines on face; text in two lines at right angles to each other, letters of first line probably facing right. OE personal name. Probably insular majuscule. Eighth to ninth century.

Peers and Radford (1943), 27–47 & figs. (General article).

UI[D] | BURG |

The text reads: UI[D]BURG, or possibly [C]INBURG, with the first line reversed, the letters facing left. CYNBURG is a recorded feminine name, and the feminine *WĪDBURG, though unrecorded, is perfectly explicable.

133 Whitby DCCXXXII

Whitby, NR Yorkshire. Now in the British Museum, London, no. W 732.

Found December 1924, at abbey during controlled excavation. 15·2 × 20·3 × 7·6 cm. Incomplete carboniferous limestone slab (millstone grit); incomplete rather deteriorated text set on one face. Latin text, formula uncertain. AS capitals. Eighth to ninth century.

Peers and Radford (1943), 27–47 & figs. (General article).

— [..]EAED[. ...] | [...]ABINFANT[. ...] | [... .]TRIXQVEVA —

The text reads: — [..]EAED[. ...] AB INFANT[. ... .]TRIXQVE VA —. It is now too fragmentary to be meaningful, though Peers and Radford made a conjectural restoration: [✠ AEL]FLEAEDA [QVAE] AB INFANTI[A CONSILIA]TRIXQVE VA[S]—,[1] presumably, though no translation is given, '✠ Aelfleaeda, who from infancy (was ?chosen) as a counsellor and [?vessel]—'.

134 Whitby DCCXXXIII

Whitby, NR Yorkshire. Now in the British Museum, London, no. W 733.

Found May 1924, in north side of abbey chancel, during controlled excavation. 10·2 × 14·6 × c. 4·1 cm. Incomplete micaceous red sandstone slab, with incomplete rather deteriorated text set on one face, probably in panel but without framing lines. Language and formula uncertain. AS capitals. Eighth to ninth century.

Peers and Radford (1943), 27–47 & figs. (General article).

— [.]VBVR[. ...] | [... .]SETIA[.] —

The text reads: — [.]VBVR[. ... .]SETIA[.] —, and is too fragmentary to be meaningful. Peers and Radford read: CVNVBVRGA, whom they identified as the wife of King Oswald, but this is highly conjectural.[2]

135 Whitchurch

Whitchurch parish church, Hampshire.

Found 1868, in inner church fabric. 55·9 × 53·3 × c. 20·3 cm. Incomplete rectangular stone with rounded head, possibly Isle of Wight Binstead stone; slightly deteriorated text set in panel in thickness over head, letters facing front of stone. Latin memorial formula. AS capitals. Probably ninth to eleventh century.

Smith, C. R. (1871), 884 & figs.; Hübner (1876), no. 165, p. 61; Browne (1884–8), 12–13; Browne (1886), 31; Allen (1887), 125 & fig.; Allen (1889), 216, 220, 221; Shore (1898), 124;

---

[1] Peers and Radford (1943), 42.   [2] Peers and Radford (1943), 43–4.

Minns (1899–1900), 171–4 & figs.; Allen (1903), 234, 236–7; Upcott (1911), 303–4 & figs.; Clapham (1930), 141; (—) (1930b), no. 19, p. 114; Brown, G. B. (1937), 254–5 & figs.; Kendrick (1938), 182–3 & figs.; Clapham (1948a), 7; Green, A. R. and Green, P. M. (1951), 53–4 & figs.; Rice (1952), 107; Pevsner and Lloyd (1967), 651 & fig.

✠ HICCORPVSFRI[.]BVRGAEREQVI | ESCITIN[.A]CE[.]SEPVLTVM: |

The text reads: ✠ HIC CORPVS FRI[Đ]BVRGAE REQVIESCIT IN [PA]CE[M] SEPVLTVM, '✠ Here lies the body of Fri[ð]bvrg, buried in peace'. FRIÐBURG is a recorded feminine name. The stone has a rough base and probably stood upright. Although the text is oddly positioned, it is likely to be primary.

136–7 Wimborne I and II

Wimborne, Dorset. Now in the British Museum, London, nos. 1927.4-4.5 and 1927.4-4.6.[1]

Found 1926–7, at Witchampton Manor with other uninscribed pieces during controlled excavation. I: 8·3 × c. 5·1 × c. 1·9 cm. II: c. 2·2 × c. 2·5 × c. 1·3 cm. Incomplete decorated whale-bone chess pieces blackened by fire, with incomplete slightly deteriorated texts set sideways on face, letters facing left. Language and formula uncertain. AS capitals. Date uncertain, possibly late or post-Conquest.

Dalton (1927), 90–1 & fig.; Dalton (1928), 77–86 & fig.

I: — [.A]TRAS: |

II: :CL —

The texts read: — [.A]TRAS and :CL —, but are too fragmentary to be meaningful. It is rare for chessmen of any date to be inscribed, and the reason for one or two pieces being so is unclear. The text or texts might be personal names, but they are unlikely to be OE. Dalton read I as SATRAS, derived from Hindi CHATURANGA, 'chess', though the ME form is SCAC(H)US.[2]

138 Winchester I

Winchester, Hampshire. Now in the care of the Winchester Excavation Committee, no. RF 1160.2 (= WS 104.2).

Found August 1965, *in situ* on Old Minster site, during controlled excavation. 43·2 × c. 152·4 × c. 50·8 cm. Coped stone with slightly deteriorated text set without framing lines on face. OE memorial formula. AS capitals. Late tenth to eleventh century.

Biddle (1966), 325 & fig.

1 Piece I is the bottom portion of a major piece, perhaps a king; piece II may be the top of the same piece, and so the two pieces are entered as one.   2 Dalton (1928), 82.

✠ HERL[*I*]ÐG[*V*.]N[. :]*EORLESF*/*EOL*/*AGA* |

The text reads: ✠ HER L[I]Ð G[VN]N[I :] EORLES FEOLAGA, probably '✠ Here lies G[vn]n[i], Eorl's companion', though there are other possible readings of G[VN]N[I], and the following word-division could be only accidental marks. FEOLAGA, 'companion', could have legal significance in the context. GUNNI and EORL are recorded names of ON origin, although EORL is only recorded as a name in one other source, the twelfth century Cartulary of the Abbey of Peterborough;[1] the translations, 'the Earl's companion' and 'an earl's companion' are therefore also possible. The stone was found covering a grave which had at one end an un-inscribed carved stone, now also in the care of the Winchester Excavation Committee.

139 Winchester II

Winchester, Hampshire. Now in the care of the Winchester Excavation Committee, no. SF 523.

Found July 1965, in upper filling of ditch, during controlled excavation at Wolvesey Palace. Diam. *c.* 3·8 cm. Decorated copper alloy brooch with texts set without framing lines in panel on face; text i legible, ii slightly deteriorated, texts set upside down with respect to each other. Language and formula uncertain. AS capitals. Possibly tenth century.

Biddle (1966), 326–7.

i: EVAH✠ |
ii: IE[.]*J*/HS |

The texts read: EVAH ✠, and IE[.]JHS. Alternatively, both texts could be read laterally displaced as, EAVH ✠, and IEL[.]H[.]. Neither reading makes any sense, unless JHS is a form of the *nomen sacrum*. It is possible that the texts are blundered copies of coin-legends, inscribed for decorative purposes. On this assumption, Dolley tentatively suggested a date about the end of the first quarter of the tenth century.[2]

140 Winchester III

Winchester, Hampshire. Now in the care of the Winchester Excavation Committee, no. RF 819.

Found July 1965, during controlled excavation on Old Minster site, inside south projection of New Minster, possibly *in situ*. *c.* 22·9 × 31·1 × 5·7 cm. Incomplete stone slab, with rather deteriorated and possibly incomplete text set in panel on one

---

[1] See Robertson (1956), 74–83.
[2] M. Dolley, in a personal communication.

edge, letters towards one face.[1] Probably Latin memorial formula. AS capitals. Pre *c.* A.D. 903.

Unpublished.

V[*I*.]*A*TI N[*E*]V V M |

The text probably reads: V[IV]AT IN [E]VVM, 'May he live for ever', where [E]VVM = [AE]VVM. The text is complete as it stands, but there might be some, perhaps including a personal name, lost from the missing edge. It is not certain why the text is set on an edge and not a face of the stone. The stone is dated on archaeological evidence.[2]

141 Winchester IV

Winchester Cathedral Library, Hampshire.

Found May 1905, exterior to and east of south transept of Cathedral. Diam. 3·8 cm. Decorated circular brooch, probably bronze, with rather deteriorated text set in panel but without framing lines on face, letters laterally displaced and in relief. OE personal name. AS capitals. Probably tenth century.

Grueber (1908), 83–4 & fig.; Vaughan (1914), 7–9; Wilson, D. M. (1964), 7–8, 35.

HE*R E*[. . .] |

The text reads: HERE —, presumably the recorded first element of a name. The centre of the brooch is probably a coin copy: there exists a similar coin of Edward the Elder with the name HEREMŌD.[3] On this numismatic evidence, Dolley dated the text to the end of the first quarter of the tenth century.[4]

142 Winchester V

Winchester, Hampshire. Now in the care of the Winchester Excavation Committee.

Found September 1964, during controlled excavation on Old Minster site. Nine clay bell-mould fragments, varying from *c.* 3·5 to 15·5 cm., falling into four groups. All fragments concave with laterally displaced texts probably set in panels or framing lines, uncertain which way letters face. Possibly Latin, formulae uncertain. AS capitals. Pre A.D. 994.

Biddle (1965), 255; Biddle (1968), 31.

[1] For convenience the illustration shows the text reading from left to right.
[2] M. Biddle, in a personal communication.
[3] Grueber and Keary (1893), 98 & pl. viii, no. 6. This is preserved in the British Museum, BMC no. 102.
[4] M. Dolley, in a personal communication.

Group i: two fragments from the shoulder of a bell, with slightly deteriorated relief lettering, respectively nos. SF 798 and SF 799 (= RF 177).

— [Q]V —
— TA —

Group ii: four fragments from the shoulder of a larger bell, probably c. 76 cm. at the shoulder, with legible lettering, no. SF 784.

— ISC —

Group iii: two fragments with illegible lettering, nos. SF 791 and SF 794.
Group iv: a number of uninscribed fragments.

The texts are all too fragmentary to be meaningful. They are dated on archaeological evidence to pre A.D. 994, and Biddle suggested that they might be from the castings of bells for the rebuilt Old Minster of A.D. 971–80.[1]

143   Workington

Workington, Cumberland. Lost.

Found 1926, in Curwen vault, St Michael's parish church, during controlled excavation. Length 36·8 cm. Red sandstone shaft, with one end rounded, one end rectangular; rather deteriorated text set in panel on rectangular end.[2] Probably OE personal name. AS capitals. Date uncertain.

Mason and Valentine (1928), 59–60 & fig.

O S I[. . I]D |

The text reads: OSI[..I]D, presumably a personal name, though its exact form is uncertain; ōs- is a recorded first element.

144   Wycliffe

In the possession of C. U. Peat, Esq., of Wycliffe Hall, near Darlington, NR Yorkshire. Set into an interior wall of the Hall.

Found 1778, by road from Wycliffe to Greta Bridge. 48·9 × c. 19·1 cm. Incomplete carved stone cross-shaft; incomplete and highly deteriorated text set in panel but without framing lines on visible face. OE memorial formula. AS capitals. Probably eighth to ninth century.

Gough (1806), III, fig. opp. p. 340; Haigh (1856–7), 520; Haigh (1857), 156; Stephens (1866–7), 476E; Hübner (1876), no. 187, p. 68; Stephens (1884b), 149; Allen (1889), 214, 221; Stephens

---

[1] Biddle (1965), 255.   [2] The description, etc., is taken from Mason and Valentine (1928), 59–60.

(1894), 13; Searle (1897), 97; Chadwick (1901), 83; Collingwood, W. G. (1907), 413; Collingwood, W. G. (1912), 128; Collingwood, W. G. (1915a), 289; Dahl (1938), 10–11, 188; Page, R. I. (1958), 149; Cowen and Barty (1966), 61–70 & figs.

[.]BA[.A] | [...] | [...]FTE | [R:]B[ER]E | HTV[IN]I: | BECVN[:] |
  [AE]FTE[R..] | —

The text reads: [.] BA[DA ... AE]FTE[R :] B[ER]EHTV[IN]I : BECVN [: AE]FTE[R] —, probably '[✠] Ba[da] (? set this) in memory of B[er]ehtv[in]e, a monument in memory of —'. The names BADA and BEORHTWINE are recorded. The text is interpreted by comparison with OE memorial texts.

145 Yarm

Yarm, NR Yorkshire. Now in Durham Cathedral Library, no. 50.

First mentioned May 1878, in Yarm. 66× c. 30·5× 19·1 cm. Incomplete carved stone shaft with incomplete slightly deteriorated text set without framing lines but in panel on one face. OE memorial formula. Insular majuscule. Eighth to ninth century.

(—) (1869–79), lxxxii; Haigh et al. (1881), 47–52 & fig.; Stephens (1882), 112–18 & figs.; Stephens (1884a), 189–93 & figs.; Stephens (1884b), 132–3 & figs.; Allen and Browne (1885), 343; Browne (1886), 32; Frank (1888), 35–6, 46; Allen (1889), 218, 221; Hodges (1894), 196 & fig.; Stephens (1894), 13; Browne (1897), 161–2 & fig.; Haverfield and Greenwell (1899), no. L, pp. 112–15 & figs.; (—) (1900b), 69 & figs.; Stevens (1904), 50; Collingwood, W. G. (1907), 413; Collingwood, W. G. (1912), 128; Conway (1912), 193; Collingwood, W. G. (1915a), 289; Browne (1916), 24 & fig.; Howorth (1917), III, 31–2 & fig.; Collingwood, W. G. (1927), 61–2, index; Elgee, F. and Elgee, H. W. (1933), 198; Ross (1933), 152; Dahl (1938), 18, 193; Page, R. I. (1958), 151–2; Page, R. I. (1962), 903; Cramp (1965a), no. 50, p. 7.

— [M]BEREHC | T✠SĀC✠ | ALLA✠SIGN | UMAEFTER |
  HISBRE/ODERA | [S]SETAE✠ |

The text reads: — [M]BEREHCT ✠ SĀC ✠ ALLA ✠ SIGNUM AEFTER HIS BREODER A[S]SETAE ✠, '—[m]berehct ✠ the priest ✠ Alla ✠ set up this monument in memory of his brother ✠', where sĀc = OE SACERD or Latin SACERDOS. sĀc presumably refers to Alla, though it is not certain which man is the subject of the sentence. ALLA is a recorded name of ON origin, while SIGNUM is a unique Latin borrowing. The last two words could alternatively be read, ungrammatically: BREODERA[S] SETAE, 'set up this monument in memory of his brothers', but this is less likely.

146 York I

Set into the easternmost interior pillar of the north aisle of the unused church, St Mary Castlegate, York.

Found 1868–70, possibly 1871, in fabric of east wall. 49·5 × 38·1 × c. 12·7 cm. Incomplete sandstone slab, with incomplete rather deteriorated text set on visible face. Mixed OE/Latin, dedication formula. AS capitals. Tenth to eleventh century.

Haigh (1870), 50–6 & fig.; Hübner (1876), no. 175, p. 64 & fig.; Collingwood, W. G. (1909), 151–2, 203, 207–8 & fig.; Collingwood, W. G. (1912), 123; Collingwood, W. G. (1915a), 290; Ekwall (1930), 20–1; Elgee, F. and Elgee, H. W. (1933), 225; Clapham (1948a), 7; Raine, A. (1955), 194; Dickens (1961), 333–4 & fig.; Tillott (1961), 392–4.

— [..]:M[*I*]N*STERSET*[...] | [.]*ARD₇GRIM₇ÆSE*:O[...] |
MANDRIHTNESHÆ[....] | *CRISTES*[7]*SC̄AMA*[.......] |
E[:]*MARTINI*:*7SC̄EC*[.....] | [.]*TI₇OMNIVMSCŌR*[*V*...] |
[.*S*]*ECRATA*:*EST*:*AN*[...] | [.]*VISIN*:*VITA*:*ET*[...] |
[.]*AERIOÞEM*[. ...] | [. ..*Æ*]*R*[*Æ*]*TSI*[. ...] —¹

The text can be plausibly reconstructed: — [...] : M[I]NSTER SET[TON ...]ARD 7 GRIM 7 ÆSE : O[N NA]MAN DRIHTNES HÆ[LGES] CRISTES [7] SC̄A MA[RI. 7 SC]E [:] MARTINI : 7 SC̄E C[...]TI 7 OMNIVM SCŌR[VM CONS]ECRATA : EST : AN[...]-VIS IN : VITA : ET[...] —, '—[...]ard and Grim and Æse raised (this) church in the name of the holy Lord Christ, and to (or of) St Mary and St Martin and St [?Cuthbert] and All Saints. It was consecrated in the [...] year in the life of —'. The remainder cannot be reconstructed with certainty. GRIM and ÆSE are recorded names of ON origin. The abbreviated forms of SANCTUS, grammatically in the genitive or dative, show some confusion: SC̄A = SANCTA (for SANCTAE, with the abbreviation mark between the C and A); [SC]E, SC̄E = SANCTE (for SANCTI); SCŌR[VM] = SANC-TORUM. The text is unique in that it begins in OE, changes to Latin, but with the use of Þ may revert to OE at the end.

The M[I]NSTER may have been a large church, with the various saints' names referring to separate altars, or it could have been a monastery with dependent chapelries. Churches with all the above saints' dedications are mentioned in DB.

---

¹ Due to the inaccessibility of the stone, it is not always certain whether letters are lost from the end of one line or the beginning of the next. The text is therefore printed as if letters were lost only from the ends of the lines.

147 York II

Yorkshire Museum, York, no. 1.

First mentioned 1852, found St Leonard's Place, near site of St Peter's Hospital. 55·9 × 28·6 × 21 cm. Incomplete grit-stone shaft with incomplete slightly deteriorated text set without framing lines in panel on one face. Latin memorial formula. AS capitals. Possibly eighth to ninth century.

Hübner (1876), no. 176, p. 64; Wellbeloved (1881), no. 1, p. 66; Browne (1884–8), 10 & fig.; Allen (1889), 213; Collingwood, W. G. (1909), 154 & fig.; Collingwood, W. G. (1915a), 289; Dickens (1961), 333.

— [D..] | ADM[.] | MORI | AM | SC̄O | RV[M] |

The text reads: — AD M[E]MORIAM SC̄ORV[M], probably '— to the memory of the saints', where SC̄ORV[M] = SANCTORUM. The text might be incomplete at the end as well as at the beginning.

148 York III

Yorkshire Museum, York, no. 12.

First mentioned 1881, probably found after 1875 in York, though Browne said Ripon.[1] c. 17·8 × c. 17·8 × 14 cm. Incomplete carved stone slab, probably Tadcaster stone, with traces of paint of uncertain date; slightly deteriorated text set in panel on face. Latin memorial formula. Uncials and AS capitals. Possibly eighth to ninth century.

Wellbeloved (1881), no. 12, p. 68; Browne (1897), 283; Collingwood, W. G. (1909), 178, 185 & figs.; Collingwood, W. G. (1912), 123; Collingwood, W. G. (1915a), 289; Collingwood, W. G. (1932), 51; Clapham (1948a), 10 & figs.

SALVEP | ROMERITIS | PR̄SALME | TVIS |

The text reads: SALVE PRO MERITIS PR̄S ALME TVIS, 'Hail O beneficent priest according to your merits'. PR̄S = PRESBYTER and could refer to Christ though this would be unusual; in this case MERITIS might refer to Christ's suffering. The text is more likely, however, to refer to a priest. It forms a pentameter verse with internal rhyme.

149 York IV

York Minster.

Found 1829, in east wall of Minster beneath east window, during repairs. 83·8 × 38·1 × 5·7 cm. Incomplete carved magnesian limestone (Tadcaster) slab, with prob-

[1] Browne (1897), 283.

ably complete, legible text set without framing lines round figure on visible face. Latin descriptive formula, type b. AS capitals and uncial. Eleventh or twelfth century.

Poole and Hugall (?1850), 198 & fig.; Clutton-Brock (1899), 119 & fig.; Prior and Gardner (1912), 134 & fig.; Maclagan (1923), 479–85 & fig.; Clapham (1930), 139 & fig.; (—) (1930a), no. 18, p. 4 & fig.; Casson (1931), 208–13 & fig.; Saunders (1932), 88–9 & fig.; Casson (1933), 31 & fig.; Clapham (1934b), 689–90 & fig.; Clapham (1936), 152, 181–2 & fig.; Rice (1947), 7–9; Clapham (1948a), 6–13 & fig.; Saxl and Wittkower (1948), 27 & fig.; Kendrick (1949), 49; Rice (1952), 115–21 & fig.; Saxl and Swarzenski (1954), 23–32 & figs.; Hunter Blair (1956), 191; Dickens (1961), 334; Beckwith (1964), 200 & fig.; Stoll (1967), 331–2 & fig.

SC̄A | MA | RIA |

The text reads: SC̄A MARIA, 'St Mary', where SC̄A = SANCTA. The text presumably refers to the figure carving, but it is possible that it is not primary. Stylistically, the carving has been dated to both the eleventh and the twelfth centuries; the evidence on both sides was summarised by Rice.[1]

150 York V

In the care of the Superintendent of Works, York Minster.[2]

Found November 1967, during controlled excavation, in fifteenth-century grave-fill in Minster foundations, at south end of north transept. 9·8 × 12·9 × c. 14 cm. Incomplete magnesian limestone slab with incomplete legible text set without framing lines but possibly in panel on face. Latin memorial formula. AS capitals. Date uncertain.

Wilson, D. M. and Hurst (1968), 162.

— PROANI | [..] —

The text reads: — PRO ANI[MA] —, '— for the soul —'. The text lost from the beginning is likely to have been ORA or ORATE, and a personal name presumably followed. Possible traces of an incised cross remain on the face of the stone, in which case the remaining text would be in the top right hand quadrant.

151 York VI

In the care of the Superintendent of Works, York Minster.

Found April 1969, during controlled excavation, re-used in wall of grave in Minster foundations, in west aisle of south transept. 15·2 × 26 × c. 8·9 cm. Incomplete carved magnesian limestone slab, with legible, probably incomplete text set without framing

---

[1] Rice (1952), 115–21.

[2] I am indebted to A. D. Phillips, Archaeological Supervisor, York Minster, for permission to publish the newly found stones, York V, VI, VII, VIII.

lines in remaining top quadrants of cross on face. Language and formula uncertain. AS capitals. Date uncertain.

Unpublished.

✠ LEO[.] | DEI[.] —

The text reads: ✠ LEO[.]DEI[.] —, where the uncertain letters are respectively either B or R and either H or N. The first part of the text at least is probably a personal name. There is no recorded OE element *LEOR-, but LEOB- = LEOF- is well attested; the second element could then be DEI[N], a DB form of -ÞEGN, or DEI[H] = -DEIG, a DB form of -DAEG.[1] Alternatively the name could be mono-thematic followed by a Latin text DEI [H] —; the names LEOFA, LEOFE and prob-ably LEOF are recorded.[2] The grave also re-used an uninscribed Anglo-Saxon stone and contained a child burial.

152 York VII

In the care of the Superintendent of Works, York Minster.

Found May 1969, during controlled excavation, *in situ* in graveyard in Minster foundations, in centre of south transept, grave facing north–south. 175·4× c. 48·3× c. 11·4 cm. Carved grit-stone slab in three pieces, with incomplete rather deteri-orated text set without framing lines in panel at one end of face; at right angles and facing left is set RB text. Latin memorial formula. AS capitals and insular minuscule. Date uncertain.

Unpublished.

✠ ORATEPR | OANIMA | CO[S]T[A/V]N | C[...] —

The text reads: ✠ ORATE PRO ANIMA CO[S]T[AV]N C —, '✠ Pray for the soul of Co[s]t[av]n —', where about five letters are lost at the end and where the first letters in the first two lines touch each other. The name *COSTAUN is unrecorded, though COS- and GOS- are recorded OE first elements; in addition Lind recorded the ON name KOST-BERA.[3] The text is not primary and the carving on the stone is RB.

The RB text reads:[4] D(IS) M(ANIBUS) [A]NT(ONI) GARGILIANI EQU(O) | PUBL(ICO) E[X PR]A[E]F(ECTO) LEG(IONIS) VI; V(IXIT) AN(NOS) LVI | M(ENSES) VI. CLA(UDIUS) FLORENTINUS | DEC(URIO) GENER EIUS, 'To the spirits of the departed (and) of Antonius Gargilianus, of equestrian status, formerly prefect of

---

[1] Feilitzen (1937), 250, 183.   [2] Redin (1919), 51, 114, 124, 14–15.   [3] Lind (1905–15), col. 715.

[4] I am indebted to R. P. Wright, Department of Classics, University of Durham, for permission to quote his unpublished reading. For the system of transliteration used, see Collingwood, R. G. and Wright, R. P. (1965), xxxiv.

the Sixth Legion. He lived 56 years, 6 months. Claudius Florentinus, decurion, his son-in-law (set this up)'.

The stone probably had a burial associated with it. On archaeological evidence this graveyard pre-dates the Norman foundations of *c.* 1080.

153 York VIII

In the care of the Superintendent of Works, York Minster.

Found September 1968 during controlled excavation, re-used in eleventh century footing of north nave wall of Norman church. *c.* 22·9 × *c.* 25·4 × *c.* 14·3 cm. Incomplete carved magnesian limestone slab in two pieces, with incomplete rather deteriorated text set without framing lines in remaining quadrants of cross on face. Probably Latin memorial formula. AS capitals. Date uncertain.

Unpublished.

✠ HIC[...] | [...] | CES[..]ITE | M[...R]A | [...] | VVL/FH/ER[.] | QVIESC[VN]T | —

The text probably reads: ✠ HIC [...]CES[...] ITEM [...R]A[...] VVLFHER[E RE]QVIESC[VN]T —, probably '✠ Here [...] rest Vvlfher[e] —', with other personal names now lost. However it is uncertain how the words of the third and fourth lines are to be divided, and the letters RE- of [RE]QVIESC[VN]T are not visible. WULFHERE is a recorded name. The text appears to read in the order

$$\begin{matrix} 1 & 2 \\ 3 & 5 \\ 4 & 6 \end{matrix}$$

as it is shown above (cf. 46, 47 Hartlepool IV, V), but it is too fragmentary to be certain. The text appears to be incomplete at the end of each bottom line, and it could be so at the beginning also.

154 'eadward' brooch

Provenance unknown. Now in the Ashmolean Museum, Oxford, no. 1945.41.

First mentioned 1930, in possession of Messrs Baldwin, dealers. Diam. *c.* 3·2 cm. Circular decorated silver roundel, possibly brooch, with legible text in relief lettering set right round perimeter on face, letters facing inwards. OE personal name. AS capitals. Probably tenth century.

(—) (1930*b*), no. 4, p. 59; (—) (1944), 13 & fig.

✠ EADƿARDREXANGLORVM |

The text reads: ✠ EADƿARD REX ANGLORVM, '✠ Eadƿard, King of the English'. It is uncertain which king this refers to, though the Ashmolean favour Edward the Elder. The use of REX ANGLORUM suggests, however, a date from the reign of Edward the Martyr (A.D. 975–8). Dolley noted affinities with the work of the Winchester engraver responsible for the coins of the last type of Ethelred II and the first type of Cnut associated with that area, but was unwilling to date the brooch more narrowly than within the limits c. A.D. 975 to c. 1025.[1]

155 'eawen' ring

Provenance unknown. Now in the British Museum, London, no. AF 459, ring cat. no. 182.

First mentioned 1897, when acquired by BM. Diam. c. 2·9 cm. Decorated gold ring, with legible text of niello lettering on gold set right round outside of hoop. OE text, probably in part owner formula. AS capitals. Probably ninth to tenth century.

(—) (1901 a), 14; Dalton (1912), no. 182, p. 30 & figs.; Smith, R. A. (1923), 116; Oman (1931), 107 & fig.; Harder (1932), 37–9 & fig.; Page, R. I. (1964), 89–90; Wilson, D. M. (1964), no. 145, pp. 23, 27, 205–6 & figs.

✠ :EAƿEN:MIEAHSPETRVS:STANCES |

The text begins: ✠ : EAƿEN : MIE AH, presumably '✠ Eaƿen owns me' though MIE is an odd form of ME, and the feminine name ĒAWYNN is otherwise only recorded once.[2] The rest of the text is presumably Christian. Several possible interpretations have been suggested for it, perhaps the most probable being: s PETRVS : STAN CES, 'May St Peter the Rock choose (her)', where s = SANCTVS and CES = CESE, CIESE.[3]

156 'sigerie' ring

Provenance unknown. Now in the Ashmolean Museum, Oxford, no. 1901–469.

First mentioned 1850, in possession of J. Warren, Esq., bought from a travelling dealer. Diam. c. 2·5 cm. Silver ring, with legible text set without framing lines right round outside. OE maker formula. AS capitals and insular majuscule. Date uncertain.

[1] M. Dolley, in a personal communication.
[2] Gibbs (1939), 6; see also Feilitzen (1945), 79.
[3] Cf. Page, R. I. (1964), 90, for other possible interpretations.

Warren (1851), 153–4 & fig.; Warren (1853), 223 & figs.; Stephens (1866–7), 463; Smith, R. A. (1911), 349; Oman (1931), 107 & fig.

:SIGERIE/HEÐMEAGE/V/VIRCAN |

The text reads: : SIGERIE HEÐ MEA GEVVIRCAN, 'Sigerie ordered me to be made'. SIGERIE may be an odd form of the recorded SIGEHERE; MEA and HEÐ are presumably variants of ME and HET, cf. 19 Canterbury I FECIÐ = FECIT, and the discussion of it. These suggest, though do not prove, that the text may not be genuine. If it is genuine, it probably dates from late in the period.

157 'ðancas' ring

Provenance unknown. Lost.

Mentioned only 1851, in possession of Sir Thomas Beevor. Dimensions uncertain. Possibly complete, decorated silver ring, described thus: 'A silver ring, ornamented with a zigzag tooling, and the word— ✠ÐANCAS✠'.[1] OE text, formula uncertain. Script and date uncertain.

Beevor (1851), xxx.

✠ÐANCAS✠ |

The text reads: ✠ ÐANCAS ✠; it could be OE ÐANCAS, 'thanks', though its significance is uncertain. As Beevor suggested, the ring could have been given in recognition of services rendered.

158 V&A crucifix

Provenance unknown. Now in the Victoria and Albert Museum, London, no. 7943–1862.

First mentioned 1861, acquired from Soltikoff Collection. 19·1 × 14× 1 cm. Decorated gold covered wooden cross with ivory crucifix on face. Text i legible, gold lettering set in panel in glass above figure; ii highly deteriorated, set without framing lines in gold on edges of cross. Text i Latin descriptive formula, type b; ii uncertain. AS capitals. Probably late tenth to early eleventh century.

Maskell (1872), 34; Mitchell (1925), 324–30 & figs.; Goldschmidt (1926), no. 3, p. 9 & fig.; Longhurst (1926), 9–10, 74 & fig.; (—) (1930c), no. 18 & fig.; Saunders (1932), 26–7, 37 & fig.; Rice (1952), 161–2 & fig.; Stone (1955b), 41–2 & fig.; Oman (1957), 74 & figs.; Godfrey, J. (1962), 373 & fig.

[1] Beevor (1851), xxx. No other descriptive details are known, and no illustration exists.

i: IH̄SNASA | RENVS |
ii: [....]I:QVIE |
       LIGNI [...] |
       [...] |
       [...] |
       [.]LQD[.....]OETCAMIN[.] |
       [...] |
       ⊬IHS:XP̄S:AM[.........] |
       [...] |
       [...] |
       [.....]:ISIME[.] |
       [N]:ISE[......] |
       [...] |

Text i reads: IH̄S NASARENVS, 'Jesus the Nazarene', where IH̄s is the abbreviated *nomen sacrum* and the whole refers to the figure beneath. Text ii is too fragmentary to be meaningful, though some words can be made out, e.g. LIGNI, and the *nomina sacra* ⊬ IHS : XP̄S :. Mitchell suggested that the text was a list of relics originally contained inside.[1] It has been suggested that the metal setting is Ottonian, but Oman held both the figure and the setting to be English.[2]

[1] Mitchell (1925), 329.
[2] Mitchell (1925), 329, Longhurst (1926), 9–10, Rice (1952), 161–2; Oman (1957), 74.

MAPS

Map I. Distribution map of inscriptions on stone.

Map 2. Distribution map of inscriptions on material other than stone.

PLATES

1 Aldbrough

3 Ardwall

2 *a* Alnmouth

2 *b* Alnmouth

2 *c* Alnmouth

4 a   Athelney

4 b   Athelney

4 c   Athelney

5 a   Attleborough   5 b   Attleborough   5 c   Attleborough

6   Auzon

7 a   Bath

7 b   Bath

8   Beckermet

9   Billingham

10   Birtley

12 Bishopstone

11 Bishop Auckland

15 Breamore I

13 a, b, c, d Bodsham

16 Breamore II

14 a, b Bossington

17a   Brussels I, from Logeman (1891)   17b   Brussels I, from Logeman (1891)

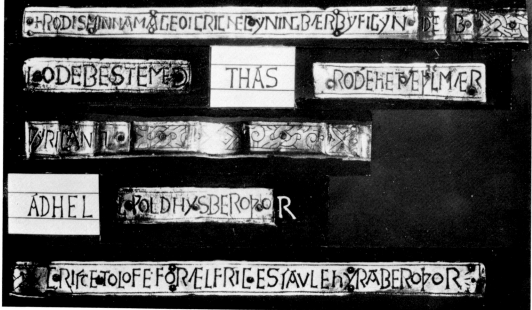

17c   Brussels I

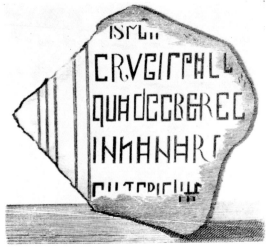

18 Caistor, from Gough (1806), II

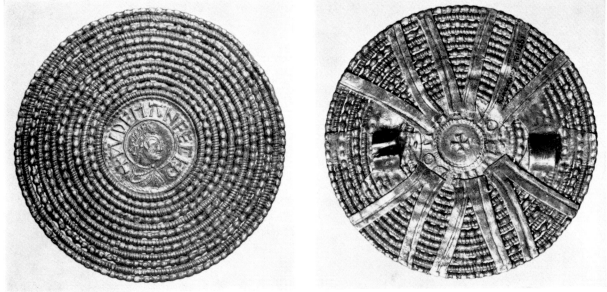

19 a   Canterbury I

19 b   Canterbury I

20 a   Canterbury II

20 b   Canterbury II

20 c   Canterbury II

20 d   Canterbury II

21 *a*   Canterbury III

21 *b*   Canterbury III

22   Canterbury IV

23 *a*   Carlisle I

23 *b*   Carlisle I

24   Carlisle II,
from Collingwood, W. G.
(1916)

25 Chester-le-Street

26 Crowland

27 Cuxton

28 Deerhurst I

29 Deerhurst II (photograph of cast)

31 Dewsbury II

30 Dewsbury I

33 Driffield, from Fowler (1869-70)

32 Dewsbury III

34 a   Durham I

34 b   Durham I

35 a   Durham II

35 b   Durham II

35 c   Durham II

36   Essex, from Braybrooke (1860),
     BM copy (see page 70)

37   Exeter

38   Eye

39 Falstone

40 Gainford

41 Great Edstone

42 Hackness

43 Haddenham

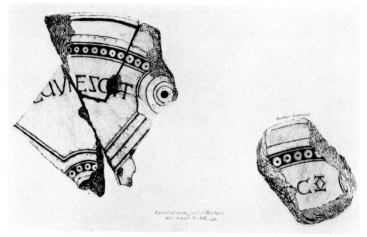

44 Hartlepool O, from a drawing of a rubbing in
the Library of the Society of Antiquaries, London

45 Hartlepool III

46 Hartlepool IV

47 Hartlepool V

48 Hartlepool VI

49 Hartlepool VII

50 Hartlepool VIII

51 Hauxwell

52 Hexham I

53 a Hexham II

53 b Hexham II

54 Hexham III
(photograph of cast)

55 Hornby I

56 Hornby II

57 Inglesham

58   Ipswich I

59   Ipswich II

60 a   Ipswich III

60 b   Ipswich III

60 c   Ipswich III

61 Jarrow I (photograph of cast)

62 Jarrow II

63 Jarrow III

64 Kirkdale

65 Knells, from Collingwood,
W. G. (1911)

66 *a* Lancashire

66 *b* Lancashire

66 *c* Lancashire

66 *d* Lancashire

67 Lancaster I

68 *a*   Lancaster II

68 *b*   Lancaster II

68 *c*   Lancaster II

68 *d*   Lancaster II

69 a Lanteglos

69 b Lanteglos

70 a Laverstock

70 b Laverstock

70 c Laverstock

71　Leake I

72　Leake II, from
Green, A. R.
(1928)

74　Lindisfarne O

73　Lincoln I

75 Lindisfarne I

76 Lindisfarne II

77 Lindisfarne III

78 Lindisfarne IV

79 Lindisfarne VI

80 Lindisfarne VII

81 Lindisfarne VIII

83 Lindisfarne X

82 Lindisfarne IX

84 Lindisfarne XIV

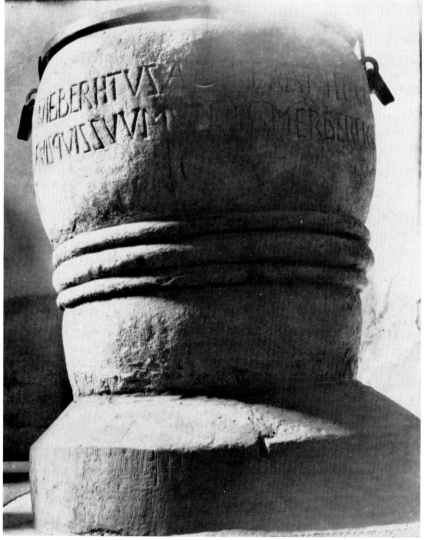

85 Little Billing

86 Llysfaen

87 London I

88 London II

89 Manchester

90 Mildenhall

91 Monk-
wearmouth I

92 Monkwearmouth II

93 Mortain, from Blouet (? 1954)

94 a   Newent

94 b   Newent

94 c   Newent

95   Norham I,
from Hutchinson (1778)

96   Norham II,
from Langlands
(1856–62)

94 d   Newent

97   North Elmham

98   Old Byland

99   Orpington

100   Pershore

101 Plymstock   102 Ripon

103   Rome I

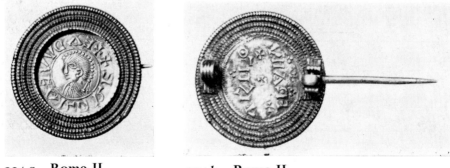

104a Rome II   104b Rome II

105 Ruthwell

106 a   Sandford

106 b   Sandford

106 c   Sandford

107 a   Sherburn

107 b   Sherburn

107 c   Sherburn

109 a   Sittingbourne

109 b   Sittingbourne

108   Sinnington, from Haigh (1879)

110 Skelton

112 Suffolk

111 Stratfield Mortimer

113 Sulgrave

114 Sutton

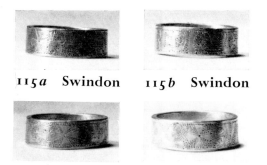

115a   Swindon   115b   Swindon

115c   Swindon   115d   Swindon

116   Thornhill

117 Wallingford I

118 Wallingford II

119 Weeke

120 Wensley I

121 Wensley II

122 Whitby O

123 Whitby II

124 Whitby III

125 Whitby IV

126 Whitby V

127 Whitby VI

128 Whitby VII

29 Whitby VIII

130 Whitby XI

131 Whitby XII

132 Whitby XIV

134 Whitby DCCXXXIII

133 Whitby DCCXXXII

135 Whitchurch

136-7 Wimborne I and II

138 Winchester I

140 Winchester III

139 Winchester II

141 Winchester IV

142 Winchester V

143 Workington,
from Mason & Valentine (1928)

144 Wycliffe

145 Yarm

146 York I

147   York II

148   York III

149   York IV

150   York V

151   York VI

152   York VII

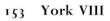

153 York VIII

154 'eadward' brooch

155 *a, b, c, d,* 'eawen' ring

156 'sigerie' ring

158   V&A crucifix

INDEX OF RECORDED INSCRIPTIONS

A. EXTANT INSCRIPTIONS BY COUNTY

ENGLAND

ENGLAND (*cont.*)

SCOTLAND

WALES

BELGIUM

FRANCE

ITALY

PROVENANCE UNKNOWN

B. LOST INSCRIPTIONS BY COUNTY

These inscriptions are said to have been in existence at some time since 1800, but are now lost. As stated in the *Introduction*, the choice of the date 1800 is purely arbitrary. Inscriptions recorded on the sole evidence of William of Malmesbury (*ob.* ?1143), John Leland (?1506–52), Samuel Pegge (1704–96), or Richard Gough (1735–1809) are excluded.

Cumberland
24 Carlisle II
65 Knells
143 Workington

Durham
44 Hartlepool O

Essex
36 Essex

Lincolnshire
18 Caistor

Northumberland
95 Norham I
96 Norham II

Yorkshire ER
33 Driffield

Yorkshire NR
108 Sinnington

Provenance unknown
157 'ðancas' ring

10-2

INDEX OF INSCRIPTIONS UNDER TOWNS OF PRESENT LOCATION, WHERE THESE DIFFER FROM FIND-PLACES

INDEX III

INDEX OF INSCRIPTIONS EXCLUDED
FROM THE HAND-LIST

This index lists doubtful Anglo-Saxon inscriptions. It includes those which have been said to be Anglo-Saxon but are excluded from the Hand-list by reference to the criteria set out in the *Introduction, 1 General*. However it excludes those which are certainly to be excluded by these criteria. As with the Hand-list entries, the inscriptions are listed under their provenances, following which are given their present locality and the nature and material of the object. These are followed by a reference, wherever possible one containing an illustration. The inscriptions are listed under three categories, depending on the criterion by which they are excluded from the Hand-list.

1. INSCRIPTIONS EXCLUDED ON THE GROUNDS THAT THEY PROBABLY DATE FROM AFTER A.D. 1100

Canterbury V, VI, Kent

Lead coffin plates in St Augustine's College Museum, Canterbury; see 21 Canterbury III. Potts (1926), 97–112 & figs.

Castle Bytham, Lincolnshire

Three stones, possibly part of a cross-shaft, in the parish church. Davies and Clapham (1926), 9 & figs.

Gloucester

Gold candlestick in the Victoria and Albert Museum, London. (—) (1930*a*), no. 38, p. 8 & fig.

Lincoln II

Lead coffin plate in the Cathedral Library, Lincoln. (—) (1850), xliv & fig.

Potterne, Wiltshire

Stone font in the parish church. Powell, W. R. *et al.* (1953), 212 & fig.

Rolleston, Nottinghamshire

Stone, now deteriorated, formerly in the parish church. Hill, A. du B. (1916), 202 & figs.

Waterperry, Oxfordshire

Three stones in the parish church. Todd (1969), 29.

Winchester VI, Hampshire

Stone in the City Museum, Winchester. Cottrill (1947), 8 & fig.

2. INSCRIPTIONS EXCLUDED ON THE GROUNDS THAT THEY ARE PROBABLY NOT FROM ANGLO-SAXON ENGLAND.

Boxmoor, Hertfordshire

Bronze brooch in the Ashmolean Museum, Oxford. Smith, R. A. (1902), 260–1 & fig.

Brussels II

Ivory book-covers in the Royal Museum, Brussels. Goldschmidt (1914), nos. 1,2, pp. 8–9 & figs.

Cologne

Ivory bishop's crozier in the Domschatz, Cologne. Goldschmidt (1926), no. 10, p. 11 & figs.

Paris

Ivory panel in the Louvre, Paris. Longhurst (1926), 23, 85 & figs.

Rome III

Stone, of uncertain location. Levison (1946), 38.

Sutton Hoo, Suffolk

Silver spoon in the British Museum, London. Kaske (1967), 670–2 & fig.

Tintagel, Cornwall

Stone cross in the garden of the Wharncliffe Arms Hotel, Tintagel. Langdon and Allen (1888), 312 & figs.

3. INSCRIPTIONS EXCLUDED ON ONE OF THE OTHER GROUNDS GIVEN IN THE *INTRODUCTION*

Bury St Edmunds, Suffolk

Lead book-cover in the Pitt Rivers Museum, Farnham, Blandford, Dorset. Wright (1852), 438–40 & fig.

Corbridge, Northumberland

Stone in the parish church. Craster (1914), 193 & fig.

Littleton Drew, Wiltshire

Stone now lost or deteriorated, formerly in the parish church. Browne (1903), 172–6 & figs.

London III

Pewter brooch in the British Museum, London. Wilson, D. M. (1964), 35, 147–8 & figs.

Middlesmoor, WR Yorkshire

Stone cross in the parish church. Collingwood, W. G. (1927), 90–1 & fig.

Provenance unknown, 'conv' brooch

Pewter brooch in the British Museum, London. Wilson, D. M. (1964), 35–6, 204 & figs.

INDEX IV

INDEX OF INSCRIPTIONS WHICH HAVE A POPULAR NAME

INDEX OF VERNACULAR PERSONAL NAMES USED IN THE TEXTS

This index is divided into 1. Old English names, 2. Old Norse names, 3. Celtic names, 4. names of uncertain etymology. Only complete names, and those incomplete ones whose etymology is fairly certain, are included. The term 'probably' refers to a reading which is only fairly certain. Some words, where the reading is certain, may or may not be personal names; these are included but prefaced with a question mark. The Old English head-words are normalised under early West Saxon spelling with ð for the dental spirant.[1] If the length of an element is uncertain it is presumed to be short.

1. OLD ENGLISH NAMES

Abbe *fem.*: probably a[bb]ae *Whitby IV*, or *Eahha *q.v.*

Āedbeorht *masc.*: a[ed]berec[h]t *Lindisfarne I*, or Aeðbeorht *q.v.*

Āedrāed *masc.*: ædred *Lancashire*, or Aeðrāed *q.v.*; *probably* edred (*twice*) *Newent*, or Ēadrāed *q.v.*

Aelfgifu *fem.*: ælfgivv *Cuxton*.

Aelfrāed *masc.*: aelfred *Athelney*.

Aelfrīc *masc.*: ælfrices *Brussels I*; ælfrici *Deerhurst I*; ælfrici *Weeke*.

Aelfwine *masc.*: *probably* ælƿynes *Lanteglos*, or Aeðelwine *q.v.*

Aeðbeorht *masc.*: a[ed]berec[h]t *Lindisfarne I*, or Āedbeorht *q.v.*

Aeðelheard *masc.*: *probably* [e. . .]ha[r]d *Lindisfarne X*.

Aeðelmāer *masc.*: æþlmær *Brussels I*.

Aeðelswīð *fem.*: eaðelsvi̇ð *Sherburn*; *probably* ed[les]u[id] *Hartlepool V*.

Aeðelweald *masc.*: aðelƿold *Brussels I*; eðilvvaldi *Eye*.

Aeðelweard *masc.*: ægelƿa[r]dvs *Stratfield Mortimer*.

Aeðelwine *masc.*: *probably* ælƿynes *Lanteglos*, or Aelfwine *q.v.*; ed[iluini] *Hartlepool III*.

Aeðelwulf *masc.*: ethelvvlf *Laverstock*.

Aeðrāed *masc.*: ædred *Lancashire*, or Āedrāed *q.v.*

*Aeðwynn *fem.*: aedvƿen *Sutton*, or Ēadwynn *q.v.*

Bada *masc.*: ba[da] *Wycliffe*.

Beorhtgȳð *fem.*: berchtgyd *Hartlepool VI*.

Beorhthelm *masc.*: biorhtelm *Sittingbourne*.

Beorhtwine *masc.*: b[er]ehtv[in]i *Wycliffe*.

*Bureðrȳð *fem.*: bvredrvð *Swindon*, or Burgðrȳð *q.v.*

Burgðrȳð *fem.*: bvredrvð *Swindon*, or *Bureðrȳð *q.v.*

Cēolfrið *masc.*: ceolfridi *Jarrow I*.

*Costaun *masc.*: co[st]avn *York VII*.

Cūðgār *masc.*: cu[d]gar *Ardwall*.

---

[1] Any doubtful cases of normalisation have been resolved by reference to Feilitzen (1937).

*Culla *masc.*: *probably* c[u]lla *Bossington*.

*Cynebad *masc.*: *probably* cyniba[.] *Lancaster II*, or Cynebald *q.v.*

Cynebald *masc.*: *probably* cyniba[.] *Lancaster II*, or Cynebad *q.v.*

Cynburg *fem.*: *probably* [c]inburg *Whitby XIV*, or *Wīdburg *q.v.*

Cypping *masc.*: kyppingvs *Stratfield Mortimer*.

*Dolgbōt *fem.*: ? dolgbot *Essex*.

Dōmfrið *masc.*: *probably* donfr[. .] *Wensley I*.

Ēadbeorht *masc.*: eatbereh[ct] *Wensley II*.

Ēadburg *fem.*: eadbvrh (*twice*) *Wallingford II*.

Ēadhyse *masc.*: adh[y]se *Ripon*.

Ēadmund *masc.*: eadmvnd *Chester-le-Street*.

Ēadrǣed *masc.*: *probably* edred (*twice*) *Newent*, or Ǣedrǣed *q.v.*

Ēadrīc *masc.*: eadri[c] *Bishopstone*.

Ēadweard *masc.*: eadᵹard *Kirkdale*; eadᵹard 'eadward' *brooch*; eadward *Deerhurst I*; eadvveard *Rome II*.

Ēadwulf *masc.*: [e]adv[l]fes *Alnmouth*.

Ēadwynn *fem.*: ædvᵹen *Sutton*, or *Aeðwynn *q.v.*

*Eahha *masc.*: *probably* a[hh]ae *Whitby IV*, or Abbe *q.v.*

Ealdrǣed *masc.*: ealdredvs *Deerhurst I*.

Ealhstān *masc.*: alhstan *Llysfaen*.

Ēanrǣed *masc.*: eanred *Lancashire*.

Ēawynn *fem.*: *probably* eaᵹen 'eawen' *ring*.

Ecgfrið *masc.*: ecfridi *Jarrow I*.

Eomund *masc.*: *probably* eo[. .]nd *Whitby VII*.

Friðburg *fem.*: fri[ð]bvrgae *Whitchurch*.

Gārmund *masc.*: *probably* [.]armvnd *Bodsham*.

Godgȳð *fem.*: godgyðe *Wallingford I*.

Godrīc *masc.*: godric *Pershore*.

Godwine *masc.*: godᵹini *Wallingford I*.

Gūðlāc *masc.*: gvthlacvs *Crowland*.

Herebeorht *masc.*: herebericht *Monkwearmouth II*.

Hrēðbeorht *masc.*: hroethberh[te] *Falstone*.

Ōsgȳð *fem.*: osgyð *Lindisfarne II*.

Ōwine *masc.*: ovino *Haddenham*, or OW Oue(i)n *q.v.*

Sigebeorht *masc.*: s[i]gebereht *Sittingbourne*.

Sigehere *masc.*: *probably* sigerie 'sigerie' *ring*.

Tondwine *masc.*: *probably* tvndvini *Hexham I*.

*Torhtswīð *fem.*: torhtsuid *Hartlepool IV*.

Wǣermund *masc.*: uermund *Hartlepool IV*.

*Wīdburg *fem.*: *probably* ui[d]burg *Whitby XIV*, or Cynburg *q.v.*

Wīgbeorht *masc.*: wigberhtvs *Little Billing*.

Wuduman *masc.*: ᵹvdeman *Canterbury I*.

Wulfhere *masc.*: vvlfher[e] *York VIII*.

Wulfmāeg *fem.*: wlfmæg *Canterbury III.*
Wulfrīc *masc.*: wlf[r]ici *Canterbury III.*

2. OLD NORSE NAMES[1]

Alli *masc.*: alla *Yarm* (*see below*)
Ási *masc.*, Ása *fem.*: æse *York I* (*see below*)
Brandr *masc.*: brand *Kirkdale.*
*Dragmall *masc.*: drahmal *Brussels I* (*see below*)
*Framvíss *masc.*: fra[m]vvis *Rome II.*[2]
Gamall *masc.*: gamal *Kirkdale.*
Grímr *masc.*: grim *York I.*
Gunni *masc.*: *probably* g[vn]n[i] *Winchester I.*
Gunnvǫr *fem.*: gvn[ᚦara] *Aldbrough* (*see below*).
Hávarðr, *ODan* Hawarth, *masc.*: haᚦarð *Kirkdale.*
Iarl *masc.*: eorles *Winchester I* (*see below*).
Loðinn *masc.*: loðan *Great Edstone.*
Oddi, *ODan* Odda *masc.*: odda *Deerhurst I.*
Ormr *masc.*: orm *Kirkdale.*
Tóki *masc.*: toki *Stratfield Mortimer.*
Tósti *masc.*: tosti *Kirkdale.*
Úlfr *masc.*: vlf *Aldbrough.*

In addition, certain names listed above as Old English may contain an Old Norse element: *dolgbot* Essex, *tvndvini* Hexham I, possibly [.]armund Bodsham, and possibly ᚦelv[a]r London II, the latter listed below. *Gvn[ᚦara]* Aldbrough is probably Old Norse, though the second element could be Old English -*waru* or a late form of -*weard*; *alla* Yarm and *æse* York I are also more likely to be Old Norse. *Eorles* Winchester I is better considered as an anglicisation of the Old Norse name *Iarl* than as a name formed from the Old English noun borrowed as *eorl*. *Drahmal* Brussels I may be either Old Norse as listed above, or be from the recorded Continental Germanic elements *drag-* and -*mahal*.[3]

3. CELTIC NAMES

OIr Muiredach *masc.*: myredah *Alnmouth.*
OW Oue(i)n *masc.*: ovino *Haddenham, or OE* Ōwine *q.v.*

---

[1] The Old Danish forms are only quoted if they seem more likely to be the origin of the recorded name than the Old Norse form.
[2] OWN *framvíss*, 'foreseeing', Bjørkman (1910), 43.
[3] Suggested by Dickins and Ross (1954), 16; see Förstemann (1913), cols. 138–9, and (1916), col. 181.

4. NAMES OF UNCERTAIN ETYMOLOGY

The following names are probably Old English but have more than two possible etymologies or are
of obscure etymology. They are quoted in the forms in which they appear in the texts.

a[l]rihc *Gainford.*
a[v]fret *Rome I.*
ælsel[ð] *Lanteglos.*
beanna *or* beanna[h] *Lindisfarne III.*
eirtig *probably Lincoln I.*
eleᵹ *Plymstock, possibly* elewynn, elewyn.
eofr[i] *Exeter.*
ethraldric *probably Attleborough.*
[g]ene[reð] *Lanteglos.*
[h]ane[. .]ev[b] *Hartlepool VII.*
leo[.]dei[.] *York VI.*
osi[. .i]d *Workington.*
ᵹelv[a]r *London I.*

INDEX VI

INDEX OF ABBREVIATIONS USED IN THE TEXTS[1]

1. LATIN

abbas: abb = abbatis *Canterbury III*; abb̄ = abbatis *Jarrow I*.

agnus dei: *probably* Ã Đ *Sherburn*.

alpha, omega: A ꞷ *Canterbury III*; A ꞷ (*upside down*) *Swindon*; A ⳹ *Hartlepool VI*; *probably* Ӿ *Weeke*.

andreas: *probably* and *Bishop Auckland*.

angli: anglorv̄ = anglorum *Deerhurst I*.

aprilis: apr *Canterbury II*; apĪ = aprilis (*gen.*) *Deerhurst I*.

assumere: asv̄pta = assumpta *Deerhurst I*.

atque: atq: *Little Billing*.

augustus: avg *Canterbury II*.

autem: avte *Deerhurst I*.

christus:[2] xpō = christo *Bossington*; xp̄i = christi *Canterbury III*; xpvs *Dewsbury II*; [x]p̄s *Durham I*;
  xp̄e = christo, *possibly with OE -e, Kirkdale*; x[ps] *Ruthwell*; xp̄s *V&A crucifix*.

commendare: commēdo = commendo *Manchester*.

december: dec *Canterbury II*.

dedicare: *probably* de[dic]atv̄ = dedicatum *Deerhurst II*.

deus: dī = dei *Brussels I, Driffield*; dō = deo *Jarrow I, Wallingford I*.

dominus: dn̄[i] = domini *Lancaster II*; *probably* d[mē] = domine *Manchester*.

draco (*OE* draca): draca *or* dracā = dracan *Ipswich I*[3]

ecclesia: eccles = ecclesiae *Jarrow I*.

episcopus: ep̄s *Deerhurst I*; ep̄ = episcopi *Eye*.

esse: *probably* ē = est *Deerhurst II*.

et: & (*twice*) *Ruthwell*.

facere: *probably* f[e] = fecit *Exeter*.

februarius: feb *Canterbury II*.

fingere: *possibly* fic = fictum est *Bossington*.

gabriel: gab *Mortain*.

gloria: glor[i]ā = gloriam *Lancaster II*.

habere: h̄[t] = habet, habuit *Crowland, or hic q.v.*

hic: h̄[c] = hanc, huic *Crowland or habere q.v.*

ianuarius: ian *Canterbury II*.

---

[1] The index contains only those abbreviations whose form is certain or fairly certain, the examples being arranged inside each head-word in alphabetical order of texts. Head-words are in the nominative singular (or plural where appropriate) or in the infinitive; the form as it appears in the text is expanded only where it is not nominative or infinitive, or if it might cause confusion. 'Latin' and 'Old English' refer to the head-words, not to the language of the texts.

[2] The origin of *xps* is an adaptation of the Greek Χριστός with Latin inflexions added.

[3] A Latin word borrowed into Old English, appearing here in an Old English text.

idem: eandē = eandem *Deerhurst I.*

iesus:[1] ihs *Dewsbury II*; [ihs] *Durham I*; ihs *Norham I, Ruthwell*; ih̄s, ihs *V&A crucifix.*

iulius: ivl *Canterbury II.*

iunius: ivn *Canterbury II.*

kalendae: k̄l = kalendas *Jarrow I*; k̄l = kalendas *Stratfield Mortimer.*

maius: mai *Canterbury II*; mai = maii *Jarrow I.*

martius: mar *Canterbury II*; mār = martii *Canterbury III.*

michael: mih *Mortain.*

millesimus: ml̄ = millesimo *Canterbury III.*

november: nov *Canterbury II.*

october: oct *Canterbury II*; octb = octobris Stratfield Mortimer.

omnis: *probably* ōmniṽ = omnium *Canterbury IV*; oms *or* oms: = omnes *North Elmham.*

orare: *probably* ōr = ora, orate *Birtley.*

paulinus: pas *Bishop Auckland, or* paulus *q.v.*

paulus: pas *Bishop Auckland, or* paulinus *q.v.*

pes: *probably* p[.] = pedes *North Elmham.*

petra: petrā = petram *Crowland.*

piscis: *probably* pis: = pisces *Dewsbury III.*

presbyter: p̄rs = presbyter, presbyteri *Kirkdale*; p̄rb *or* p̄rb: *Monkwearmouth II*; [pr]b̄ *Ripon*; p̄rs *York III.*

pro: *probably* p *Birtley, Lancaster I*; p *Norham II*; p̄ *Lancaster II.*

regina: regna *Sherburn.*

requies: reqviē = requiem *Haddenham.*

rex: rēg = regis *Jarrow I*; rx *or* rx: = rex *Laverstock.*

sacerdos: sāc *Yarm, or OE* sacerd *q.v.*

sanctus: sc̄orṽ = sanctorum *Canterbury IV*; s̄ = sancti *Deerhurst I*; scs, [s]cs *Durham I*; s *or* [sc]s = sanctus, sancti *Durham II*; sc̄e, [sc]e *Ipswich I*; sci = sancti *Jarrow I*; sc̄s, scs *(undeclined) Kirkdale*; sc̄e = sanctae *Lincoln I*; scs *(twice) Mortain*; sc̄ *North Elmham*; sc̄a = sancta *North Elmham*; scs = sanctus *or* sancti *Ruthwell*; [sc]e, sc̄e = sancti *York I*; sc̄a = sancta *York I*; scōr[vm] = sanctorum *York I*; sc̄orv[m] = sanctorum *York II*; *probably* s 'eawen' *ring.*

september: sep *Canterbury II.*

sigillum: siḡ *Eye.*

spiritus: *probably* [sp] = spiritum *Manchester.*

-bus: -bꝫ *Billingham.*

-que: q *Jarrow I.*

2. OLD ENGLISH

cyning: cn̄g *(undeclined) Kirkdale.*

in: *probably* n *Kirkdale.*

ond, and: 7 *Brussels I, Kirkdale (six times), probably Lincoln I, Orpington, York I (probably five times).*

sacerd: sāc *Yarm, or Latin* sacerdos *q.v.*

---

[1] The origin of *ihs* is an adaptation of the Greek 'Ιησοῦς with Latin inflexions added.

INDEX VII

COLLATION OF NUMBERINGS OF SERIES OF TEXTS

The following series of inscribed stones have been differently numbered on various occasions. This collation is not intended to include all numbers that have ever been allotted to the stones, but only those from the most important works.

74–84 LINDISFARNE

Hand-list[1]	Page[2]
O	—
I	—
II	I
III	II
IV	III
V	IV
VI	—
VII	V
VIII	VI
IX	—
X	—
XIV	—

91–2 MONKWEARMOUTH

Hand-list	Page
I	II
II	—

[1] The Hand-list numbers follow the numbering of Peers (1925), 255–70.
[2] All numbers refer to R. I. Page's forthcoming *Corpus of Anglo-Saxon runic inscriptions* (Cambridge).

122–34 WHITBY

Hand-list[1]	Peers and Radford[2]	Find-list[3]
O	—	—
II	10	6
III	11	688
IV	12	659
V	13	689
VI	14	305
VII	18	441
VIII	21	285
XI	15	687
XII	16	394
XIV	?26[4]	442
DCCXXXII	inscription 1	683
DCCXXXIII	inscription 2	573

In addition, Page refers to 34 Durham I as 'Lindisfarne/St Cuthbert's coffin'. The numbers of the Hartlepool stones (44–50) in both Page and the Hand-list follow the numbering of Haigh (1846a), 185–96.

[1] The Hand-list numbers follow the numbering of the British Museum *Whitby Loan Register*.
[2] Peers and Radford (1943), 27–47.
[3] Find-list of the Excavations, preserved in the Public Record Office.
[4] Whitby XIV corresponds exactly in size to Peers and Radford no. 26, but they described no lettering, only rough incisions on it.